D1701649

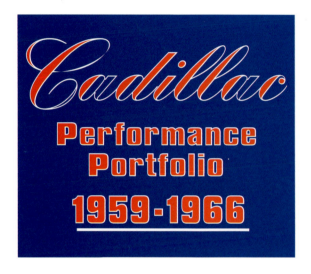

Compiled by R M Clarke

ISBN 1 85520 6641

BROOKLANDS BOOKS LTD.
P.O. BOX 146, COBHAM,
SURREY, KT11 1LG. UK
sales@brooklands-books.com

A-CAD5PP

Printed in China

ACKNOWLEDGEMENTS

Both of our books on early Cadillacs recently went out of print, they covered the years 1949-1969 and ran to 100 pages each. Due to the great interest in the finned models we have doubled the coverage of the 1959 model year in this book and increased the page count to 128 pages. The earlier finned models, up to 1958, are well covered in our new publication *Cadillac Performance Portfolio 1948-1958.*

Our books are printed in small numbers and now with over 400 titles are one of the main reference works for those that indulge in the hobby of automobile restoration. We exist because firstly there is a need by enthusiasts for this information and secondly because the publishers of the world's leading motoring journals generously support us by allowing us to include their copyright articles. We are indebted in this instance to the management of *Autocar, Automobile Topic, Car and Drivers Year Book, Car Facts, Car Life, Classic American, Modern Motor, Motor, Motor Life, Motor Trend, NZ Classic Cars, Popular Mechanics, Popular Science, Road & Track Specials, Classic & Sports Car* and *Wheels.*

We are also indebted to Tony Beadle, the motoring journalist, for his observations below and also for generously supplying our front cover photograph.

R.M. Clarke

There can be no question as to the automotive styling feature that defined the excesses of the 1950s - the tailfins of a 1959 Cadillac. Never before, or since, has such an outrageous design been used on a production automobile. Unfortunately, the flamboyance of the Cadillac bodywork has tended to overshadow the car's performance. For example, in a side by side comparison with a '59 Imperial, at 10.3 seconds the Cadillac was almost two seconds quicker to 60mph.

Although Cadillac clung on to them longer than most, with the coming of the Sixties tailfins disappeared almost as quickly as the cars accelerated away down those long, straight highways. Thanks to its 390 cubic inch, 325 brake horsepower V8, the 1960 Cadillac could still outpace its competitors in the luxury sector - hitting 60mph 1.6 seconds ahead of the Imperial and a whopping 3.5 seconds in front of the Lincoln Continental.

The mid '60s saw the coming of the 'muscle car' era and the trend for manufacturers to squeeze big V8 engines into smaller models. At the expensive end of the market, however, in those days bigger was still better and nothing expressed this philosophy better than the Cadillac. By '66 the engine had grown to 429 cubic inches and was pumping out 340 horsepower, bringing the zero to 60mph time down to way below ten seconds, and giving a top speed of around 120mph - this from a car tipping the scales at close to 5,000lbs.

The weight penalty was a direct result of the luxury and elegance expected from a Cadillac by its owner. Air conditioning, power windows, power adjustable seats, cruise control and many other accessories fitted as standard equipment also added to the purchase price, but then there's always an extra charge for first class travel, isn't there?

The opening line of an old and famous magazine advert for Cadillac began with the words: 'The Penalty of Leadership…' and during this period the company's designers and engineers worked hard to uphold the marque's tradition of excellence. With the benefit of hindsight, it might be questioned whether they fully achieved those goals or not, but Cadillac had certainly come a long way since the cars were described by one American motoring journalist as being 'terrestrial battleships'.

Tony Beadle

CONTENTS

4	Jumbo Jet - '59 Cadillac Eldorado	*Road & Track Specials*	Jan	1991
11	Tail-fin Fantasy - '59 Series 62 Convertible	*Wheels*	Mar	1988
12	Chrome, Sweet, Chrome - '59 Coupe de Ville	*Classic American*	Sept	2002
16	What Cadillac Offers in 1959	*Car Facts*		1959
18	The 1959 Cadillac	*Motor Life*	Nov	1958
20	1959 Cadillac Consumer Analysis	*Car Life*	May	1959
24	Cadillac and Imperial Comparison Test	*Motor Life*	May	1959
26	Elegant Eldorado	*Motor Trend*	Sept	1959
28	American for 1959	*Motor*	Oct 1	1958
29	Cadillac - 1960 Analysis	*Motor Life*	Nov	1959
30	Cadillac's Eldorado Brougham Driver's Report	*Motor Life*	Oct	1959
32	Gold Behind the Glitter - Series 62 Road Test	*Wheels*	Oct	1960
36	Cadillac, Still the Champ	*Car Life*	Aug	1960
39	Cadillac - Sedan de Ville Introduction	*Motor Trend*	Apr	1961
42	Cadillac	*Motor Life*	Nov	1960
44	Cadillac	*Motor Trend*	Nov	1960
46	Return of the Cadillac - Series 62	*Wheels*	Apr	1961
48	Cadillac Fleetwood 75 Imperial Limousine Road Test	*Autocar*	May 26	1961
52	1961 Cadillac Engineering	*Automobile Topic*	Dec	1960
53	Cadillac 60, 62 & 75 Introduction	*Car Life*	Nov	1961
54	Egad - A Cad! Road Test	*Modern Motor*	Jan	1962
58	'60 Cadillac Eldorado Biarritz Retrospect	*Motor Trend*	Nov	1990
61	60th Anniversary Cadillacs	*Automobile Topic*	Oct	1961
62	Eldorado!	*Classic & Sports Car*	Aug	1996
65	Cadillac Coupe de Ville Road Test	*Car Life*	June	1961
70	Caddy Produces First New Engine in 14 Years	*Popular Science*	Nov	1962
71	Cadillac gets Lighter Engines	*Popular Mechanics*	Nov	1962
73	Introducing the '63 Cars	*Car Life*	Nov	1962
74	Cross-Country - Series 62 Coupe de Ville Road Test	*Motor Trend*	Jan	1963
80	1963 Cadillac Park Avenue - Series 62 Road Test	*Car Life*	Feb	1963
84	Cadillac Owners Report	*Popular Mechanics*	June	1963
87	'64 Cadillac Makes its own Weather	*Popular Mechanics*	June	1963
88	Cadillac Series 60	*Car Life*	Nov	1963
90	Cadillac Sedan de Ville Road Test	*Motor Trend*	Mar	1964
96	Cadillac Sedan de Ville Road Test	*Car Life*	July	1964
100	Cadillac Coupe de Ville Road Test	*Autocar*	Aug 7	1964
105	Cadillac Calais	*Car Life*	Oct	1964
106	Cadillac Cruiser - '65 Coupe de Ville	*NZ Classic Cars*	Nov	1998
110	Setting the Standard - 1964 Cadillac de Ville	*Classic American*	Feb	2001
114	GM's Crown Jewel - Cadillac de Ville Road Test	*Motor Trend*	Aug	1965
118	Go West Young Man - Sedan de Ville Road Test	*Motor Trend*	Jan	1966
121	Economy Cadillac - Calais Coupe Road Test	*Car Life*	Aug	1966
126	Cadillac Owners	*Popular Mechanics*	July	1966
128	Cadillac Brougham	*Car and Drivers Year Book*		1966

JUMBO JET

THIS 1959 CADILLAC ELDORADO CONVERTIBLE IS TRULY A FLIGHT OF FANCY

BY RAY THURSBY

PHOTOS BY ROY D. QUERY

I t was the best of times, it was the worst of times, it was a period unlike anything those born later could know. On the surface, given the historian's predilection for gloomy revisionism, it was a time of colonialism, of wretched excess, of indignities and inequalities. For those who were there, it was a time of pride, of discovery, a time that promised to be the starting point for a better future. It was 1959. . . .

To understand the Cadillacs of the day, it is necessary to understand the environment that nurtured them. Today, the 1959 Caddies seem gross and inefficient of materials and resources, overblown; they are now relics of a dead past, which we have, it is said, replaced with something better. The mere fact that a 1959 Cadillac Eldorado convertible—one of 1320 built—can be considered an exotic by *anyone* is more a function of changing times and attitudes than of intrinsic worth or rarity. Neither applies; this is an artifact, a 4-wheel memoir.

Consider: The United States of the late Fifties was a strong nation, a place in which everyone knew who were the Good Guys and who wore the black hats. The Russkies might have beaten us into space, but we'd catch up. We always did. The moon wasn't so far away; neither were the rest of the planets. Future technology meant picture phones, color TV for all, cars that rode on air cushions, personal helicopters. Oil? How could we ever run out? There was lots to go around. Even if the Arabs had nationalized the fields and refineries once owned by Texas oil barons, they still had to sell their Black Gold. To us.

And America built the best cars. Sure, there were a few wackos who bought strange little German beetle-cars, and funny sports cars from Europe, but Mr and Mrs America weren't interested. Detroit, Kenosha and South Bend

■ **At the height of the Fifties' jet era, the Cadillac sported a tall appendage that suited it. Of course, you could get much the same view standing behind an F-86. . . .**

were keeping them happy. Mom and Pop had an Olds 98 in the driveway of their ranch-style suburban home; they could afford both house and car, even though Pop was the sole breadwinner in the family. Junior was sending off for Honest Charley's latest catalog of speed and customizing parts, and sweet-talking the old geezer down the block who had a 1951 Ford that he might sell. Sis was dating the high school football hero, whose parents had given him a Chrysler 300 for making the Big Touchdown.

It seems a fantasy today, but that was part of the reality of 1959. Not for everybody, of course, but for a good percentage of the population. Hard-working citizens, aspiring for something better around the corner, using American Know-How, felt they could do anything.

Lest we forget, the Japanese Threat at that point came from cars like the Datsun Bluebird and Prince Skyline. Lee Iacocca was just some guy at Ford who probably wouldn't have recognized a Toyopet if it had run over him.

Cadillac was Pinnacle; the embodiment of

the American Dream, a reward for making it big. You hit the Big Time, you bought a Caddy—as simple as that. It was what it had to be to suit the tastes of the era; it was what its designers wanted it to be.

"It was a wonderful, naive time when we did what we wanted," recalls Dave Holls, a GM designer who worked on the 1959 Cadillacs. "There were no clinics, no market researchers. The young people [of GM design] were in control." Though the 1959s are not Holls's favorites ("I prefer the 1960 Fleetwood; it was cleaner and had less chrome"), he remains enthusiastic about the forces and personalities that guided their creation.

"We had our clay models for 1959 finished in late 1956. Harley Earl—GM's design chief—was in Europe at the time; Ed Glowacke was in charge of the Cadillac studio. Then we saw the first 1957 Chryslers. They were light and fresh in appearance; we thought that, for the first time, Chrysler had outdone us. We started a revolution, scrapped the existing clays, broke

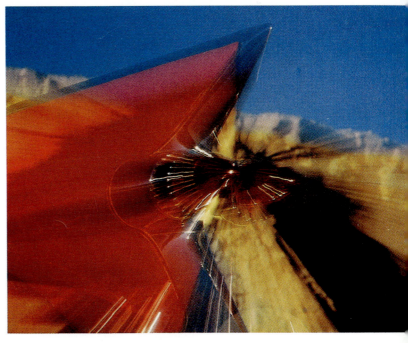

all the rules in the place, did these outlandish cars and had them in production in two years. They were so outrageous, even we were a little bit embarrassed by them."

Outlandish, yes, but still clean, and a far cry from the overdone, over-chromed GM barges of 1958, of which, paradoxically, Cadillac's were at the same time the most flamboyant and cleanest. "The 1958 Cadillac would have been as garish as the Buicks and Oldsmobiles, but Ed Glowacke wouldn't have it. He could have been fired for scraping off all the bright trim, but he did it anyway. He was great."

Glowacke was, like many of his GM contemporaries, as enthusiastic about tasteful sports cars as you and I. "When I went to work for Ed in 1952," Holls recalls, "he was racing a Siata 1100. It was white with a blue top, and he towed it to the races behind a white Cadillac, which also had a blue top."

In any case, the 1959s were different, and a far cry from Harley Earl's concept. "Nobody knew what Earl would think of our 1959s when he returned from Europe. We asked ourselves, 'Will he go through the roof?' He had to back these designs in front of GM management if they were to go into production. We ended up in the courtyard [at the GM design center] with our 1959 design models and the 1957 Chryslers side by side. Earl was shocked; he didn't say anything. Then he looked at the Chryslers and said, 'They really stumbled onto something. He approved our designs, but after that he felt the place had passed him by."

Despite their appearance, the 1959 Cadillacs were not quite clean-sheet designs; some com-

promises were required by GM management. "All 1959s shared the same uppers, from Cadillacs to Chevrolets. Roof stampings and glass were identical on all. Moreover, we had to use the same front doors. The Buick's was the most radically sculptured, and its shape dictated the arc of the Cadillac's downswept rear fender. We had proposed a more conservative sweep that made the fins look smaller, but this is what we wound up with."

Ah, tailfins. They're the first thing one notices when approaching a 1959 Cadillac today. Great, rising expanses of sheet metal, evocative of the jet planes that served as inspiration for a generation of designers, they draw the eye from the body form itself, in a rising line to their chrome-plated peaks. The pointed taillight lenses, serving as stylized jet exhaust flames, accentuate the overall impression of flight captured and held on the ground.

The sheer bulk of the car casts twice the shadow of my own late, lamented 1959 Hillman Minx, taking up far more space on the

road than a 6-passenger conveyance should ever occupy. That's more than 5000 lb of car sitting there, much of the weight made up of exterior sheet metal.

Sheer size does not, however, automatically mean gracelessness. The Cadillac's lines *are* masterful; they flow beautifully, with character and a sense of purpose. There's continuity of theme in every line and detail, from the "landing lights" (that aircraft influence again!) in the lower front bumper ends that echo the dual-headlight treatment, to the repeating of the grille's textures on the flat panel below the trunk lid. The huge hood, fender, door and rear deck stampings appear seamless, interrupted only by necessary cut lines.

In short, this is a design that is far better than its detractors (and many of its current fans) would want to admit. Today, it is attractive; when new, it was a knockout. Give Dave Holls the last word on the Cad's exterior: "It was a high-water mark in flamboyance. It may have shaken traditional Cadillac buyers, but it at-

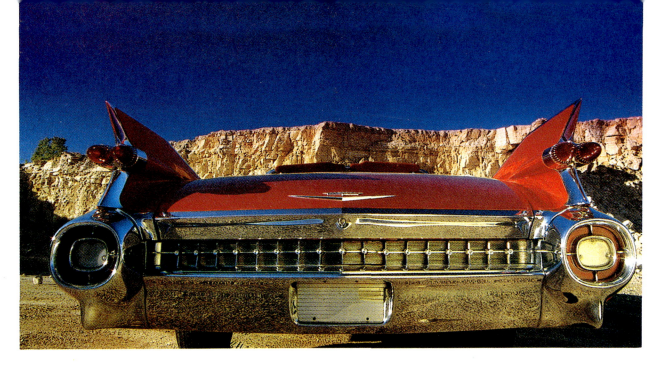

tracted new, more extroverted types."

Inside, the 1959 is no more restrained, and no less attractive. The wide, comfortable bench seats were upholstered in a semi-tuck-and-roll pattern and would carry six real people. Passengers had only the knobs of the AM radio to distract them; the driver, naturally, had more.

But not much. Aside from the two pedals, a thin chrome shift lever sprouting from the steering column, and a thin-rimmed plastic wheel (dished, with a chrome bullet at its center), there was little to command the Cadillac pilot's attention. Three dials—a horizontal speedometer, fuel (from E to F) and temperature (from C to H) filled the instrument pod, flanked by chrome knobs for headlights and cigarette lighter. Two large plain panels below the instruments carried controls for vent, heat and defroster. A group of small switches, also chromed, were situated in the dogleg under the left windshield pillar; these controlled the wipers and electric window lifts.

Driving this behemoth is neither exciting nor terrifying. Its 325-bhp V-8 produces enough torque to get it off the line smartly, and it will carry its occupants in great comfort down the highway. In the manner of the time, the power-assisted steering requires only fingertip pressure to guide it through its three turns lock-to-lock, and the brakes seemed capable of at least one panic stop. I avoided sports-car roads while piloting the car, in deference to its aged wide whitewall "super-cushion" tires and in recognition of its intended use but found little to complain about under normal conditions. Just the opposite, in fact. I *liked* it. Dramatic, comfortable, and quite well-assembled, the 1959 Cadillac is a monument to style and pride, and to an age of flair.

As Dave Holls says, "It was a wonderful time in America." And the Cadillac was there. ■

1959 Cadillac El Dorado Convertible

SPECIFICATIONS

Price	na
Curb weight	5060 lb
Wheelbase	130.0 in.
Track, f/r	na
Length	225.0 in.
Width	80.3 in.
Height	54.4 in.
Fuel capacity	21.0 U.S. gal.

ENGINE & DRIVETRAIN

Type	ohv V-8
Bore x stroke	101.6 x 98.4 mm
Displacement	6382 cc
Compression ratio	10.5:1
Horsepower, SAE gross	345 bhp @ 4800 rpm
Torque	435 lb-ft @ 3400 rpm
Carburetion	3 Rochester 2-bbl
Transmission	3-sp automatic
Final-drive ratio	3.21:1

CHASSIS & BODY

Layout	front engine/rear drive
Brake system, f/r	drum/drum, vacuum assist
Wheels	na
Tires	8.20 x 15 bias-ply
Steering type	recirculating ball, power assist
Suspension, f/r	upper & lower A-arms, air springs, tube shocks/ live axle on trailing arms, upper A-arm, air springs, tube shocks

PERFORMANCE

0–60 mph	est 10.6 sec
Standing ¼ mile	est 18.2 sec
Top speed	115

na means information is not available.

RETROSPECTIVE

PETER BATEMAN

TAIL-FIN FANTASY

The '59 Cadillac Series 62 Convertible was the ultimate mobile boudoir

NO SOONER had John Keats' 1958 book *The Insolent Chariots* pointed out the follies of America's love affair with the motor car than the 1959 Cadillac convertible appeared. We needed to look no further. The Series 62 Convertible Coupe was precisely the insolent sort of chariot Keats was talking about.

Twenty five years later, Brock Yates' book *The Decline and Fall of the American Automobile Industry* argued that the US makers had given too much attention to styling and not enough to real engineering. The finger pointed again. The '59 Caddy convertible was the kind of styling extravaganza Yates was referring to.

Without doubt, this is the de-finitive land yacht, the ultimate mobile boudoir. On its 3300 mm (10 ft 10 in) wheelbase is a body which must surely have been the pinnacle of late '50s over-the-top styling, 5715 mm (18 ft 9 in) long, the car weigh-ing some 2170 kg (42 cwt) and powered by a 6.4 litre (390 cu-bic inch) 242 kW (325 bhp) V8, at that time one of the world's largest production engines.

Its vast grille – once de-scribed as a 'glittering cliff of chrome' – was echoed by a smaller replica across the back bumper. The car had not only power brakes and power steering, but power roof, with a single dashboard button to raise or lower the convertible top. It had seats which ad-justed electrically for reach,

height and tilt ('six' ways', by Cadillac's arithmetic). It had not only dual headlights, but dual tail lights. And above all – literally – it had those tail fins.

They were used on all the '59 Caddies other than the hand-built Eldorados, and were not really that much lar-ger than the fins of the '58 models. But for 1959 the fins also incorporated the bulletted pairs of tail-lights. It was daring and spectacular. But it was hardly unexpected. Cadillac had introduced bold rear fins as part of its complete restyle of the 1957 range, and had used rocketship fins as early as the '55 Eldorados. Distinc-tive rear fender treatments went even further back, to the first of the truly post-war

Cadillacs in 1948, with small but unmistakable finlets.

The story goes that these finlets – 'rudder-type styling' was Cadillac's terminology – were devised to make sure post-war Caddies would look different to the rest of the Gen-eral Motor's stable. The deri-vation, however, probably goes back even further, to the very early 1940s when GM's styling supremo Harley Earl had some GM stylists study one of the first P38 Lightning fighter planes. From this inspiration – long tail booms, bold fins, ag-gressive scoops – came a strong and enduring source of GM styling themes.

The 1948 Cadillac dealers were worried about the first fin-lets, but the public loved them. Those trick tails became pro-duct identification of the very best kind, as Cadillac started its successful post-war move to increase sales without los-ing its hard-earned reputation for quality and luxury. In 1949, after 47 years of manufactur-ing, Cadillac built its millionth car. By 1959 it had built a mil-lion more, and in a record year the '59 became Cadillac's best-selling convertible.

Looking at the cars, it's easy now to say that the packaging had become the product. Yet how ironic it was in Cadillac's case, because the company had a magnificent engineering history. It demonstrated new standards in precision manu-facture in 1910, introduced the electric starter-motor in 1912, the first production V8 in 1915, the synchro gearbox in 1929, a production V16 in 1930.

But post-war its engineering does seem to take the back seat. We have to do some dig-ging to discover that the 1959 models introduced self-dipping headlights and inert-gas shock absorbers. And the 1959 models' engines were descended from a trend-setting oversquare ohv V8 introduced in 1949, and their automatic transmissions were four-speed overdrive.

Of course, the tail-fin era couldn't last, and for 1960 Cadillac (and the rest of the in-dustry) was more restrained. Perhaps America realised it had been living its fantasies in public. But they are fantasies which still have strong appeal. If you wanted a 1959 Series 62 Convertible Coupe today you would have to pay more than $US80,000 for an average example. You could have bought one new for $5455.

Graham Howard

Chrome
sweet
chrome

Words and Photography: Erik Stigsson

Never mind turning sows' ears into silk purses, how about transforming this former rats' nest '59 Cadillac Coupe DeVille into a stunning paragon of automotive beauty? One very determined Swede managed, **Erik Stigsson** *has the story …*

CONNY Sjölund from Vännas in Sweden enjoys restoring cars as much as owning them. That's probably why Conny felt the need to restore this 1959 Cadillac Coupe DeVille. Several car restorers had backed off when they saw the Cadillac's condition, but Conny bought it and started to restore it from the frame upwards.

Some years ago, having finished a total restoration on a 1959 Chevrolet Bel Air four-door sedan, Conny was ready for a new project. At that time this Cadillac coupe was up for sale in Tavelsjö, a town close to Vännäs. Conny went and took a look at the car and

found that not only was the body rusted out, but the engine had not been run for the last 20 years. Even the seats were on their way through the rusted-out floor, so it was no surprise to discover that several potential buyers had already backed off when they saw the condition of the car.

'Of course I realised that it would take a lot of work to get the Cadillac back in shape again, but I fell in love with its once-beautiful Wood Rose metallic colour – I just couldn't stop myself from buying it.'

Before Conny could lift the body from the frame he had to make new sills. The car was so rusty that the body would have literally split into two if he hadn't fitted new sills before lifting it off the chassis. With the body out of the way, Conny stripped the chassis down to its bare rails. Having repaired all the rust damage, it was sandblasted and painted, then reassembled as a rolling chassis. All the parts that were in bad shape were replaced with new ones before it was finally ready.

'I believe that the car wasn't used much before it was laid up. I could see that several parts of the chassis were still in good shape, for example the whole front end was still in very good unrestored condition,' explained Conny.

Then it was time to continue with the body. Everything was taken off the body and Conny made notes of where and how each part was placed and fitted. These notes are very important to have when you put the car together again. Then it was time to fix the rest of the rust on the body. The whole floor had to be replaced and there was also lots of rust in the boot and on the lower parts of the rear quarters. When all the bodywork was completed the car was sprayed in primer and was resprayed in the original colour, Wood Rose metallic.

While the car was at a local body shop, Conny had time to rebuild the original 390cu.in. engine and it now has its original 325 ponies back! The Hydra-Matic transmission looked like it was in good condition so Conny just changed the oil and filter, since which its run perfectly.

Prior to Conny owning it, the Cadillac had been home to a number of rats, so the original interior was in pretty poor condition. The only thing to do was to strip the seats down to the bare frames and then build them up again from scratch. Conny ordered original materials from the US and then made up the fantastic interior himself: 'There was a lot of work to do on the interior but I'd challenged myself to do as much work as I could on the car, so I persevered.'

Since this is a '59 Coupe DeVille, electric windows and electric seats are standard, although this particular model has the optional six-way power seats; four-way power seats were standard on the '59 Coupe DeVille. Conny's Cadillac also has its original radio with a power antenna that still works. For originality's sake, Conny also decided to use the old-style crossply tyres that are taller than modern radial tyres and since this car is from the Fifties, whitewall tyres are more or less a must.

For lots of people a '59 Cadillac is the ultimate dream car. It was for Conny too, but that dream has now become reality, although it took plenty of blood, sweat and tears along the way before this old Cadillac was restored to its former beauty. As they say: 'Good things come to those who wait'!

CADILLAC

LAST YEAR'S STORY

Production: 121,786 (1958 model run)
Down from 146,840 in 1957 (154,631 in 1956)

Sales: 88,111 (first 8 months 1958)
Down from 96,054 in 1957 (99,007 in 1956)

Position in industry: 9th in sales
Unchanged from 1957 (Unchanged from 1956)

Summary: A good year despite the down trend. Percentage of industry production increased from 2.36% to 2.88%.

Series Sixty-Two Two-door Hardtop

Cadillac's flat-roof four-door hardtop is called the four-window Sedan de Ville. Like the people in Kansas City (according to the song) fins have "gone about as far as they can go."

Fleetwood Sixty Special Four-door Sedan

Those of you who don't trust your wives to drive the new Cadillac can buy the Fleetwood Series Limousine. There's a lot of the Rolls-Royce flavor in the way the roof drops down to the belt line at the rear. In a different sense from above, when you own this car, you've "gone about as far as you can go."

What Cadillac offers in 1959:

Cadillac must have willingly given up the funeral-directors' business. After all, you don't go to a funeral in a car that looks like a rocket.

Its chest-high tailfins are the raciest, rashest design on the road today and they just don't seem to fit a funeral.

Over-all, the new car is slightly shorter than its most popular 1958 models (although the new styling makes it appear longer). All models, except the Seventy-Five, are 225 inches long. Wheelbase on all (with the same exception) is 130 inches. Height has been reduced sharply and some body styles are as much as 5.5 inches lower.

The engine now has 390 cubic inches, increased from 365 by a longer stroke. Compression ratio is up to 10.5 to 1. Horsepower, too, is up, now being 325 with 345 on the "Q" engine (standard on Eldorado models, optional on others). Actually the only difference between the standard engine and the extra-cost "Q" engine is carburetion. The "Q" has three two-barrel carburetors instead of one four-barrel carburetor. This is the same difference as having a big flyswatter and an extra-big one—both will do the job.

Hydra-Matic has been simplified by the removal of the rear pump. The main purpose of this pump was to turn over the engine should the car have to be pushed to start. It was suddenly realized that people don't often push Cadillacs to start them, so the pump has been dropped. As a result, there is a slight increase in economy because it took gas to spin the pump.

The smaller steering wheel gives a more sporty feel.

Handling has been improved markedly. There is less "load" on the power steering, and this, plus the lower center of gravity, makes it feel better.

Connecting rods and pistons are aluminum. The connecting rod is new, of course, to accommodate the enlarged stroke. The intake manifold has been redesigned to provide better breathing. A new choke stove for the carburetor reduces the normal choke time on cold starts from 2.5 miles to 0.8 mile. This will reduce gas consumption, but more importantly, it will prevent loading up and the resultant embarrassing hard starting.

Just announced is the new $13,000 Eldorado Brougham. Built in Italy by Farina, the Brougham is the lushest thing to come down the pike. It is racy, yet dignified. It has a royal bearing that reminds one of the Bentley and the Rolls-Royce. Yet it doesn't look like yesterday the way those British classics do. This car is dignified enough for the funeral.

16

CADILLAC Specifications
(All data in inches except as noted)

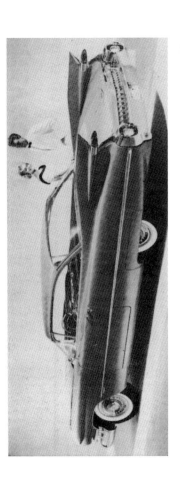

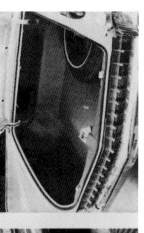

Rear window of the Sixty-Two two-door hardtop curves high into the postage-stamp roof.

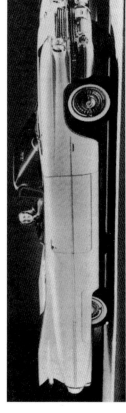

Dashboard instrumentation is deeply recessed so it doesn't reflect on the compoundly wrapped windshield.

Cavernous describes the trunk. It is finished off so well that it looks like another passenger compartment.

Series Sixty-Two Convertible Coupe

Artist's drawing of the Eldorado Brougham. This exclusive model is built by Farina of Italy.

GENERAL

	Series 62 / Series 60	Fleetwood Series 75
Wheelbase	130.0	149.8
Over-all length	225.0	244.8
Over-all width	80.2—Series 62 / 81.1—Series 60	80.2
Over-all height (loaded)	56.2	59.3
Over-all steering ratio	18.9 to 1	18.9 to 1
Wheel turns, lock-to-lock	3.75	3.75
Wall-to-wall turn circle	48.4 ft.	54.0 ft.
Curb-to-curb turn circle	47.0 ft.	49.2 ft.
Shipping weight	4835 lb.—"62" / 4890 lb.—"60"	5490 lb.—"75"
Minimum road clearance	5.9	7.0

ENGINE

	All Series
Bore & stroke (inches)	4.00 x 3.875
Displacement (inches)	390.0
Standard compression	10.5 to 1
Optional compression	None
Standard horsepower	325 at 4800
Optional horsepower	345 at 4800 (Standard on Eldorados)
Standard torque	430 at 3100
Optional torque	435 at 3400 (Standard on Eldorados)
Oil capacity	5 qt.
Water capacity with heater	19.3 qt. (20.8 qt. Series 75)
Gasoline capacity	21 gal.
Fuel recommended	Premium
Rear axle, handshift	None
automatic transmission	2.94 to 1, 3.21 to 1—Eldorados, 3.36 to 1—"75", (3.77 opt.—"75")
overdrive	None

INTERIOR DIMENSIONS
(All Four-door Sedans)

	Series 62	Series 60	Series 75
Headroom, front	34.8	35.0	36.2
rear	33.2	33.0	34.8
Seat height, front	9.4	9.5	8.5
rear	14.2	13.8	13.1
Steering wheel to seat	4.9	4.9	5.4
Legroom, front	45.6	45.5	43.9
rear	45.3	43.6	Not applicable
Shoulder room, front	60.5	60.1	60.5
rear	59.1	59.1	58.8
Hiproom, front	64.6	64.6	65.4
rear	64.4	64.4	60.1

BODY STYLES AVAILABLE

	Series 62	Eldorado	Series 60	Series 75
2-door hardtop	X	X		
2-door convertible	X	X		
4-door sedan	XX	Brougham	X	Limousine
4-door flattop sedan	XX			

Determined to retain top spot in the luxury car field, Cadillac has made major appearance and technical changes in its cars for 1959. Styling especially is more different than in recent years and engineering modifications are aimed at improving already approved factors.

THE 1959 CADILLAC

STYLING

NO SECOND look will be necessary to identify Cadillacs for 1959 as completely new cars. They retain some basic styling resemblance to earlier models, but to much less a degree than has been true for some years. The process of evolutionary change hasn't been discarded completely but it definitely has been accelerated.

One familiar Cadillac trademark now missing is the "Dagmar" front bumper with its rubber-tipped, bullet-shaped guards. The new design, slightly less massive in appearance, is set low across the front of the car and has parking and turn signal lights set deeply in oval recesses.

The grille has a texture somewhat reminiscent of the egg-crate types long used by Cadillac but fender and hood changes make its shape completely different.

The hood now extends to the fender crown; the dividing line parallels the crown molding on the fender.

The greenhouse, or roof and window area, has been changed considerably. Front corner posts are more upright, do not have the reverse angle slope that has characterized past models. Rear roof pillars flow back and down to the deck, no longer slant forward sharply to the leading edge of the rear fenders.

Glass area has been greatly increased —the most ever used by Cadillac. There is more than 450 square inches more glass area in the 62 series sedan than in the same 1958 model, for example.

Rear view of new Cadillacs is dominated by pronounced fins. Pods mounted on each side of these fins contain stop, turn signals and taillights. Large back-up lights are mounted in chrome housings at the outer edges of the huge rear bumper. A small grille section, similar to the one at front, is set above the bumper.

All models again this year are hardtops, without a center roof pillar, but a new four-window sedan body style has been added in two series.

The four-window sedan has four side windows with a large wraparound rear window. The standard sedan has six side windows, including two small ones at rear, and a normal rear window.

The 1959 Cadillac line consists of six series of cars: five standard series (60, 62, 63, 64 and 67) which feature 12 body styles and the Eldorado Brougham series with just the one custom sedan body style.

There is more standardization of dimensions between series than in the past. Except for Brougham and eight-passenger Fleetwood models, all have a 130-inch wheelbase and overall length of 225 inches. Overall height varies according to body style, but is much lower than last year in all cases.

The 62 sedan is just 56.2 inches high, compared to 59.1 inches for the same model last year. The 62 four-window sedan is even lower—53.7 inches! Fleetwood 60 Specials are down from 59.1 to 56.2 inches also and Eldorado Biarritz models have dropped a full four inches— from 58.4 to 54.4.

Despite these decreases in overall height, interior dimensions have not changed greatly from last year. In 62 sedans, for example, front headroom is 34.8 inches compared to 35 inches last year; rear headroom has been decreased from 34.9 to 33.2 inches. Front legroom has gone up from 45 to 45.6 inches and rear legroom is 45.3 inches compared to 45.2 in 1958.

ENGINEERING

Engineering changes by Cadillac for 1959 include more powerful engines; a new shock absorber design and other sus-

PRONOUNCED FINS dominate rear view. Pods mounted on each side of fins contain stop, turn signal and taillights. Small grille section, similar to front, sits above bumper.

pension modifications aimed at smoother, more stable ride; improved power brake and steering systems, and a number of alterations made necessary by the new body design.

Cadillac's V-8 is basically similar to the 365-cubic-inch powerplant used in 1958 but displacement has been increased to 390 inches by lengthening its stroke from 3.625 to 3.875 inches. Stroke remains four inches. Compression ratio has been raised from 10.25-to-1 to 10.5-to-1.

These changes have upped horsepower ratings from 310 at 4800 rpm to 325 at 4800. (Torque has gone from 405 to 440 foot pounds at 3100 rpm.) This is for standard engines equipped with four-barrel carburetors.

Another version of this V-8, using three two-barrel carburetors, is again being offered. It is rated at 345 hp at 4800 rpm. This "Q" engine is standard for all Eldorados, optional for all other models.

Automatic choke control has been moved into the exhaust area of the intake manifold for quicker response and an automatic temperature compensator incorporated for improved idle operation. Intake manifolds have been redesigned with larger passages and exhaust valve shape has been streamlined for improved fuel flow.

Cadillac engineers are enthusiastic about their new shock absorbers for 1959. They are unique in that they have enclosed plastic bags of Freon-12 replacing the air normally used in conventional shocks!

The bags of Freon-12 fit in the chamber above the shock absorber piston. The captive gas can't escape to mingle with shock absorber fluid—as sometimes hap-

pens with conventional units—and thus hinder efficient shock absorber action.

Otherwise, Cadillac's standard steel suspension is similar to that used in 1958 models. Coil springs are used at all four wheels, with four-link trailing arms at rear. One arm on each side attaches to frame outriggers and runs back to the axle, positioning it laterally. A control yoke attaches to the differential cage and is hinged to a rear frame crossmember.

This design permits ready installation of optional air suspension (air springing is standard only for Broughams) at the factory. This suspension system is essentially the same as in 1958, but new valving and other refinements have been incorporated as a result of a year's experience. The accumulator tank design has also been changed from a long slim shape mounted horizontally to a short, squat type mounted vertically.

Only important brake change is a new direct-acting power brake booster of larger capacity than last year. A new rotary valve giving improved response and a larger capacity pump are used in Cadillac's power steering system; this results in an overall steering ratio of 19.1-to-1 and faster steering. Turn circle diameter, however, has increased on most models from 43.4 to 47 feet.

Standard rear axle ratios have been lowered numerically from 3.07 to 2.94-to-1. (Air conditioned cars and those with "Q" engines will use 3.21 axles.) This should help economy but will probably cancel out any performance advantages of the bigger, higher torque V-8. Axle gear teeth design has been changed to quiet gear noise.

Just how the changes for 1959, par-

ROOF AREA of the two-door Cadillac is kept to an absolute minimum. Sweeping front and rear windows cut the top to dimensions not much larger than a card table.

DASH AND CONTROL area still bespeaks the quality that has made GM's big production the coin of the luxury realm. Appointments are plush, interior comfort is high.

ticularly the styling, will affect sales will be interesting to follow. Whether the more abrupt break with the past will make more owners feel their earlier models are obsolete and spur them to buy new Cadillacs, or whether they will rebel at the less conservative approach remains to be seen. ●

CADILLAC

By JIM WHIPPLE

THE LONG, low, sleek lines of the 1959 Cadillac not only tell you that it's a brand-new body but may also give a clue to the fact that it's a much changed car in all respects. Don't worry, it still has all the quality of material and perfection of assembly and finish that have pretty much made it the standard against which other cars are measured. But, the '59 Caddy is quite a bit different from the solid, high-crowned models of years past.

It looks lower and *is* lower. Sedans have dropped from 58 and 59 inches to 56 inches in overall height, while some of the hardtops are down to 54 inches—as low as any car in the industry, barring the Corvette and Thunderbird. Headroom has been shaved a little too—from a roomy 34 and 35 inches down to 33 and 34 inches.

Seat-cushion heights have dropped, too—in some models as much as three inches. The front seat on the

Sixty Special sedan, for example, is 9½ inches above the floor. A seat as low as this would have seemed out of place in anything but a sports car just a few years back.

Rear cushions have been dropped less in relation to the floor in sedans due to the fact that designers have been able to lower the floor without interference from the wasp-waisted, X-type frame.

The transmission housing and drive-shaft tunnel take up just a bit more of the passenger compartment than in '57 and '58 models and have limited the size and comfort of the center-of-the-seat areas somewhat. Seating positions—particularly in the front compartment—require more stretch-out and less sit-up than the higher seats. For driver-comfort I found the six-way power seat a real boon.

In the Coupe DeVille test-car I was able to maneuver into a very comfortable position by powering the seat all the way to the rear of its travel, elevating it for proper

vision and tilting it forward to find the most comfortable reach. Cadillac's designers have left no surface uncushioned and made all details work for passenger comfort.

PERSONALITY

The new, lower bodies have helped change Cadillac's road personality as well as make it one of the sleekest looking jobs that ever came down the pike. The center of gravity is lower and as a result—even though little change has been made in the suspension—the car is more stable and handles better than last year's model. And the '58 handled very well indeed. Now that Cadillac's weight has been brought as close to the road as that of its competition, it turns out to be a very stable, road-hugging car.

I took the Coupe DeVille out into a favorite test area of mine, an almost deserted and forgotten stretch of sadly beat-up and broken concrete. It's a road on which almost no engineering

Cadillac
is the car
for you

if... You want the most desired car in the U.S.

if... You want the inner satisfaction of knowing that you own the best all-around engineering job to come out of a U.S. auto plant.

if... You like the idea of a really luxurious car that does not sacrifice anything in roadability or ease of handling.

if... You're interested in getting all the quality and fine workmanship you're paying for.

CADILLAC SPECIFICATIONS

ENGINE	V-8	"Q" V-8
Bore and stroke	4 in. x 3.875 in.	4 in. x 3.875 in.
Displacement	390 cu. in.	390 cu. in.
Compression ratio	10.5:1	10.5:1
Max. brake horsepower	325 @ 4800 rpm	345 @ 4800 rpm
Max. torque	430 @ 3100 rpm	435 @ 3400 rpm
DIMENSIONS		
Wheelbase	130 in.	
Overall length	225 in.	
Overall width	80.3 in.	
Overall height	53.7 in.-56.2 in.	
TRANSMISSIONS Hydra-Matic		

At $13,075 factory A.D.P., there is no optional equipment on this Eldorado Brougham—everything is standard. Only 4-door hardtop is available.

Distinctive front end of Cadillac balances twin headlights with dual parking lights. Hood is extra wide for easy engine access.

Distinctive high fins of '59 set off the Cadillac on any street. Thin roof overhangs huge rear window.

skill at all was wasted when it was built some 35 years ago. There are four solid miles of serpentine curves of varying radius—most of 'em tight —all of which are banked in the wrong direction. When this road is lightly powdered with snow or sleeted over, it takes everything you've got to keep out of the ditches at 20 mph.

I took the Caddy over this stretch —happily dry at the time—at 40 to 55 mph, holding the transmission in third gear at all times. The tires screamed 'till it sounded like the zoo at feeding time, but 5000 lbs of well-balanced Cadillac stayed right where my fingertips put it. The initial response when swinging from a left-hand curve to a sharp right was the mushy beginning of a dive—or plowing—when the rapid transfer of weight from one side of the car to the other squashed the soft tires and caused a slight roll effect until the tire was compressed enough to resist. Raising the pressure from an underinflation of 24 (26 is recommended) to 28 lbs. sq. in. not only cured it, but gave the car an amazing feeling of rock-solid stability.

This trip over the serpentine gave me a great deal of respect for Cadillac's power steering—improved this year with a rotary valve. It's the best

power steering in the business today. The engineers at GM's Saginaw Division have managed to overcome all power-steering problems. The touch on the wheel is feather-light, yet not so delicately responsive that you feel in danger of swerving when you apply sudden pressure. There is good feedback of road feel in that you can pretty well gauge how much you need to increase the turn-angle of the front wheels to overcome the understeer tendencies. There is also good self-centering action—a function of front-end geometry sometimes blotted out by power steering.

In short, Cadillac power steering gives perfect two-way communication between driver and road—never interfering, and helping the driver just as much as he needs and no more.

RIDING QUALITIES

Cadillac's ride has been good in most recent years—especially in the area of control of dip and bounce. When the new coil-spring rear suspension first came out, the resultant riding qualities weren't up to those provided by the long leaf springs of earlier models. This year however, they've really hit the mark. The car

rode as level as any I've ever driven, including the fabulous Citroen DS-19. Bumps in the road displace the wheels most of their length of travel before the body begins to rise gently for a short distance.

Without a detailed analysis, let me simply say that I feel Cadillac's ride is now the best in the luxury—or any other—price field. The competition is terrific and comes very close, but this year, for the first time in recent years, Cadillac is the best.

The '59 engine is somewhat larger, displacing 390 inches instead of 365. Horsepower is up only 15—now rated at 325—but torque, the real measure of working power in the mid-speed ranges, has been increased. This has enabled Cadillac engineers to lower the numerical ratio of the rear axle to 2.9 so that the engine turns over more slowly. As a result, the engine ticks over lazily at 35 or 40—giving surprisingly high mileage and making no audible sound.

Hydra-Matic transmission, standard on all Cads, is the best of the automatics, for my money. It has positive action in four well-spaced ratios, yet the changes between them are butter-smooth and can only be noticed under full-throttle acceleration.

The big, smooth-running Cad engine

At left is the Fleetwood Sixty
Special hardtop sedan, stylized
by convex scoop on rear side panel.

Instrument panel features cruise
control at upper left, driver can
select desired speed and maintain
it without any accelerator pressure.

is the other half of a perfect power team. Its high ratio provides easy, quiet, economical cruising, yet can be dropped into third for rocketlike acceleration either by flooring the throttle at any speed below 65, or by moving the selector lever to third position at part-throttle. This move provides a nice boost in power for hill-climbing without wasteful, overpowering full-throttle operation.

Driver vision is excellent over the smooth, flat hood, providing you have adjusted the power seat properly. Instrument layout has been improved and somebody up there at Cadillac listened to our previous pleas and toned down the chrome around the dials, which had proved annoyingly dazzling in past years.

The workmanship throughout the Cadillac, whether it be paint finish, fit of trim or upholstery, is the best currently available on a production automobile this side of the Atlantic, and after all, what more can you say than that?

SUMMING UP

Cadillac is a large, superbly engineered and beautifully built automobile that's hard to fault in any respect.

CADILLAC CHECK LIST

5 CHECKS MEAN TOP RATING IN ITS PRICE CLASS

Category	Description	Checks
PERFORMANCE	Although Cadillac does not top its class in acceleration or all-out power, its exceptionally smooth-running and quiet engine gives smooth, powerful and flexible performance in all speed ranges.	4
STYLING	Personal opinion is everything in this category. We feel that the sweeping contours and mercifully chrome-free surfaces of Cadillac make it one of the most beautiful cars we've ever seen—but we have our doubts about those fins and the "ice-tray" grilles.	4
RIDING COMFORT	By a narrow but discernible margin, Cadillac has the best ride in its class and in the industry. It is extremely soft yet not overly mushy, it is very well-controlled yet not harsh, and vibration is nearly non-existent.	5
ROADABILITY	Cadillac has improved roadability, coming very close to the best in its class. Its behavior is precise and predictably safe at all times.	4
INTERIOR DESIGN	The questionable advantages of a lower silhouette and the undoubted benefits of a lower center of gravity are the result of space taken from the important vertical dimensions that have made exit and entry more difficult than before. Body width and legroom leave nothing to be desired for all but center of seat passengers.	4
EASE OF CONTROL	Top-notch power steering, easy-acting power brakes and a well-balanced suspension system, plus flexible Hydra-Matic make the Cadillac surprisingly light and easy to handle for a 5000-lb car.	5
ECONOMY	Hydra-Matic and a well-engineered power plant will give the conservative driver surprisingly good mileage per gallon of premium fuel. Mileage will not quite equal the fabulous 17 and 18 miles-per-gallon performance of some earlier models.	4
SERVICEABILITY	The Cadillac isn't a particularly easy car to service and service will not be cheap if it's properly done, however, the amount of servicing required has been lower than average in recent years.	4
WORKMANSHIP	There is hardly an area throughout the car, be it upholstery, paint, trim or operation of hardware and controls, which cannot be described simply as "The Best."	5
VALUE PER DOLLAR	Cadillac has had the lowest depreciation in its field for years. There are waiting lists for used Cadillacs. This year's models live up to the quality of past years in every way. For those who can afford it, the Cadillac is a top transportation buy.	5

CADILLAC OVERALL RATING... 4.4 CHECKS

1959
ROAD TEST

WHERE there once was a wide range of choice in upper bracket American-made luxury cars, the field in recent years has been reduced to just three names: Cadillac, Lincoln and Imperial. This trio is likely to remain unchallenged by any domestic newcomer, at least in significant volume, and each make seems to have a promising future.

The chief objective in this limited class, aside from the prestige of driving a more costly vehicle, is massive luxury, supported by a higher degree of quality. On the massive luxury point there is some threat from the middle priced cars which have constantly been raising their stand-

1959 it has undergone major changes that accompany a new design. Only unaltered components are the engine, which has been carefully refined over a 10-year period, and the pioneer Hydramatic transmission.

The rest of the chassis was new in 1958 and its principal distinguishing feature is the cruciform or "hourglass"-type frame. Although air springing is available, the test car had the traditional coil and A-arm in front, matched by coils with trailing links at the rear.

In a straight line at moderate speeds, or in city cruising, the Cadillac is masterfully smooth. Flaws are noted only at high speeds, when some swaying motion sets in, and in fast corners when the tires protest loudly as the heavyweight goes through a bend. Under certain conditions on rough roads it appeared that the frame was actually flexing, as the car developed an overall quiver. During hard acceleration runs there was no wheel spin.

Fuel consumption was creditable for a

car of this size. While the average for all driving was 11.7 mpg, with cautious operation during one phase of the testing a top of 22 mpg was registered for 150 miles from the center of a metropolitan area.

Cadillac's strongest claim to superiority is its unmatched feeling of luxury and quality. When riding in this car, the almost soundless operation coupled with rich materials and fine assembly produce the desired effect: you know that this is an expensive and luxurious automobile. One is never in doubt.

The interior is Cadillac's best to date. The instruments are the most legible of any GM car, deeply recessed in padded cavities. Electric latches, not an exclusive feature, permit locking of all doors with one switch, which is surprisingly handy and convenient.

Imperial in its 1959 model has some advantages. The major one is better handling qualities, although not as good as some of the lighter Chrysler Corporation

CADILLAC AND IMPERIAL

ards. As yet, however, the prestige trio is more secure in its position than any other category of U.S. cars.

The real differences between these cars are often subtle and slight. Performance is relatively adequate by today's averages, with no apparent effort at outstanding accelerating ability in keeping with the conservative requirements of dignity. Distinctive features are largely on the surface, a matter of styling and appointments rather than extreme basic design.

Two of these luxury cars, a Cadillac four-door hardtop of the most popular series, and the rarer Imperial convertible, were recently tested. While two such body types were certain to produce different results, they do make an interesting study.

Cadillac is the more noteworthy this year, not only because it still is the undisputed leader in this class, but because in

CADILLAC FRONT AND REAR is massive as ever, but sleeker. The flamboyant fins are as controversial as they were 10 years ago.

IMPERIAL LOOKS GOOD but needs greater distinction from the Chrysler line in order to match its rivals in the luxury class.

One is nearly all-new—and one is not. But the differences that count are not revolutionary features. Solid luxury is the word

a heavy steel plate X-member assembly for the convertible body type. It is this and similar strengthening elsewhere that adds to the car's weight.

The Imperial's handicap in its field is not that it is a lesser car, which it positively is not, but that it is a comparatively new name alongside Cadillac and Lincoln. Some years will be required to develop its personality. Another limiting factor is Imperial's close relationship with Chrysler —much closer than, say, Cadillac is to Buick or Lincoln is to Mercury. A greater separation is necessary for prestige and distinction.

Cadillac, in 1959, unquestionably remains the leader in this exclusive class and it has earned the right again through production quality and engineering of details. Imperial may be more roadable and may even possess some advantages in style, and in performance potential, but these are almost secondary factors. Magnificent massive luxury is the mark. ●

vehicles. Nonetheless it corners well, travels at high speeds with a surer degree of control.

The acceleration figures for the test convertible do not reflect the normal ability of the Imperial, which in lighter body types would be a second or two quicker.

The Imperial, of course, is much the same car it was in 1958. The minor facelift included lowering of the headlights and locating them in the dual chromed pods which project forward of the front fender. The grille has been dressed up so that it no longer consists of the simple patterns of straight bars. In general, the alterations have not improved the appearance of the car, and it might have been better left as it was in the preceding year.

The instrument panel is definitely less desirable than 1958, when it was a more logical arrangement. Night reading of dials is easier than by daylight.

Frame of the Imperial is conventional boxed outside frame rails, universal in Chrysler products, with the addition of

Test Data

Test Car: 1959 Imperial
Body Type: Convertible
Basic Price: $5773
Engine: V-8
Carburetion: Single four-barrel
Displacement: 413 cubic inches
Bore & Stroke: 4.18 x 3.75
Compression Ratio: 10.1-to-1
Horsepower: 350
Horsepower per cubic inch: .84
Torque: 470 lb.-ft @ 2800 rpm
Engine speed: 2000 rpm @ 60 mph
Test Weight: 4910 lbs. without driver
Weight Distribution: 55 per cent on front wheels
Power-Weight Ratio: 14.02 lbs. per horsepower
Transmission: Torqueflite
Rear Axle Ratio: 2.93
Steering: 3½ turns lock-to-lock
Dimensions: overall length 226 inches, width 81, height 57, wheelbase 129
Springs: Torsion-bar front, leaf rear
Gas Mileage: 11.5
Speedometer Error: Indicated 30, 45 and 60 mph are actual 32, 46½ and 61 mph, respectively
Acceleration: 0-30 mph in 4.0 seconds, 0-45 in 7.2 and 0-60 in 12.2

Test Data

Test Car: 1959 Cadillac
Body Type: Four-door sedan
Basic Price: $5498
Engine: V-8
Carburetion: Single four-barrel
Displacement: 390 cubic inches
Bore & Stroke: 4 x 3.875
Compression Ratio: 10.5-to-1
Horsepower: 325 @ 4800 rpm
Horsepower per cubic inch: .83
Torque: 430 lb.-ft @ 3100 rpm
Engine speed: 2200 rpm @ 60 mph
Test Weight: 5160 lbs. without driver
Weight Distribution: 52 per cent on front wheels
Power-Weight Ratio: 15.8 lbs. per horsepower
Transmission: Dual Range Hydramatic
Rear Axle Ratio: 2.94
Steering: 4 turns lock-to-lock
Dimensions: overall length 225 inches, width 81, height 56, wheelbase 130
Springs: Coil
Gas Mileage: 11.7
Speedometer Error: Indicated 30, 45 and 60 mph are actual 26½, 39 and 52 mph, respectively
Acceleration: 0-30 mph in 3.8 seconds, 0-45 in 6.4 and 0-60 mph in 10.3

"Quiet elegance" is the way Cadillac describes the instrument panel of the Eldorado Brougham. Instruments are well clustered, recessed, raised closer to eye level. All equipment is powered and is standard, including windows, ventipanes, steering, brakes, seats and door locks. Other standard features include "cruise control" and air conditioning.

ELEGANT

Custom-designed and custom-built, Cadillac's Eldorado Brougham continues as a limited production car—for the "not-so-limited" few.

A new (and necessary) innovation is in the rear quarter panel window. As the rear door is opened, the window slides into a recess for easier passenger entry. As the door is closed, it returns to its original position. The window can also be operated in the normal manner from the inside.

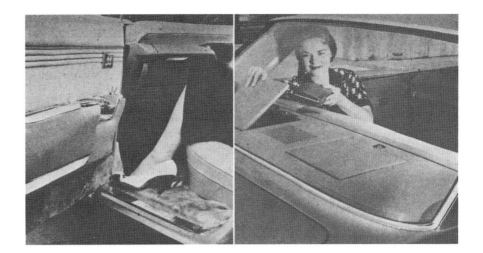

Interior appointments of the Brougham shout quality, from the mouton carpeting, to the broadcloth upholstery, to the courtesy lights, to the way that the car is finished. Extra storage for small, valuable items is possible in two lockable compartments in the package shelf behind the rear seat. (It's a safety feature, too.)

ELDORADO

IN STYLING, CRAFTSMANSHIP, interior luxury and attention to every detail, the Brougham has no peer. It is the true monarch in Cadillac's realm of motoring majesty for 1959." So said James M. Roche, general manager of Cadillac, when this GM division introduced the car at the Chicago International Auto Show in January of this year.

Until recently, we had to take him at his word, for these $13,075 luxury cars were as scarce as the proverbial hen's teeth. Now, however, we have been able to look over a virtual bevy of them that were being prepared for customers in the special shop set aside for this purpose in Detroit. And we'll have to admit: styling, craftsmanship and interior luxury are all far better than on most any car we've seen.

The cars get their beginning at Cadillac, where the parts are built, pre-assembled, crated and shipped off to Italy. There, Pinin Farina drops on the body he has built for it, installs the interior, finishes it off and sends it back to Detroit. Final touch-up, including finish painting, polishing and tune, is given to the cars and then they're whisked away to dealers for delivery to lucky customers.

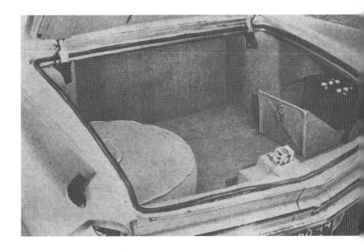

The entire trunk of the Eldorado Brougham is covered with a nylon frieze material, including the decklid, the spare tire (laid horizontally) and the fold-down cover over the battery. Though the trunk is not as great in cubic space as some cars, it still holds ample luggage.

CADILLACS for the coming year have striking styling features, notably the "rocket" tail and dummy rear grille seen on the series 62 coupé below, and the massive frontal treatment and the curved pillars flanking a huge wrapround and wrapover screen seen in the four-door sedan on the right.

AMERICANS for 1959

CADILLAC

MORE power is provided for buyers of 1959-model Cadillacs, a new V-8 engine having the swept volume enlarged from 5,980 c.c. to 6,375 c.c. by a ¼-in. increase in piston stroke. Running with a 10½/1 compression ratio, in place of the 10¼/1 used last year, this bigger engine is catalogued as giving 325 b.h.p. in normal form with one four-choke carburetter, whilst a "Q" engine with three twin-choke carburetters provides another 20 b.h.p. and a slight torque increase. The extra engine displacement has allowed a 2.94/1 top gear to be standardized, in place of the 3.07 ratio used last year, so that there should be little increase in fuel consumption.

Use of an X-type chassis continues, as does the optional self-trimming air suspension which is an alternative to four coil springs. More consistent riding is claimed to result from use of non-foaming hydraulic shock absorbers of telescopic pattern, in which Freon-12 trapped inside a plastic sleeve replaces air as the expansion medium. Detail improvements have been made in the power steering, power brakes and automatic choke, all designed to make driving easier.

Pictures show the shape of these 1959 Cadillacs, which are produced as the simplest "60 series," a more luxurious "62 series" which includes the Eldorado models, and a

"Fleetwood 75 series" of formal 8-seaters on long-wheelbase chassis. More glass area is featured by all models, and the optional heating and air-conditioning (refrigeration) systems are improved to give greater rear-seat comfort in extremes of weather. Cruise Control which will govern the car's cruising speed at any desired level on motorways is optional, as are electric door locks and an electrically lifted boot lid.

1959 CADILLAC SPECIFICATION

Cylinders	..	V-8
Bore	..	101.6 mm.
Stroke	..	98.4 mm.
Cubic capacity	..	6,375 c.c.
Piston area	..	100.5 sq. in.
Valves	..	Pushrod o.h.v.
Compression ratio		10.5
Max. power (gross)	325 or 345 b.h.p.	
at	..	4,800 r.p.m.
Max b.m.e.p.	..	167 lb. sq. in. at 3,100 r.p.m. or 169 lb. sq. in. at 3,400 r.p.m.
Top Gear ratio	2.94 1 (3.21 on Eldorado, 3.36 or 3.77 on limousines)	
Wheelbase	10 ft. 10 in. (limousine, 12 ft. 5¼ in.)	
Overall length	18 ft. 9 in. (limousine, 20 ft. 4¼ in.)	
Overall height	4 ft. 5¾ in. to 4 ft. 11¼ in.	
Turning circle..	47 ft. (limousine, 49¼ ft.)	
Brake lining area	..	210.3 sq. in.
Tyre size	..	8.00-15 (Eldorado, 8.20-15)
Top gear m.p.h. at 1,000 r.p.m. 28.7 (with 2.94 axle ratio)		
Top gear m.p.h. at 1,000 ft./min. piston speed	..	44.5

DE SOTO face lifting for 1959 is the first new season's programme to be announced from the Chrysler group of companies. An innovation which will be welcome on such low-built cars is the use of seats which swivel through 40° to facilitate entry or exit, and the push-button control fashion is extended from the automatic transmission to the interior heater. Also standardized is an oval steering wheel, power steering being optional. On the technical side, there is a new combination of the existing torsion-bar front suspension with pneumatic rear springs which are self-adjusting to suit whatever load is being carried. Most powerful of a range of alternative engines is the Adventurer V-8 developing a gross power output of 350 b.h.p.

WHEN a product is recognized as "The Standard of the World" by consumers and competitors alike, that product has arrived at a very enviable position in the marketplace.

In the case of domestic automobiles, the Cadillac motor car has attained such a summit only because the people responsible for its continued success have never stopped striving for a superior machine. And, for 1960 they're still at it!

Cleaner and more subdued than the 1959 car, this year's Cadillac is probably the most handsome version of the marque ever offered. The overall styling has been toned down from last year with a less radical fin treatment at the rear and a new grille.

The latter is a slightly convex plane with a series of bright-metal "dots" or jewel-like ornaments, set into a field of vertical and horizontal bars. It presents a tasteful front exposure when coupled with dual headlamps and a massive, projected one-piece bumper.

The side panel sheet metal treatment is basically the same, varying only as to trim application from model to model. On the more expensive Biarritz version and also on the Seville, a thin chrome side moulding accentuates the lines and the body contours.

Another luxurious note is the addition of a fabric top for the 60 Special series. The top is of a grained material, dyed to match the body colors and outlined by a narrow molding, edged in chrome.

The rear end is distinctive on all models with a new "back grille" treatment and a very attractive taillight cluster. The rear fins have lost their "moon rocket-ish" feeling and now follow the Brougham lines with a sharp concave line that pierces upward and outward at the fender's end with a taillight lens set into the curvature.

Inside, the 1960 Cadillac is just as you'd expect it would be: Plushy and fully adorned with devices to make Cadillac owners a very happy, comfortable breed. A large array of upholstery fabrics and leathers are offered.

In keeping with a General Motors' trend for 1960, more foot room for the front seat's center passenger is available in this year's Cadillac. This space is achieved by a thinner, narrower transmission case that allows a lower, narrower tunnel hump. The new tunnel is one inch less in height and three inches less in width than last year's.

The 1959 lineup of 13 models is carried over into 1960 with basically the same dimensions remaining on all series. The only variance in size is the width with 80.2 inches being the norm last year as compared to 79.9 inches for 1960.

In the engineering area, two new items are of interest. The first is a vacuum released parking brake, a "first" for Cadillac and the industry.

The new anchor works in such a way that the brake is released automatically when the car with engine running is put in gear. With such an arrangement it is now impossible to drive the car with the brake even slightly applied, as is the case with a completely manual unit.

The other significant mechanical item worth mentioning is the rear brake assembly that now employs finned, extended rear drums coupled with larger rear wheel cylinders.

The finned drums of course dissipate the heat faster than conventional units and, because of their extended casting, they can now employ the larger cylinders, thus reducing front brake load.

A general "smoothing over" of the engine to achieve quieter performance and a few minor changes and improvements in an already velvet ride, complete the car's mechanical advances for 1960. ●

1960 ANALYSIS
CADILLAC

DIMENSIONS COMPARED (in inches)

	Car	Wheelbase	Length	Height	Width	Front Tread	Rear Tread
1960	Cadillac	130.0	225.0	56.2	79.9	61.0	61.0
1959	Cadillac	130.0	225.0	56.2	80.2	61.0	61.0

NOTES—Dimensions above are of the 1959 and 1960 Sixty Two Series sedan.

ENGINES

Cubic Inches	Type	Compression	Carburetors	Torque	Horsepower
390	ohv V-8	10.5	4-barrel	430	325
390	ohv V-8	10.5	three 2-barrel	435	345

NOTES—All models are equipped with Hydramatic transmissions. Series 60, 62, Seville and Biarritz are available with rear axle ratios of 2.94 or 3.21. The Fleetwood 75 is offered in ratios of 3.36 or 3.77.

THIN, TAIL-INCLOSED taillights show close resemblance to the plush Brougham once again. Back-up lights and exhausts share gun-implacement-type berths within the confines of the rear fender extremities.

Cadillac's
ELDORADO BROUGHAM

AMERICA'S COSTLIEST CAR, the Cadillac Eldorado Brougham has never before been subjected to impartial analysis. Though it has 345 hp, weight of special equipment slows its performance.

by John Lawlor

TWO STORAGE COMPARTMENTS, recessed into the shelf behind the rear seat, typify the details to be found in the Brougham. Each holds almost a cubic foot and can be individually locked.

FABULOUSLY expensive automobiles are not only interesting in themselves, they provide exacting standards by which lesser vehicles can be judged. Thus, MOTOR LIFE has published reports on such cars as the Continental Mark II, the Rolls-Royce Silver Cloud and, now, the Cadillac Eldorado Brougham.

The Brougham was made available by George Barris, the well-known customizing and paint expert, who had just given it a beautiful pearlescent green finish for the new owner. Time did not permit a full road test but the car was driven over as many road surfaces as possible and basic performance figures were recorded.

Essentially, the Brougham is a regular Cadillac with a custom-built body and most every known item of special equipment included as standard.

The body is a Cadillac design with a Fleetwood label but is actually built by Italy's Pinin Farina.

Barris pointed out several details of Farina's workmanship to the test crew. Seams are hammer welded without the use of solder, potential rust spots have been filled with sealer, the chrome trim is made from brass castings and protective flanges

TRIPLE CARBURETOR ENGINE, also used in Eldorado coupe and convertible, is buried under plumbing for accessories. Small two-cylinder motor at lower left is air suspension compressor.

under the car prevent the rocker panel scraping on steep driveways.

As one would expect, the hood, trunk and doors all fit perfectly. Tolerances along the panel edges do not vary a fraction of an inch.

The trunk, though smaller than usual, is fully carpeted with matching covers for the spare tire and battery, which balance each other at opposite sides of the compartment.

When a rear door is opened, the quarter window slides back a couple of inches to allow more room for entry and exit. The usefulness of this feature was proven on the test car when one of the windows jammed and made it noticeably more difficult to pass through the narrow door opening.

The windshield design revives conventional pillars, anticipating a feature that will be seen on many '60 and '61 cars. Arched well into the roof, it measures a full three feet at the center.

From the front seat, this massive expanse of glass loses much of its glamour. There are annoying reflections in the upper corners and the sun warms the legs of occupants even with the air conditioner going full blast.

The interior, upholstered in a soft broadcloth, is full of mysterious little storage compartments and warning lights. The instrument panel is stock, supplemented by a dazzling array of controls for all the accessories.

Some of the earlier Brougham's most elaborate features, such as the power-operated hood and deck lids, have been abandoned on the new model.

The Eldorado engine is a triple carburetor version of the familiar Cadillac V-8, producing 345 hp at 4800 rpm, and the rear axle ratio is 3.21-to-1. The only chassis modification has been the substitution of air bags for the coil springs.

Despite 20 added horsepower and lower gearing, the weight of the Brougham's custom body with all its power equipment resulted in a 0-to-60 time of 11.7 seconds, 1.4 seconds slower than the standard 62 sedan tested earlier this year.

It was interesting to note a difference in performance with the air conditioner on, 0-to-30 in 4.7 seconds against 4.5 with it off, an indication of the power it takes to keep cool.

The ride was extremely smooth. The air suspension took the roughness out of just about any surface at any speed. When the car crossed railroad tracks, for example, they were heard more than felt.

There was a slight floating sensation at cruising speeds, but a much milder one than on softly-sprung conventional car.

At no time was there the frame quiver that has been experienced on other Cadillac test cars, though a slight rumble was noticed at about 50 mph, possibly due to inadequate undercoating.

Otherwise, the noise level was quite low. Aside from the air conditioning blower, the hum of the tires on the pavement was about the loudest thing to be heard.

In general, the car felt like what it was, a refined Cadillac. Would it be worth the $13,075 asking price? To those who appreciate extremely fine workmanship and the prestige of exclusive styling, yes. These are the Brougham's prime advantages over a regular Cadillac, since the latter can be almost as lavishly equipped.

More than anything else, the Brougham pointed out the value to be had in today's lower priced cars. There is simply not the difference that once existed between the cheapest models and the most expensive. ●

ELEGANT INTERIOR features luxurious broadcloth upholstery, has extra clock mounted behind front seat, red warning lights to indicate door is open. Instrument panel is stock Cadillac.

DISTINCTIVE BROUGHAM STYLING, enhanced by a special Barris paint finish, was created in Detroit though body construction is by Italy's Pinin Farina. Non-wraparound windshield design, easing front seat access, is sure to be seen on other cars in near future. Mounted on standard 130-inch Cadillac wheelbase, car measures same 225 inches overall length as stock 62 sedan.

CADILLAC COMMENTS

GOLD
BEHIND THE
GLITTER

Fast, comfortable, well made and nice to drive, the Cadillac is something unexpected out of Detroit, reports ex-American car critic, PETER HALL.

Low, long and with enormous fins, the Cadillac is an immensely impressive car, but really too big for Australian city use, in spite of power assistance for everything.

I HAVE sneered with the best of them at the juggernauts of North America.

I have looked with distaste and a superior curl of the lip at the dollar-grin, at the acreage of chromium and the misshapen, vulgar fins.

But recently I came face to face with the greatest juggernaut of them all and reeled from the most monstrous grin — that spreading across the wide flat face of the newest Cadillac to reach Australia.

I was forced to admire the great quality of the finish, the strange, twisted dignity it gained through sheer size.

Then I got what is one of the rarest occurences in the history of Australian motor journalism — a full-scale road test of the monster Cadillac.

At the end I was forced to withdraw from my sneering attitude. Don't get me wrong, I still believe the grin is an affront to good taste, the size

is unnecessary and wasteful and the glamor concept not in keeping with the dignity of a great motor car.

Because that is what I am forced to admit — the Cadillac is undoubtedly a great car, probably one of the finest 10 automobiles built in the world today, certainly the best sedan built in North America.

The Cadillac I tested was a Series 62 six-light hardtop sedan first registered (brand new) in Australia last December. A new model of the Series 62 has been released in America since then, but it is identical mechanically to the one I tested and **has only** minor bodywork modifications to distinguish it as a new model.

The Series 62 is the basic range of Cadillacs and is available as normal four door sedans, convertibles and the hardtop. More expensive Caddies (as the natives know them) range up to the El Dorado Brougham, leather-trimmed with a polished stainless steel roof that sells in the USA for

as much as a Ferrari (about 14,000 dollars).

Very few Cadillacs ever make their way into Australia and some of the ones that have done so in the past have done so more-or-less under the lap of the law. So how this one arrived is quite an interesting story.

Apparently General Motors sent the car to this country for a special client (no one will say who, but it may have been a diplomat) but once it arrived here, it proved unsuitable (I believe the true story is that it should have been colored white but that GM made the mistake of sending a black one and the customer would not have it.)

Whatever really happened, GM-H here obtained a Customs' clearance to sell the car in this country. It was bought by well-known radio and TV star Bob Dyer for his almost equally well-known wife, Dolly. They loved the machine, but it was just too big both for Dolly to drive around

prize for being the most accurate car speedometer I have ever driven behind. Most of the instruments were warning lights, including one that stayed on until the handbrake was released.

The "hand" brake, incidentally, was foot-operated in much the same manner as on the current model Ford Fairlane and Custom in Australia. It is a pedal on the floor, smaller than the footbrake but operated in the same way. A small catch is pressed by the foot to release it. A very powerful brake, it would undoubtedly be most useful in the emergency of the main system failing.

Vision was magnificent through the vast windscreen and windows. From the aesthetic point of view you can take or leave the soaring fins at the back, but they have the advantage from the driver's point of view that he knows exactly what the monstrous rocket-like rear end of the Cadillac is doing.

On test the car handled remarkably well. It had the solid, level ride one would expect from a vehicle with a kerb weight of 43 cwt, but none of the floating on rubber cushions feel that is pretty standard equipment with American cars especially when, like the Cadillac, they have coil springs all round.

This Cadillac was rock-steady on all surfaces. At one stage of the test I took it over a bad, disused railway crossing at more that 100 mph with three other passengers on board. Apart from a barely perceptible nose-down action as it hit the deep bump, the car showed no signs at all of the terrific whack with which it must have hit the depression.

On corners its stability was as surprising as its firmness was on straight highways and corrugated back roads.

crowded Sydney and to fit into the already well-supplied Dyer garage. By the time they sold it, the car was barely run in.

I came across it a few days after well-known car auctioneer Jack Linacre drove it down from Sydney. He put it into the hands of Rhodes Motors, the Melbourne Cadillac agents who sell a lot more Holdens than Caddies, and in between it being shown to starry-eyed prospective buyers, I was handed the keys.

The massive car had done just on 2000 miles and was, in every respect, showroom new. Jack Linacre (who was tempted to cancel his recently lodged order for a new Thunderbird and sell his 1955 Cadillac to keep this one) had even polished underneath the wings.

My first surprise was at the high quality of the Cadillac's finish. There was not a blemish on the black duco, not a panel even a fraction out of place and having looked at quite a few recent model high-priced American machines, that was quite a surprise. The doors shut with a nice clunk, there was no sign of a hit-or miss welding job.

The interior was luxuriously appointed in a glamorous, but not over-showy way. The upholstery was thick, silver tinted plastic, closely pleated and resembling cloth in appearance. The seat edges and door coverings were a light grey plastic to contrast with the dominant black tonings. The floor was covered with rich, thick, black carpet.

All the best American effort-saving devices were in profusion. Every window, including the quarter vents, was operated by a push button. There were four cigarette lighters, four ash trays, door handles that formed part of the arm rests and a superb rear vision mirror that was adjustable inside the car.

The front seat lacked a centre arm rest and the glove box could have

been larger but the tinted glass all round covered any other sins in the sunny Melbourne weather.

The second great surprise came when I tried to manoeuvre the huge vehicle out of Rhodes' kennel-size upstairs showroom. The steering was so light I nearly sent the Caddy spinning around in an expensive circle. The power operating the steering system would be just about as effective as any I've ever sampled.

The driving position was utterly comfortable. The big wheel sat nicely in the lap, the huge brake pedal and accelerator were perfectly placed and everything needed to operate the car (including a row of six buttons for all the windows) was at my fingertips.

The instrument cluster was set back in a huge, slightly-raised cavity right in front of the driver. The speedo was a massive, easy-to-read affair graduated to 120 mph. It takes the

Instrument layout is typically American, but the speedo was almost dead accurate, according to tester Hall.

Caddie has four doors, uses hardtop style body. All windows are electrical.

CADILLAC COMMENTS—GOLD BEHIND THE GLITTER

Plenty of room was needed to get it around tight corners fast but that was due to its great size not to any lack of inherent cornering ability. It would be stretching things too far to suggest that the Caddy cornered like a sports car, but it did corner incomparably better than anything else we have seen from Detroit for many years.

Part of the Cadillac's handling secret was its superb power steering which included something which other power steering systems lack — directness. The Cadillac division of General Motors seem to have accepted the obvious — that with power available to take all the effort out of turning a big car, there is no reason to have ridiculously low steering box ratios and steering wheels that need to be madly wound to get from lock to lock.

The Cadillac's was as direct as anyone could want and also permitted just that small amount of road feel to be transmitted from the front wheels to the driver's hands — the feel that makes the difference between a driver's car and just another hunk of transport.

The automatic transmission was one of the best ever to come to Australia. The Hydramatic system, based on the first General Motors' system which became available just before the Second World War on Cadillac, it is standard equipment in America now on Cadillac and Oldsmobile.

It differs from every other system by having four speeds and two different "drive" settings.

They are together on the selector quadrant, but one is for city work and fast, short hauls; the other is for high speed cruising.

The first position uses only the three lower gears and takes the car well over the 100 mph mark. It also keeps each ratio in operation to a higher speed. If needed, for more sustained full-blooded acceleration.

The other position tends to conserve engine revs and petrol (using it, Jack Linacre got 18 mpg on a fast run from Sydney to Melbourne) by bringing in fourth gear, which is actually an overdrive, at high speeds. On my maximum speed runs, this "top" ratio came in at about 90 mph. It was quite an uncanny feeling to sense the gears shifting automatically below the floor at that speed.

The other positions on the selector quadrant are quite normal — park, neutral, low and reverse.

The Cadillac's performance, as you can see by the figures, was little short of sensational. Remember, this car weighed 43 cwt unladen and all the performance figures were taken with four aboard, none of them remotely approaching the midget class in size.

The secret of that is in the sheer brute force in the 325 bhp 6.4 litre engine. The surprise here was that it delivered its power in such utter silence, with such luxurious smoothness.

The power brakes equal the car's performance. No discs either, just massive drums with more than 210 square inches of lining area.

It is high and brassy and not the most beautiful car in the world, but the Cadillac would be hard to beat on the scores of performance, comfort, driving ease and sheer impressiveness.

However, this could easily be the last really big Cadillac for many years since Detroit is having a shrinking campaign which, for 1961, has short-ende the immense Caddie by some nine inches.

Apparently the influence of compact cars has been so great that the long suffering American public has decided that its full sized cars are too big. Now they want the big cars to be more manageable, shorter and easier to use around town with pretty much the same kind of performance and effort-reducing equipment.

Just how the Caddie will look in a couple of years time remains to be seen, of course. Following previous GM practice it will include all the expensive goodies which eventually find their way onto the cheaper cars in far less costly form.

Unlike so many American luxury cars, the Cadillac's place on the US market seems highly secure financially. Throughout the world it is a symbol of good living and success.

Few cars conjure such visions of rather gawdy luxury as the Cadillac. In days gone by it lived in the same class as Packard, Lincoln, Stutz and Rolls-Royce, but now Packard is no longer with us, nor is Stutz. Lincoln has become a medium priced branch of the Ford family. Rolls-Royce and Cadillac are the surviving members of the group and represent pretty much the same thing on different sides of the Atlantic.   #

Specifications:

MAKE:
Cadillac series 62, four-door hardtop.

AVAILABILITY:
Only one in Australia.

PRICE:
About £7000.

ENGINE:
Cylinders, eight; pattern, V8; valves, over-head, pushrod operated; **bore and stroke, 4 x 3.875 in**; capacity, 390 cu in (6400 cc); compression ratio, 10.5 to 1; bhp, **325 at 4800 rpm**; capacity fuel tank, 17½ gallons.

TRANSMISSION:
Hydramatic automatic with four ratios; rear axle ratio, 2.94 to 1.

SUSPENSION:
Front, independent by coil springs; rear, live axle, coil springs.

BRAKES:
Hydraulic, servo-assisted drum brakes, 210 sq in lining area.

STEERING:
Power assisted. Turning circle, 47 feet.

ELECTRICAL EQUIPMENT:
Voltage, 12; standard equipment includes electrically operated windows, four cigar lighters, four headlights, flashing turn indicators, clock, electric screen wipers.

WHEELS AND TYRES:
Type, pressed steel discs; tyre size, 8 x 15.

DIMENSIONS:
Wheelbase, 10 ft 10 in; length, 18 ft 9 in; width 6 ft 8 in; height, 4 ft 8in.

Performance:

TOP SPEED:
115.38 mph

ACCELERATION:
Standing quarter mile, average 18.2 sec; best time, 18.1 sec; through gears, 0-30, 3.6 sec; 0-40, 5.6 sec; 0-50, 6.8 sec; 0-60, 10.6 sec; 0-70, 12.0 sec; 0-80, 18 sec; in drive, 20-40, 3.4 sec; 40-60, 4.6 sec.

SPEEDOMETER CALIBRATIONS:
Variation throughout the entire speed range was never more than 4.5 mph.

FUEL CONSUMPTION:
Overall on hard test: 12.1 mpg.

WEIGHT:
43 cwt at the kerb.

TEST CONDITIONS:
Weather, cold, no wind; road dry; surface, non-skid bitumen.

TEST CAR FROM:
Rhodes Motors, Elizabeth Street, Melbourne.

THE standards of judgment in the three-car luxury field—Cadillac, Imperial and Lincoln—must be rightfully high to match the $5000 to $7000 price range. These three cars don't offer any more practical transportation than the fast, capable and comfortable cars of the medium-priced field such as Olds, Mercury or the Chrysler Windsor. Therefore they must have some extra margin of value to attract and justify that extra couple of thousand dollars that buyers are willing to pay. Let's look at some of the differences between the luxury three and the mediums.

First of all the luxury cars are larger. Wheelbases are longer and overall lengths are greater. This stretchout provides practical benefits in return for the greater bulk of car. Rear seat legroom is greater and rear doors are, (in some cases), wider, permitting easier entry and exit. Trunk space, too, is generally greater than on the mediums, although the larger cross section tires take up more room.

The big luxury cars do give a ride that's more comfortable than the average medium priced car, although anyone who could seriously fault the Olds, Mercury or Chrysler's riding qualities must be nearly as sensitive as the legendary princess who felt the uncomfortable rose petal beneath the nine mattresses. Be that as it may, the upholstery on the top ticket jobs is a bit softer and a bit more luxurious beneath one than the cushions of the mediums.

Then, too, there is the generally quieter operation of the three luxury cars due to more and better soundproofing. There are also more luxury details such as ash trays and cigar lighters at every seat, power operated trunk lids, radio antennae, and front vent windows, as well as rear arm rests and the like.

The upholstery on these luxury bracket cars is, as always, a sensuous delight   CONTINUED

BEST CAR BUY Luxury Price Field

cadillac
still the champ

to loll on. However, having spent so much effort to achieve comfortable cushioning it always puzzles me why none of the three major carmakers provide reclining seatbacks and headrests as do Studebaker, American Motors and a number of foreign cars.

To get down to the difficult business of choosing between the Lincoln, Cadillac and Imperial, the differences in quality are less this year than they have been in the last several years. Lincoln has perfected its engineering so that production of its large unit body no longer poses quality control problems that troubled the car in 1958. Imperial, too, has improved production standards so that there are very few sources of discontent from a car properly prepared for delivery by the dealer.

Of course, for this year none of the three cars has received major body or engineering changes, though Lincoln has a new curved backlight and rear roofline, Cadillac a milder fin, rear bumper and grille treatment, and Imperial a new grille, new rear fenders and rear deck plus considerable change in exterior trim. However, all three cars are basically unchanged mechanically. All have the same big, quiet engines as they used last year. Many refinements have been made all in the direction of detail improvement, reliability and trouble-free-operation.

cadillac

Continued on page 47

MORE THAN ANY OTHER single Detroit car, Cadillac has come to symbolize those things that the luxury class stands for. The road test conclusions indicate that this is largely justified. Strangely, Cadillac also has the most conservative overall design of any car in the luxury field. Undoubtedly the reason for this is that Cadillac long ago won its spurs as a prestige car and no longer needs to use startling gimmicks or garish ornamentation to make the car different.

The test car, a Sedan de Ville, was a four-door hardtop which Cadillac identifies as a six-window model. Essentially all closed Cadillacs are hardtops, the main difference being in the roof style. A four-window style has a flat roof with a bigger rear window. Rounding out the line are two convertibles and the limousines.

Cadillac has only one powerplant this year, the 390-cubic-inch V-8 that has been revised several times since it first appeared in 1949. There have been no basic changes this year except that no options are offered; the triple two-barrel version of last year has been dropped. The four-barrel version of the test car produces 325 hp at 4800 rpm and 430 lbs.-ft. of torque at 3100 rpm.

The rear axle ratio was 3.21-to-1. Three other gearsets are available, 2.94, 3.36 and 3.77. However, Cadillac does not encourage interchanging the ratios and flatly states that the 3.21 is mandatory when equipped with air conditioning.

When the acceleration tests were finished, Cadillac proved to be the best performer of the three, but only by one-tenth of a second at the 0-60-mph mark. Judged by a broader scope of cars, it falls into the moderately better performers. Of course, the luxury class no longer is rated against the hot cars, and Cadillac's performance is normal for its class.

Along with its better performance and higher gearing, the Cadillac turned in what is usually considered normal gasoline economy for its class. The 8-to-12-mpg average, however, is considerably lower than most standard-size sedans.

Cadillac's most obvious quality is a good ride with reasonably good stability at high speeds. Stability is considerably improved over last year, when the car had a tendency to wallow at highway speeds.

The better stability can probably be traced to a redesigned front suspension. Last year the wishbone-type arm was held rigid at three points — steering knuckle

CADILLAC

A NEW TREND TO CONSERVATIVE LUXURY

and two places on the frame. This year Cadillac engineers have connected the lower control arm at one place on the frame and on the steering knuckle. A diagonal tie strut is used to control fore-and-aft deflection of the front wheels.

Besides helping improve the stability and ride, the new suspension design made it possible to move the front brake drums into the air stream. By adding fins onto the extended drums, greater cooling results. Since the wheel cylinders are larger, brakes are more efficient, with less fade.

Each year Cadillac adds some kind of additional sound insulation. This year there is a new rubber support for the intermediate propeller shaft bearing and all the joints in the suspension are made through rubber bushings, which act as road noise isolators. So complete is the insulation, in fact, that engineers had to add a copper strap from the suspension to the frame to keep tire static out of the radio.

All this insulation actually made little difference inside the passenger compartment. In last year's test, no mechanical noises were detected, and this year the same proved true. Inside, only the loudest of outside noises ever came through when the windows were rolled up.

Power steering is standard equipment and has practically no feel of the road. At any speed all driving is done visually, with no road shocks to tell the driver what is happening. There has been a change in the power unit so that even less effort is now required. Another change in the steering geometry (the steering circle is three feet less) makes the car more maneuverable. This has been fairly effective, and getting into and out of tight parking spaces is noticeably easier.

Cadillac has a new body this year, but the styling is so close to last year's that most of the design benefits could easily be overlooked. At the front door the dogleg has been eliminated, greatly improving entry and exit. But a more important change is in the rear door, which is six inches wider and opens 7½ inches farther. This makes getting into and out of the back seat exceptionally good, in fact, probably the easiest of any domestic four-door sedan. This is a major quality in a luxury sedan, where the back seat is often as important as the front.

Cadillac's back seat is one of Detroit's roomiest, with more than generous legroom. In front the dimensions are only average, although ample. The upholstery padding was firmer than any other car in Cadillac's class, although this in no way interfered with comfort. In fact, for most drivers on long trips the firmer padding was preferred. The upholstery material was only average for the luxury class (there are 112 others available, ranging up to the most expensive fabrics), but it was durable, attractive and well fitted.

Along with its conservative interior, Cadillac has a conservative dash panel and

Driver control buttons are arranged in practical and extremely convenient layout. Nearly all controls can be operated with left hand, and many of these without moving arm from the armrest.

driver controls — although there are more controls than are found on the average sedan. However, the layout is extraordinarily practical. Without moving his left arm from the armrest the driver can open the door, lock or unlock all doors, open or close any window or either front vent, adjust the front seat six ways or adjust the outside rear view mirror. Within easy reach of his left hand the driver can also set the Cruise Control to a desired speed and turn on the lights, air conditioning or windshield wiper. On the right are only three controls ordinarily used when driv-

Cadillac's engine compartment is exceptionally crowded. Notice components placed in front of radiator.

ing: radio, heater and ignition. Once the radio is on and the volume adjusted, stations can be changed with a foot control. This means that the right hand is seldom necessary for any adjustments. This is an excellent arrangement; since most people are right-handed, it is only natural to assume that driving would be safer if the left hand is removed from the wheel.

The glove compartment is new this year and has been designed like a bin. This, Cadillac claims, makes it virtually impossible for anything to roll out. But since it is so small, it is practically impossible to get enough in it to worry about the contents spilling out.

Another new interior feature is the steering wheel, which is 16 inches in diameter, one inch smaller than last year. The smaller wheel is possible, no doubt, because of the more effective power steering, but is also a psychological factor in making the interior seem larger.

One accessory, the power deck lid lock, is a switch inside the glove compartment. It works slightly different from other similar devices, in that it unlocks the trunk and only raises the deck lid slightly. Even though the trunk space is rated high in cubic capacity, it is not as efficiently laid out as it could be — and lacks the deep well arrangement of many other GM standard-size sedans.

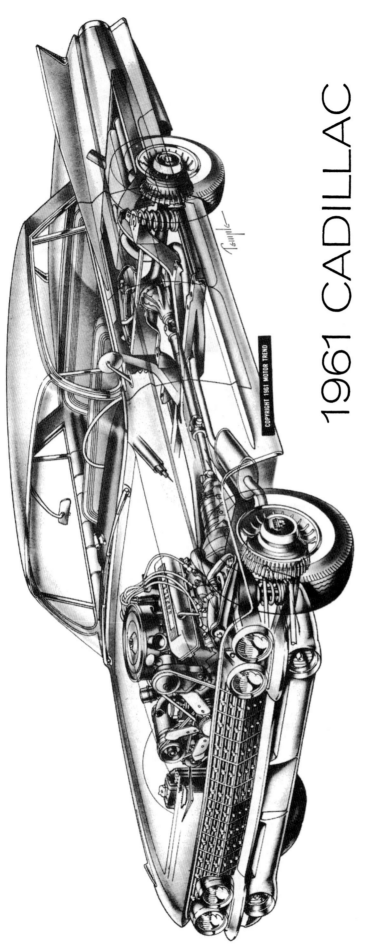

1961 CADILLAC

COPYRIGHT 1961 MOTOR TREND

TEST CAR: Cadillac Sedan de Ville
BODY TYPE: 4-door hardtop
BASE PRICE: $5498

OVERALL LENGTH: 222 inches
OVERALL WIDTH: 79.8 inches
OVERALL HEIGHT: 56.3 inches
WHEELBASE: 129.5 inches
TREAD, FRONT/REAR: 61 and 61 inches
SHIPPING WEIGHT: 4710 lbs.
STEERING: 3.7 turns lock-to-lock
TURNING CIRCLE: 43 feet curb-to-curb
GROUND CLEARANCE: 5.3 inches

SEATING CAPACITY: Six
FRONT SEAT
   HEADROOM: 34.3 inches
   HIPROOM: 59.7 inches
   LEGROOM: 45.6 inches
TRUNK CAPACITY: 17 cubic feet

TYPE: Ohv V-8
DISPLACEMENT: 390 cubic inches
BORE & STROKE: 4.0 x 3.8
COMPRESSION RATIO: 10.25-to-1
CARBURETION: Single 4-barrel
HORSEPOWER: 325 @ 4800 rpm
TORQUE: 430 @ 3100 rpm
TRANSMISSION: Automatic
REAR AXLE RATIO: 3.21

GAS MILEAGE: 8 to 12 miles per gallon
ACCELERATION: 0-30 mph in 3.8 seconds,
               0-45 mph in 6.7 seconds and
               0-60 mph in 10.4 seconds
SPEEDOMETER ERROR: Indicated 30, 45 and 60
               mph are actual 29.5, 44
               and 58.5 mph respec-
               tively
ODOMETER ERROR: Indicated 100 miles is
               actual 96.5 miles
WEIGHT-POWER RATIO: 14.5 lbs. per horse-
               power
HORSEPOWER PER CUBIC INCH: .834

CADILLAC AND PRESTIGE have been synonymous for years. Perhaps more than any other car, the line represents luxury to the general public. This year, as might be expected, the changes are mostly refinements and are slanted primarily towards promoting passenger comfort, convenience and luxury.

There are, however, slight indications that Cadillac is somewhat influenced by today's trends toward smaller cars. Overall length has been reduced by three inches under last year's 225 inches. Height, however, has been increased from .1-inch to 1.7 inches on various models. And although wheelbase and width remain the same the turning circle is now 43 feet, three feet less than last year. These changes are not startling, to be sure, but they perhaps prove that the current compact car thinking is making minor, but significant, inroads with standard size cars.

Passenger comfort is an important commodity at Cadillac and although exterior length is less, the legroom inside has been increased slightly. Another comfort development was made by increasing the seat bench height and redesigning the seat

comes about as a result of the new front suspension and a redesigned body structure. The new structure permits the reduction of several mounts in the center of the body, eliminating points of noise and vibration transmission from the chassis to the body. There is also a new-type rubber support for the propeller shaft, adding to the smoothness of the driveline.

Besides being quieter, the 1961 Cadillac should be easier to steer. The power steering pump is new and more powerful, so less effort is required in steering or parking.

Inside this year's Cadillac are several changes in keeping with the overall luxury theme of the car. For example there are 24 new upholstery combinations, making a total of 113 choices, which should be enough variety to suit any taste. The instrument panel and cluster are newly designed and although it won't be extremely noticeable, the steering wheel is one-inch smaller in diameter this year. The glovebox is now of the bin type which makes it virtually impossible for anything to roll out. But perhaps the most important interior development will be on the convertible. Bucket seats will be available for the first time. They remain optional on the Biarritz.

COUPE DE VILLE

position for a better angle. Due partly to the increase in height and partly to a lower floorpan there is also more headroom inside.

Perhaps the most noticeable change in the passenger compartment is something which is a direct result of the new styling. The windshield still slopes rearward but the dogleg has been eliminated. This, along with other design changes, made it possible to design the rear doors to open an additional 7.5 inches. Since the rear doors are also six inches wider, entry and exit should be much easier. Another interior dimension that has changed as a result of styling is the carrying capacity of the trunk, which has been increased to 18.25 cubic feet, nearly two cubic feet more than was available last year.

Cadillac, a car with many accessory options, will not confuse anyone with engine options—there are none. The 390-cubic-inch ohv V-8 is relatively unchanged this year. The performance ratings, 325 hp @ 4800 rpm and torque, 430 ft. lbs. @ 3100 rpm, are the same, as is the compression ratio, 10.5-to-1. This is the four-barrel carburetor version from last year. Not available in 1961 is the triple two-barrel carburetor model that was previously offered.

Other mechanical changes are mostly refinements, but one important development is the lubricaton-free chassis.

Cadillac's front suspension is new. One of its major features is a lower control arm and an adjustable strut rod to control fore-and-aft deflection of the front wheels. With this new suspension it was possible to move the front brake drums into the air stream. The brake drums now have fins for greater cooling results, but perhaps the most important brake development is that the wheel cylinder is now larger, increasing hydraulic leverage between master and wheel cylinder.

Cadillac, which was probably as well insulated from the road as any American-made automobile, has made several changes to make the passenger compartment even quieter. Part of this

CADILLAC

SIX-WINDOW SEDAN

CONVERTIBLE

FLEETWOOD SIXTY SPECIAL

*'61 keynote is still luxury—
more room, greater comfort*

Accessories have always been extra-important on luxury cars, and Cadillac has made a few changes this year. A new rear window defogger is now available and a new type non-slip differential is being offered. But the most important change in the accessory line-up is a new method of operating the air conditioning and heating system. Both units can now be turned on at the same time. This might seem a little odd at first—heating and cooling the passenger compartment at the same time. But in cold, rainy weather it will be possible to warm the air at lower levels while the air conditioner is cooling and dehumidifying the air at breathing level. ●

1961 CADILLAC

Engines

Cubic Inches	Type	Compression Ratio	Carburetors	Torque	Horsepower
390	V-8	10.5:1	4-bbl.	430	325

Notes: Only one engine is offered for all Cadillacs in 1961. Same engine was standard last year, but there was an optional Eldorado 345-hp using three 2-bbl. carbs available, which has been dropped.

Dimensions Compared (in inches)

	Car	Wheelbase	Length	Height	Width	Front Tread	Rear Tread
1961	Cadillac 60, 62	129.5	222.0	56.0	79.8	61.0	61.0
	Fleetwood 75	150.0	242.0	59.1	80.6	61.0	61.0
1960	Cadillac 60, 62	130.0	225.0	56.2	79.9	61.0	61.0
	Fleetwood 75	149.8	244.8	59.3	79.9	61.0	61.0

Notes: In 1960 the Eldorado series had a number of dimensional differences from other Cadillacs. In 1961 the Eldorado's specifications are largely identical to the 60 and 62 series.

CADILLAC

a decrease in length and option offerings

CADILLAC'S LEADERSHIP in tle luxury class of U.S. cars is undisputed. As such it undoubtedly is a kind of bellwether, a fact which makes its 1961 major changes in design direction of particular interest and significance.

The net results of these changes are shorter cars, simplification of engine options and a retrenchment in the special series offerings that in the past have been a conspicuous feature of the Cadillac line.

The mark of a domestic prestige car in general, and with Cadillac in particular, until now has been impressiveness from massive size. For the new model year, however, the Cadillacs are approximately three inches shorter than in 1960. The 1961 Cadillacs, outside the limousine category, are 222 inches long, compared with 225 inches of the preceding models. And even the limousines have been shortened from 245 inches to 242.

None of the car's other exterior dimensions have been signif cantly altered. Where there are differences from 1960, they amount to no more than fractions of an inch. Widths of the different series and body types average out to close to 80 inches, overall height 56 inches.

The engine picture couldn't be simpler. There is just one Cadillac engine for all series, a 390-cubic-inch V-8 rated at 325 hp. This is the same plant that served most Cadillacs last year, with a four-barrel carburetor. Not available are any higher horsepower options, such as the 1960 345-hp unit that used three two-barrel carburetors. All series, of course, have the Hydramatic automatic as the standard transmission with a 2.94 axle ratio, except the limousines, which use a 3.36 gearing.

There are three series of 1961 Cadillacs: the Fleetwood 60.

the 62 and the 75 limousine series. The basic body types are similar to those of preceding model years, with one very notable exception.

Gone are the super-luxury cars that represented the ultimate in prestige. The famed Eldorado series of the 1950's has been reduced to the position of a name only for one version of the 62 series. And dropped entirely is the limited-production Eldorado Brougham that once had a $10,000-plus price tag. The top-of-the-line now is the Fleetwood 60 Special, which in 1961 has special styling characteristics.

It was Cadillac that led the GM parade several years ago into the age of the full-wrap windshield that also resulted in elbow or dogleg front pillar that seriously interfered with easy and graceful front-seat entry and exit. This design defect has now been remedied by adopting a new pillar that slopes, rather than forming a sharp angle, and is the most satisfactory solution.

Cadillac also has devised doors that are wider and swing open further for the 1961 models. New interior feature is a glove box of the bin type.

Engineering innovations include the crankcase ventilation device for California cars; a chassis that is claimed to be completely lubrication-free; and despite the aforementioned unchanged dimensions, except the reduction in body length, the effective turning circle of the car has been trimmed by a full three feet down to 43 feet.

The 1961 Cadillacs, therefore, emerge as more "compact" cars, using the term in an especially broad sense, and certainly more maneuverable. A short step but definitely in a different direction.

/MT

Instrument panel of the 1961 Cadillac is newly designed with emphasis on greater visibility and easier operation. Shown below are the Sedan de Ville and Biarritz convertible of the "Sixty-Two" series.

Initial shipment of Caddies is limited to cheaper and smaller Series 62. Imported as left hand drive cars, they are yet to be converted.

Return of the CADILLAC

After many years of absence, Cadillac cars are now being sold again in Australia. Prices range £6000 upwards, depending on the styling you choose.

By PETER HALL

JUST before the Second World War came to upset the normal way of life in Australia there were few cars made anywhere in the world that could not be bought off the showroom floor by those who had the cash or were a reasonable credit risk.

Among the more popular of the fancy cars, in circles where there was enough lucre to justify more than just an idle thought about such matters, was the American-built, and always fully-imported, Cadillac.

Melbourne and Sydney Cadillac admirers, in particular, were well catered for by Rhodes and Lober's, respectively. Of course, many other General Motors dealers — especially in wealthy country areas — had the franchise to sell Cadillacs and their close but unfortunately late relation, La Salle.

In a land where Rolls-Royce was and is, clearly the greatest symbol of worldly success, the Cadillac never achieved quite the status in eyes of the general populus as it did in its home country and among the Arabs.

But it did well and Rhodes, Lobers and numerous other GM dealers

were dissatisfied with the fact of war for other reasons as well as the patriotic ones.

They had high hopes when the war ended that things would return at least to pre-war normal.

But things were not to be so rosy. A tremendous world-wide demand for new cars and a simultaneous shortage of them limited severely the numbers of cars that could be brought into Australia, either in bits or wholly made up overseas.

As far as Cadillac was concerned, few were made in the first year or two after hostilities ceased and those that did come off the production line were quickly gobbled by the hungry American market.

Then, when production increased and it may have been possible to order a few dozen for Australia, government policy here resulted in almost a total ban on the importation of luxury American cars. Dollars were very, very scarce.

A few Cadillacs did find their way to our shores during the 1950s, but most of them were bought by Australians who had dollar funds of their own in America or by American nationals who were working in

Australia for a time and brought the cars with them. They were often eventually sold here. A few were sneaked in under the Custom's Department's nose, but the department was not slow in seizing them.

So, at least in the Cadillac Fan Club, the first big news of 1961 was that Cadillac cars were back in the showrooms of Australia and were available to sale without any risks of Her Majesty's Customs taking an unwelcome interest in them after they were bought.

More accurately, the cars were available in two Australian show-rooms — Rhodes in Melbourne and Lobers in Sydney, who had languished through 20 years of non-Cadillac existence brightened some-what, in both cases, by possession of Holden franchises. Blow-softeners, as you might say.

The buyers who came to the showrooms to inspect the first shipment did not actually stampede. Inquiry was reported to be good and a surprisingly large number of orders were written considering the period of crippling sales tax and credit restriction.

Rhodes were so confident they would do well with Cadillac after the 20-year famine that they imported half a dozen in the initial for stock on spec.

Most of the Cadillacs which had arrived at the time of writing were from the relatively small Series 62 range.

Long (18½ feet), lavish and very glamorous in the American style, they retail at slightly under £6000 including the new 40 percent sales tax.

RETURN OF
THE CADILLAC

The price is almost a pleasant surprise for many potential Cadillac owners who thought more in terms of £7000 or £8000. They forgot (or never knew) that Cadillac prices in the United States range from as low as the medium price bracket (about 4000 dollars) right up to 13,000 dollars plus for extraordinarily lavish Eldorado Brougham which, among other things, has an unpainted stainless steel roof.

An absolute retail price has not yet been fixed for the Cadillac in Australia, because neither Rhodes nor Lobers have yet converted any of the cars from left to right drive.

They have decided to do their own conversions and are joining forces to the extent of swapping expert personnel and exchanging know-how. A Rhodes executive told me they were allowing a generous sum for the conversion and would pass on the almost inevitable savings when the actual cost was finalised, to the customer.

Final price of the car should be between £5850 and £6000.

For that money the Cadillac buyer will get a powerful, luxurious motor car with almost every aid to lazyman's driving that America has yet invented.

He will get a massive 390 cubic inch overhead valve V8 engine that develops something over 300 bhp on the SAE figure. (The American engine had a compression ratio of 10.5 to 1 and develops 325 bhp at 4800 rpm. The models exported to Australia have been fitted with 8.75 to 1 export engines and develop an unknown amount of horsepower on that ratio.)

He will get power steering, a four-speed Hydramatic automatic transmission that is probably the best automatic available in the world today, power-operated windows and front seat and a magnificent fully-automatic American radio.

Other sumptuous features of the car include four cigarette lighters, thick black carpet and black and grey synthetic upholstery.

During a brief drive of a brand new Cadillac that had had no service other than a wash since it left the ship, I found it was everything a Caddy is expected to be — easy to drive, a crowd puller and very comfortable indeed.   #

Much desired by Australians in the years since the war, the Cadillac is now back on the market. Prices are high, ranging upwards from £6000.

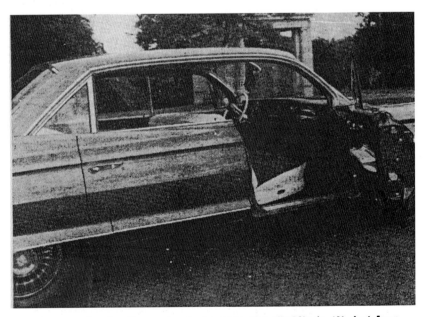

In the popular hardtop sedan body style, this Caddie is 18½ feet long, has huge V8 engine of 390 cu in capacity. Transmission is four speed.

CADILLAC
Continued from page 38

Continued from page 38

These three are about equally easy to drive, that is until you get into dense traffic and close quarters where their king-size dimensions make maneuvering difficult. But for sheer control on winding roads, all of them are surprisingly nimble. Flawless power steering systems and power brakes make light work of the maneuvering.

To summarize my point then, the differences which put one of these three cars ahead of the other are qualitative —a matter of fit, finish and workmanship—rather than quantitative, as measured by ride, handling, or performance. On this basis, Cadillac is my pick, as the differences between it and Imperial or Lincoln are all in the way it is made, not in the way it performs.

Cadillac's paint job is as near to perfection as any in this country, while the quality of metal finishing and the fit of panels and trim strips is unequalled. Squeaks, rattles, loose handles and latches, sloppy trunk lining, jagged metal edges or poorly cut carpets just don't show up on Cadillac. The Cadillac's grille, for example, is as well fitted together as the halves of a watchcase. The upholstery is without peer on this side of the Atlantic.

In short, when you buy one of the cars in the luxury field you pay for quiet, ease, a superb ride and easy handling. You also pay for something extra in the way of quality, something that earns high prestige and justifies high price. There is more of this true quality of product in the Cadillac than can be found in either of its competitors. This in our opinion makes it a best buy. **END**

CADILLAC FLEETWOOD 75
Imperial Limousine

The world's largest production car is a nine-seater which moves quietly at any speed up to 120 m.p.h.

IF sheer size were the greatest virtue in a motor-car, then the Cadillac Fleetwood 75 would take top honours. It covers 136 sq. ft. of roadway, this area deriving from a length of 20ft 4·8in. and a width of 6ft 8in. In height, however, this truly great car could just clear a hypothetical very low bridge which would stop, for instance, a Hillman Minx. There are other U.S. cars with larger engines than the Fleetwood's 6·4-litre vee-8, but the 325 (gross) h.p. which it provides nevertheless can whisk this 2½-ton limousine beyond the reach of many of today's sports cars.

Those who keep abreast of annual styling changes in the U.S. will notice at once from the accompanying photographs that the car under review was a 1960 version. When it was kindly offered for test by a private owner, Mr. J. C. Bamford, the decision to go ahead with a full test on last year's model seemed justified for the following reasons. No example of the 1961 type is likely to become available for testing, and in so far as it might affect performance figures, the mechanical specification remains unchanged. When the 75 was handed over to *The Autocar* it had just received a comprehensive check by the sole importers of Cadillacs Lendrum and Hartman Ltd, of Buick House, Albemarle Street, London, W 1, after covering its first 1,000 miles since new. At the outset it must be admitted that one of this particular car's most interesting features, the full air suspension system which was optional in 1960, is not available on the latest cars.

When first confronted with the task of driving away the big Cadillac, especially when surrounded by members of the concessionaires' staff who are familiar with it, one has only to keep in mind that its size is relative, and that it is dwarfed in turn by most lorries and motor coaches. Even so, one might be forgiven some slight apprehension that handling such a conspicuously outsize car would be a major embarrassment in city traffic and no light responsibility on British country roads.

There are unobtrusive hand grips at each side of the steering wheel, which has long horn pushes recessed in its spokes. The quadrant speedometer is deeply recessed and free from reflections, the interior mirror has a dipping reflector, and the wide sun vizors can be swung to any angle

In practice, the Cadillac follows the tradition of fine cars in seeming to grow progressively smaller and smaller the farther one drives it, although the problem of finding a parking site in town naturally remains. It has a precision and ease of control which make it simpler—and much more enjoyable—to drive than many a car of lesser dimensions.

All Cadillacs have the same size and type of engine, although there are options of compression ratio and carburation. In this case it was the standard unit with a 10·5-to-1 compression ratio, supplied with super premium fuel through a single four-choke Carter carburettor It had the G.M. Hydra-Matic four-speed automatic transmission incorporating two hydraulic clutches, which is also common to all Cadillacs. Whereas current Cadillacs have wishbone-and-coil front suspension and rigid back axles with coil springs, on the test car the steel springs were replaced by rubber bags of the rolling pack mitten variety, primed with compressed air from an engine driven pump.

Nine people can travel in the Cadillac, three of these on two wide auxiliary seats which fold away when not required beneath the partition dividing the front and rear compartments. This can be sealed off completely by a full-width panel of curved glass, which is raised or lowered electrically

48

by a switch placed in each side armrest of the back seat.

As the main purpose of this car is centred round its luxurious passenger compartment, in which two people can travel in such space and comfort as befits a car costing over £7,600, it merits a more comprehensive description than usual. It is entered through deep doors which leave a clear opening from an unusually low floor level almost to the roof top—well above the upper window line, in fact. The doorway is unaffected by the rear wheel arches and is therefore rectangular, and the floor has only a shallow, although fairly wide hump over the transmission. A soft woollen cloth of excellent quality is used to trim the seats, the lower door panels and other vertical faces, and a smooth mock-leather of matching tone covers the deep sills below the windows and glass division. In such a modern vehicle this seems much more appropriate than polished wood.

There is a thick underfelt beneath the loop-cord carpeting, and a neatly applied woollen nap cloth lines the roof. The back seat is deeply cushioned and comfortably shaped, but better support against cornering forces would be given were the centre folding armrest wider; it could with advantage also extend a few inches further along the cushion. Moreover, on long journeys one would appreciate some form of padded headrests in the rear quarters. At either side of this seat are recesses including rather unresilient, flat elbow rests and controls for various services. The sketch on page 846 shows those on the right; they include temperature and fan regulators for the heating and ventilation system and an overriding switch for the radio housed in the front compartment. Stations are selected by pressing a button which sets in motion a self-seeking mechanism. On the left are switches for the side window lifts and the division, plus a cigar lighter and ashtray.

Of two pairs of interior lamps, one is lit automatically when a door is opened. For extra ventilation, the rearmost side windows can be slid back a few inches, each by a simple lever which also locks the window securely when it is closed.

Cool or heated air is blown into the car through neat grilles recessed in the body sides next to the seat cushion. There are carpeted footrests on the floor, hinged to fold back out of the way and adjustable for two positions in use; even in the long reach position, however, they still allow too little stretch for most people. In each door is a rather tight pocket for maps and papers, and what appears to be a door pull also slides horizontally to release the lock, a device rather less practical than it is neat. For passengers riding on the folding occasionals there are, mounted in the division, two ashtrays with cigar lighters flanking a clock.

Trimmed in slippery black leather, the one-piece front seat includes a folding central armrest and can be adjusted fore-and-aft electrically. Yet it cannot go back far enough to suit anyone of more than, say, 5ft 9in. tall, and is contoured and angled to encourage a slouch rather than an alert, upright driving posture. Otherwise, everything is made as easy for the driver as he could wish. For instance, when the engine is running, the foot-applied parking brake is released automatically by a vacuum device from the induction system, as soon as the transmission lever is moved from Park or Neutral into any driving selection. It also has a manual release lever. Since modern parking brakes are often unable to hold cars on a 1-in-3 test hill, it was perhaps surprising to find no such difficulty with the heavy Cadillac. It has, of course, the transmission lock as an additional safeguard.

Three-speed Wipers

All the driver's controls are shown in the diagram on page 846, but some of them call for further comment. There is a three-speed selector for the screen wipers, which also start up automatically when the button for the washers is pressed but have to be switched off manually. The wiper arcs do not meet in the middle of the screen, leaving a wide unswept V, but the blades still wipe efficiently when the car is travelling fast. In our opinion the long horn-push buttons recessed into the steering wheel spokes are as neat and convenient as any, and we also liked the small tell-tale repeater lamps above the headlamp fairings, flashing in unison with the direction signalling lamps.

There is an external mirror on the driver's door which can be adjusted by a lever inside the car. The driver also has switch controls for both front door windows as well as the adjacent hinged quarter-lights. Just above his left knee is a cable control marked *Air Lift;* this is used to reduce the labour of jacking the car, or to increase ground

Left: Long but rather shallow, the boot loses considerable space to the spare wheel, and its counterbalanced lid can be opened only with a key. Newer cars have a different treatment of the rear lamp clusters and bumpers.   Right: With the occasional seats folded away there is a wealth of space. The passenger on the right controls the admission of warm or cool air through two grilles; one can be seen low down behind the door

Left: The seats are trimmed in a soft cloth, quilted and buttoned, and the folding occasionals are wide enough together to carry three. Right: Here the unusually deep door openings and low floor level are shown. When open, each front door shows a red reflector for safety at night

clearance when wishing to reverse over a kerb, for instance.

In almost every respect the mechanical behaviour cf the Cadillac conforms with the highly civilized luxury of its appointments. Thus the big vee-8 starts first time, soon idles with scarcely a sound or tremor, and responds to a light throttle opening by moving the car off quickly and in near-silence, with barely perceptible gear changes. Alternatively one has only to press the accelerator right down to make it rocket away with astonishing verve, the engine making some commotion only near peak revs in the lower ratios.

From a standstill 50 m.p.h. can then be reached in 8·3sec, 80 in 19·7 and 100 in 34·4—figures which need no further comment to emphasize them except, perhaps, to say that they were achieved on a damp surface which caused no apparent wheelspin. On the M1 motorway the Cadillac cruised at a true 100 m.p.h. with less mechanical or wind noise than any car we can remember. Moreover, during its maximum speed runs it reached a true 120 m.p.h. in one direction, still without vibration or other symptoms of stress. Moreover, at such speeds it ran true as an arrow, with no call for steering corrections. Doubtless the relatively long wheelbase and the stabilizing tail fins contribute towards this behaviour.

Pulling a large and heavy car at very high speeds inevitably runs through the fuel supply rather quickly. From this point of view the most logical cruising speed for motorways seems to be about 80 m.p.h., at which 14 to 15 miles would be covered per gallon, the tank holding 17½.

Smooth Automatic Changes

With this Hydra-Matic transmission there are three selections for the four forward ratios. Drive gives fully automatic changes up and down according to the throttle position and the torque being transmitted through the rear wheels; in addition, there are holds for second and third gears, the latter being particularly useful for check braking from speeds below about 64 m.p.h. The second gear hold allows 48 m.p.h. to be reached before third engages automatically, whereas with D selected this change cannot occur above 40 m.p.h. In addition, there is the customary kickdown switch whereby a lower ratio can be selected instantly from certain speeds for a burst of acceleration; a kick-down engagement is not quite so smooth as one made with the manual selector. There is full engine braking in every gear, an important asset of Hydra-Matic. As would be expected, the Cadillac moved off from rest on the 1-in-3 test gradient without any hesitation.

Much of the pleasure of driving this car derives from its powered steering gear, which is beyond criticism except for the occasional strange behaviour of this particular car when one was manœvring at less than a walking pace and with the engine turning at idling speed. It would sometimes "hunt" until the engine was speeded up, the system

delivering its power assistance in brief bursts. The gearing is reasonably high, with 3·6 turns of the wheel from lock to lock for a turning circle between kerbs averaging 51ft, which likewise is not unreasonable. Although very little effort is required, there is positive feel without any severe reactions, and the self-centring action is also quick. One soon acquires such confidence in the ability to place this 6ft 8in. wide car accurately that country lanes are entered without undue qualms. It is, of course, a disadvantage that the Fleetwood 75 is made only with left-hand drive.

In its native country the Cadillac is prevented by law from reaching such speeds as are possible in Europe. Thus it is understandable that its braking system has to be treated with discretion, and assisted where possible with the gear selector. When these limitations are realized and respected, brake fade can be held at bay and fast averages maintained in safety. Moreover, it should be recorded that the latest 75s have an increased braking area and hence a greater reserve. The pedal pressure required is light, and unless overworked the brakes are stable directionally and progressive in action. When they are applied while the car is being reversed, the shoes are adjusted automatically to compensate for wear.

With any car the suspension characteristics are partly dependent on the rigidity or otherwise of its structure, and the General Motors design engineers deserve congratulation for having combined great beam stiffness in a long vehicle with a very shallow floor indeed. Only occasionally over poor surfaces were tremors felt through the body, and it was totally free from rattles and creaks. While the springing is very soft, it allows little roll and fore-and-aft pneumatic levelling devices exert a strict control over pitching. The combination of a low springing rate and a long wheelbase occasionally leads to an unexpectedly sharp reaction over sharp dips and humps, but it is quickly damped. While such a car is unlikely in the ordinary way to be driven to the limit of its cornering powers, it was found that considerable liberties could be taken without embarrassment from a predominant but not acute tendency to understeer.

Below the efficient headlamps, and recessed into the bumper pressings, are two fog lamps as well as combined parking lamps and signal flashers. The engine lies well back from the complex grille, and the underbonnet layout generally is functional rather than elegant

The U.S. Royal tyres gave excellent adhesion on dry and wet roads, and were not prone to squeal. It was agreed that when travelling four-up the front seat gave the more restful ride with regard to road wheel suspension, with rather less vertical movement than occurs at the back. Nevertheless, it would be difficult indeed to find a more comfortable carriage for a long journey.

Among the many extras for an already very comprehensively equipped car are automatic beam setters for the paired headlamps, a photo-electric cell dimming these when it picks out the lamps of an oncoming car, and raising them again when this has passed. An adjustable speed governing device named Cruise Control is another unusual gadget.

It is always fascinating to sample the best that any country's motor industry can produce. Certainly the United States are well and truly represented with this fine Cadillac.

CADILLAC FLEETWOOD 75

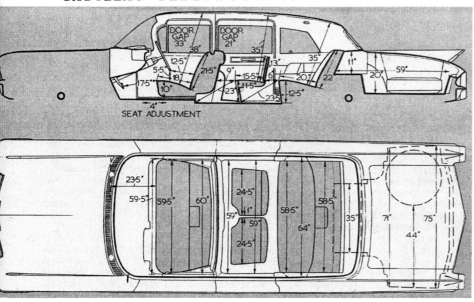

Scale ⅛in. to 1ft. Driving seat in central position. Cushions uncompressed.

DATA

PRICE (basic), with 8-9-seat limousine body, £5,375.
British purchase tax, £2,240 14s 2d.
Total (in Great Britain), £7,615 14s 2d.

ENGINE: Capacity, 6,384 c.c. (389·8 cu. in.).
Number of cylinders, 8 in 90 deg. vee.
Bore and stroke, 101·6 × 98·4mm (4·0 × 3·87in.).
Valve gear, overhead, pushrods and rockers. Hydraulic tappets.
Compression ratio, 10·5 to 1.
B.h.p. 325 (gross) at 4,800 r.p.m. (b.h.p. per ton laden 121).
Torque, 430 lb. ft. at 3,100 r.p.m.
M.p.h. per 1,000 r.p.m. in top gear, 25·2.

WEIGHT (with 10 gal fuel): 50·6 cwt (5,670 lb).
Weight distribution (per cent); F, 52·2; R, 47·8.
Laden as tested, 53·6 cwt (6,006 lb).
Lb per c.c. (laden), 0·94.

BRAKES: Type, Delco Duo-servo hydraulic, power-assisted.
Drum dimensions: F and R, 12in. diameter; 2·5in. wide.
Total swept area, 377 sq. in. (140 sq. in. per ton laden).

TYRES: 8·20—15in. U.S. Royal tubeless.
Pressures (p.s.i.): F, 26; R, 26 (normal). F, 32; R, 32 (fast driving).

TANK CAPACITY: 17·5 Imperial gallons.
Oil sump, 10 pints inc. filter.
Cooling system, 35 pints.

DIMENSIONS: Wheelbase, 12ft 5·8in.
Track: F and R, 5ft 1in.
Length (overall), 20ft 4·8in.
Width, 6ft 8in. Height, 4ft 11in.
Ground clearance, 6·9in.

PERFORMANCE

ACCELERATION TIMES:
Speed range, Gear Ratios and Time in Sec.

m.p.h.	3.36 to 1	5.21 to 1	8.57 to 1	13.31 to 1
10—30	—	—	4·1	—
20—40	—	5·8	4·1	—
30—50	8·8	5·8	—	—
40—60	9·7	5·6	—	—
50—70	10·4	6·5	—	—
60—80	11·3	—	—	—
70—90	12·1	—	—	—
80—100	15·0	—	—	—

From rest through gears to:

30 m.p.h.	..	3·9 sec.
40 ,,	..	5·8 ,,
50 ,,	..	8·3 ,,
60 ,,	..	11·2 ,,
70 ,,	..	15·1 ,,
80 ,,	..	19·4 ,,
90 ,,	..	25·4 ,,
100 ,,	..	34·4 ,,

Standing quarter mile 18·1 sec.

MAXIMUM SPEED ON GEARS:

Gear			m.p.h.	k.p.h.
Top	(mean)		116·5	187·6
	(best)		120·0	193·2
3rd	..	..	70	113
2nd	..	..	48	77
1st	..	..	14	23

TRACTIVE EFFORT (by Tapley meter):

	Pull (lb per ton)	Equivalent gradient
Top	250	1 in 8·9
Third	410	1 in 5·4
Second	630	1 in 3·4

BRAKES (at 30 m.p.h. in neutral):

Pedal load in lb	Retardation	Equiv. stopping distance in ft
25	0·45g	67
50	0·78g	38·7

FUEL CONSUMPTION (at steady speeds in top gear):

30 m.p.h.	23·4 m.p.g.
40 ,,	20·1 ,,
50 ,,	18·8 ,,
60 ,,	17·1 ,,
70 ,,	15·6 ,,
80 ,,	13·5 ,,
90 ,,	10·5 ,,
100 ,,	7·7 ,,

Overall fuel consumption for 1,069 miles, 10·9 m.p.g. (25·9 litres per 100 km.).
Approximate normal range 9-14 m.p.g. (31·3-20·2 litres per 100 km.).
Fuel: Super Premium grades.

TEST CONDITIONS: Weather: Dry, overcast. 10-15 m.p.h. wind.
Air temperature, 60 deg. F.

STEERING: Turning circle:
Between kerbs: L, 52ft 3in. R, 49ft 10in.
Between walls: L, 55ft 3in. R, 52ft 10in.
Turns of steering wheel lock to lock, 3·6.

SPEEDOMETER CORRECTION: m.p.h.

Car speedometer: ..		10	20	30	40	50	60	70	80	90	100	110	120
True speed ..	..	10	19	28	38	48	57	66	75	85	94	106	116

DATA (Continued)

ELECTRICAL SYSTEM: 12 - volt; 70 ampere-hour battery.
Headlamps: Four-lamp system, total 150 watt main beams, 100 watt meeting beams.

SUSPENSION: Front, wishbones, air springs and separate hydraulic dampers.
Rear: live axle located by longitudinal radius arms below and triangular member above. Air springs and separate hydraulic dampers.

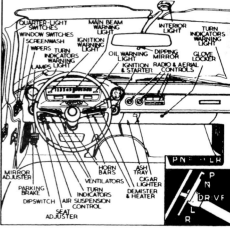

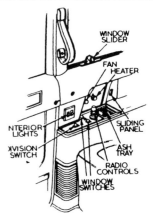

1961 Cadillac Engineering

In any discussion pertaining to the mechanical and engineering qualities of the 1961 Cadillac, the key words must be *greater comfort*. Much has been done to make operation of the 1961 Cadillac even more pleasant for all occupants.

The 1961 body is more convenient to get in and out . . . head room is increased, as is leg room . . . and seating comfort is increased with greater chair height.

Additionally, important advancements have been made in ride, handling ease, quietness of operation and braking.

Entrance and exit convenience is improved as a result of the forward sloping windshield pillar, by a rear door that opens seven-and-one-half inches further, by moving forward the center stub pillar, by narrowing the rocker step-over, and by increasing door opening heights.

Considerable improvement is made in head room, leg room and seating comfort. Here is how this has been accomplished. The chassis and frame modification permit lowering of the front floor, giving greater chair height for improved seating and greater leg room. Seat cushions are deepened. The tunnel is narrower and lower, resulting from the repositioning of the engine and transmission.

The continuing ride developments come from the new front suspension and structural advances possible with the new body.

Additional improvements in ease of handling result from the increased boost from the new steering pump. So less effort is required in steering or parking. Also, the car is more maneuverable—turning in a 43 foot circle, three feet less than last year.

Still another form of comfort—quietness and smoothness of operation—has advanced even further in 1961. This comes about as a result of the new front suspension and the improved body structure. The new structure permits the reduction of several mounts in the center of the body, eliminating points of noise and vibration transmission from the chassis to the body. A new type rubber support for the propeller shaft bearing adds to quietness and smoothness of the drive line.

As regards braking improvement, greater gains have been made than the substantial progress of last year. And this, too, is related to the new front suspension. The new suspension design permits the moving of front brake drums into the air stream. By adding fins onto the extended drums greater cooling results. This permits use of a larger wheel cylinder with shorter stopping distances and greater freedom from pull and squeak.

Other engineering advancements on the 1961 Cadillac include a lubrication free chassis, a new windshield wiper system covering 15 percent greater wiping area, a single exhaust system for greater life and an anti-smog kit that will be standard on all California bound cars and optional elsewhere.

Another option offered for the first time is a rear window defogger.

In the rear compartment of Cadillac sedans, the rear door swings open an additional 7½ inches and is 6 inches wider. The narrower step-over sill adds inches to the usable width of the floor, thanks to the improved body structure.

In the all-new Cadillac front suspension, the lower control arm is connected at only two points: one at the steering knuckle, and one at the frame as compared to three points on previous models. To stabilize the front suspension, a diagonal tie strut is used with each lower suspension arm.

Entrance and exit convenience in the 1961 Cadillac is improved as a result of sloping the front windshield pillar, eliminating the dog leg.

CADILLAC 60, 62 & 75

CADILLAC 4-DOOR SEDAN DE VILLE

The apogee, in the eyes of the world of American cars-manship, the Cadillac carries on without much change for 1962. Cadillac hasn't liquidated tailfins completely, unlike many of its contemporaries, but a new grille and headlight configuration is deemed to achieve a more massive, broad-shouldered look.

All Cadillacs are powered by the tried-and-true 390-cu. in. V-8 engine which produces a smooth 325 bhp at a quiet 4800 rpm. A novel feature is the cornering light which throws a beam of light sideways to light the way around a turn whenever the directional signal lever is actuated. The Cadillac also incorporates a dual braking system with separate master cylinders for front and rear brakes. This is in addition to the normal parking/emergency brake.

The steady hand of the styling experts is also discernible in a new roof line with, in some models, the fashionable and elegant blind rear quarter pane.

CADILLAC 60, 62 & 75	
Wheelbase (in.) ... (Fleetwood 75: 149.8)	129.5
Over-all length .... (Fleetwood 75: 243.3)	215.0–222.0
Width .... (Fleetwood 75: 80.6)	79.9
Weight (lb.)	4780
Brake Area (sq. in.)	221.8
Engine: V-8, ohv, 390 cu. in. (4.0 in. bore x 3.88 in. stroke), 10.5:1 compression ratio.	
Horsepower: 325 @ 4800 rpm **Torque:** 430 @ 3100 rpm	
Transmission: 4-speed automatic	
Axle Ratio(s): 2.94 (3.36 or 3.77 on Fleetwood 75)	

CADILLAC 2-DOOR COUPE DE VILLE

HANDLING is amazingly good for such a big car: only 3½ turns lock-to-lock, and she's very stable on corners.

EGAD—A CAD!

1961 Cadillac swamps you with comfort and gadgetry, yet performs like an outsize sports car, reports David McKay

A CADILLAC "de Ville" pillar-less sedan—favorite of film stars, business tycoons, U.S. trade-union bosses and Middle East oil sheiks—found its way into my unaccustomed hands the other week.

I admit I was somewhat awed at first by the size of the car (18¼ feet long, over 6½ feet wide) and the responsibility (a rare, privately owned car "on test" is very different to a run-of-the-mill company demonstrator).

The Caddy was handed over to me by one of its chauffeurs, who gave me a run-down on the masses of knobs, switches and levers.

It was a Friday afternoon, and the thought of suddenly being turned loose in this £6000 "land liner" on the wrong side of town, and having to negotiate the city and the Harbor

ENGINE bay is poorly finished, in contrast to rest of car — and the 6½-litre V8 is almost invisible under its burden of ancillary units.

54

Bridge before reaching a safe anchorage at home, was almost too much.

But the garage staff, who had gone to the trouble of filling the huge tank with 100-octane fuel and checking over the engine, stood by expectantly, waiting for me to blast off.

I couldn't let them down; so, with great trepidation—disguised, I hoped, with great nonchalance—I edged into the traffic stream and away.

As soon as I became accustomed to the incredibly direct steering (3½ turns lock-to-lock), made even more surprising with power assistance, and the excellent manoeuvrability for such a vast car, I relaxed and enjoyed it.

I began to look around and at once felt like a fish in a bowl. It was knock-off time in the city, and I could have filled the Caddy a dozen times over, judging from the welcoming smiles we got from admiring passers-by.

But I had work to do—the Caddy was for testing. I pulled alongside a Bentley and was amazed to see how low the Caddy was in comparison. The other car towered above us like a double-decker—a quality double-decker, of course.

Cook's Tour

Safely home, I got my first chance to inspect the car without interruptions.

Apart from its tailfins — so sharp that I was afraid a bumptious Morris Minor was going to impale itself on them at one stage — the Cadillac has good, clean lines, enhanced by its pillarless construction, and is free of the garish chromework once favored by its makers.

I lifted the bonnet ("hood" to a Caddy driver) — without, I might add, needing to release any catch inside the car. You'd have thought General Motors would provide an internal bonnet lock on their most expensive product!

What I saw underneath didn't tally with my expectations, either. The engine, for all its 325 horses, looked like any other big American V8, decidedly lacking in finish. The only difference was in the larger-than-usual number of ancillaries crowded into the compartment.

At the same time, however, it impressed one as the sort of engine that would stand up to the abuse of some illiterate sheik, such as I had met driving earlier Cadillac models in Irak, back in 1955.

The array of ancillaries is really something. In addition to the normal equipment, it includes units to operate power steering and power brakes — plus a miniature powerhouse to supply energy for the electrically-controlled doorlocks, windows, seats, warming and refrigerating plants, radio aerial, and so on.

PILLARLESS look goes well with long, low body.

MAIN SPECIFICATIONS

ENGINE: V8, o.h.v.; bore 101.6mm., stroke 98.4mm., capacity 6392c.c.; compression ratio 10.5 to 1; maximum b.h.p. 325 at 4800 r.p.m.; maximum torque 430ft./lb. at 3100 r.p.m.; single 4-choke downdraught Carter carburettor, mechanical fuel pump; 12v. ignition.

TRANSMISSION: G.M. Hydra-Matic 4-speed, with special lever position to restrict drive to the three lower ratios; overall ratios—1st, 11.6; 2nd, 7.5; 3rd, 4.5; top, 2.9 to 1.

SUSPENSION: Front independent, by coil springs and tie-struts; coil springs at rear; telescopic hydraulic shock-absorbers all round.

STEERING: Recirculating-ball type, power-operated; 3½ turns lock-to-lock, 45ft. turning circle.

WHEELS: Pressed-steel discs, with 8.00 by 15in. tyres.

CONSTRUCTION: Separate tubular centre X-frame.

DIMENSIONS: Wheelbase 10ft. 9½in.; track, 5ft. 1in. front and rear; length 18ft. 6in., width 6ft. 7in., height 4ft. 8in.; ground clearance 5in.

KERB WEIGHT: 45cwt.

FUEL TANK: 17½ gallons.

PERFORMANCE ON TEST

CONDITIONS: Fine, cool, no wind; dry bitumen; two occupants, 100-octane fuel.

BEST SPEED: 110 m.p.h.

STANDING quarter-mile: 18.6s.

MAXIMUM in indirect ratios: 1st, 30 m.p.h.; 2nd, 60; 3rd, 85.

ACCELERATION from rest through gears; 0-30, 3.0s.; 0-40, 5.0s.; 0-50, 7.4s.; 0-60, 11.0s.; 0-70, 14.6s.; 0-80, 19.0s.

HILLCLIMB: 2min. 33s.

MOUNTAIN CIRCUIT: 50 m.p.h. average.

BRAKING: 31ft. to stop from 30 m.p.h. in neutral.

FUEL CONSUMPTION: 12.2 m.p.g. overall.

PRICE: On application (approx. £6000 with tax)

SHARP in more ways than one — that lower fin threatens shins of unwary pedestrians. *BELOW:* Driver's armrest contains controls to work all windows and doorlocks.

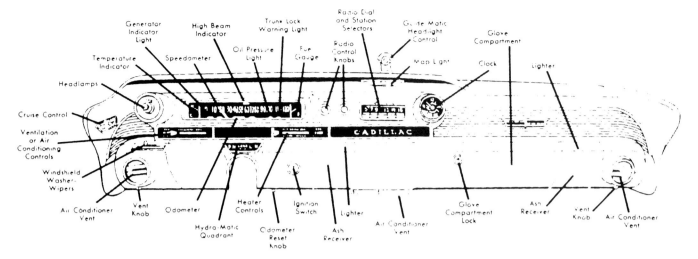

Generator Indicator Light — High Beam Indicator — Trunk Lock Warning Light — Radio Dial and Station Selectors — Guide-Matic Headlight Control — Glove Compartment — Temperature Indicator — Speedometer — Oil Pressure Light — Fuel Gauge — Radio Control Knobs — Map Light — Clock — Lighter — Headlamps — Cruise Control — Ventilation or Air Conditioning Controls — Windshield Washer-Wipers — Air Conditioner Vent — Vent Knob — Odometer — Hydra-Matic Quadrant — Heater Controls — Odometer Reset Knob — Ignition Switch — Ash Receiver — Lighter — Air Conditioner Vent — Glove Compartment Lock — Ash Receiver — Vent Knob — Air Conditioner Vent

CADILLAC

Together with the automatic transmission, all this would probably absorb at least 100 of the engine's horses.

Closing the bonnet, I made an excursion to the back of the car and lifted the boot lid. The cavern under it looked roomy enough to carry a Goggo Dart as a tender.

The big spare wheel, carried flat on the floor, had no cover to protect luggage; but there was a tag on the boot lid, telling you what to do if you got a flat tyre—other than call your nearest Caddy dealer.

The Inside Story

I closed the boot and went and sat inside the car. This, after all, is what a Caddy owner sees most of—and I'll go on record as saying I've never been in a better interior.

Seats are vast, with ample space for six big occupants—and leg-room in the rear compartment is quite exceptional for these days. There are individual armrests, and cigar lighters and ashtrays within easy reach of everyone (a lighter and a tray are built into each rear door).

Upholstery is of fine silk fabric, leather-faced. Leather and polished stainless steel take the place of the wood trim used in "quality" English cars; it's like the difference between a lush apartment in Manhattan and a London club.

Windows go up or down at the touch of an electric switch built into each door, the pushbutton radio (standard equipment) plays with perfect tone and has an electrically operated telescopic aerial.

In contrast to some earlier Caddies, the dash treatment isn't overdone—the Cadillac lettering is neat and restrained, the rather small steering wheel beautifully made.

But the instrumentation is positively primitive. All you get is a speedo, plus gauges for water temperature and fuel—warning lights cover the rest, as they do on the cheapest English or Continental cars.

That's the only fault, though: rest of the equipment couldn't be more generous or efficient.

LUSH leather padding, stainless steel, deeply-dished steering wheel and a mass of controls (see sketch above). But instruments are few, and accelerator uncomfortably close to parking footbrake. BELOW: Boot is huge— so is the spare wheel, which surely should have a cover to protect luggage.

CADILLAC

The press-button, instant-action screenwasher and three-speed wipers (overlapping, mark you) should keep the huge tinted screen clear as crystal in anything but a deluge.

Two separate air-conditioning systems — heating/demisting and refrigeration—work perfectly, and adjustable angled slats allow you to direct the warming or cooling airflow to almost any position inside the car.

Driver's Angle

The range of seating adjustments is so varied that anyone—long or short, fat or thin—can select the ideal driving position for his frame.

And it's done with incredible ease, by operating electric controls which raise or lower the front seat, move it to and fro, tilt it up or down, until you are satisfied.

I found several comfortable positions, depending on my driving mood. But I also found my rear vision somewhat limited by the smallish internal mirror and was glad of the external mirrors—the left-hand one being adjustable from inside without lowering the window!

One other complaint on the score of visibility: the sloping windscreen pillars are on the thick side by modern standards. But this was probably deemed necessary to ensure that the roof is adequately supported in the absence of central pillars.

The selector panel for the four-speed Hydra-Matic transmission lists two "drive" positions; the left-hand one gives the full four speeds, while the right-hand position cuts out high gear and is recommended for use in hilly country (for the sporting owner?).

The Caddy, of course, is normally a left-hand drive vehicle. The conversion to right-hand drive has been done very neatly, except for one thing: The foot-operated parking brake is set too close to the throttle and tends to crowd the driver's all-important right foot, which does all the work in "automatics."

It's a pity that such an obvious point should have been overlooked, especially when the designers have taken such pains to make the driver comfortable. They've even provided him with remote controls to lock or unlock all doors and raise or lower all windows without ungainly reaching.

Along with all these gimmicks, which fascinated both me and my three-year-old daughter (she was a sucker for the disappearing aerial), there's a magic-eye headlight dipper, which automatically puts your headlights on low beam when you meet other traffic at night.

This control is so sensitive that once it politely dipped our headlights to a reflective road sign!

On the Road

Being conscious of the car's value, I handled it somewhat sedately during the four-day test period. Even when going over my regular mountain course, I tried to forget my sporting instincts, pretending I was a tycoon in a hurry—well, a moderate hurry—and kept to the four-speed side of the transmission quadrant.

John McKittrick, who logged the run for me, was amazed at the big car's agility—but had he been driving he'd have realised just how simple it was to hurl 45cwt. of Caddy through the bends.

The 3½ turns lock-to-lock, plus power steering, plus a gross 345 b.h.p., plus a commendably flat and stable ride, made my job easy.

A limited-slip diff—offered as optional equipment, according to the factory's surprisingly scanty instruction book—would have helped greatly up the hill; but even so, the heavy car shot up the climb in 2min. 33sec. to the accompaniment of appropriate jet noises.

Despite my restrained driving, it recorded 50 m.p.h for the circuit—an average many saloons would envy. Had I used the three-speed drive position and given the car its head, I am sure it could have averaged between 52 and 53 m.p.h.

On a long-distance run, say Sydney to Adelaide, I would imagine the Caddy would really shine, and any sort of car would have to motor really hard to keep up with it.

I used the normal 24lb. pressure in the big 8.00 by 15in. tyres—but for sustained speeds in excess of 75 m.p.h a pressure of 28lb. is suggested. Obviously, G.M. had turnpike derbies in mind when giving this advice.

With the windows shut, 80 m.p.h was quite silent, and even the maximum of 110 gave little indication of our velocity.

It was only when braking from speeds "over the ton" that the brakes seemed a trifle worried. Over the mountain circuit, where high speeds aren't possible, the brakes coped with the great weight uncomplainingly.

Perhaps G.M., who can obviously make a car that's equal to any in the world, will follow the proud Daimler-Benz factory's example and fit the unbeatable British disc brakes to make this fine chariot even better than it is.

And it IS a fine chariot — make no mistake about that. The ride, the handling, the overall performance and comfort — plus such minor detail touches as a warning light that goes on when you open the boot, and red reflectors inside the doors, to warn other traffic when these are opened — show what Detroit can achieve when it wants to, and when cost is no object.

To all this you can add a surprisingly moderate thirst for petrol. I thought we'd be lucky to get 10 m.p.g. from such a heavy car with massive 6½-litre engine, but consumption worked out at 12.2 m.p.g., despite the arduous test course.

No wonder the Cadillac is the world's top-selling "car of distinction."

FOOTNOTE: This particular car had previously been running on premium-grade pump petrol until recently — and disliking it. It now normally uses a mixture of methylbenzine and super (1 to 3), but for this test we fed it 100 octane fuel.

The chauffeurs report the Caddy to be a different car on either MB or 100-octane — not surprising, considering the engine's 10.5 to 1 compression ratio!

●●●

R E T R O

A SCULPTURED BEAUTY FROM THE ERA OF EXCESSIVE CHROME AND ROOF-HIGH TAILFINS

'60 CADILLAC

There'll never be another time in the car business like that of the late '50s. It was an era of unabashed decadence, a few brief years when sensibility was thrown to the wind and form allowed to progress independent of function. We were flying high in style and spirit, and our automobiles were there as four-wheeled versions of the American Dream.

And although we now shake our heads in disbelief at many of those flamboyant designs, there were a few truly beautiful cars that emerged from the glitter bowl of sparkle seat cushions, bombsight hood ornaments, and tri-tone paint. The "aircraft look" that spawned the swept-back styling and P-38-inspired tailfins of the understated '49 Cadillac had progressed into the "rocket look" of Eisenhower-era autos, culminating in tasteful cars such as the '57 Chevy and '59 Pontiac. (The less tasteful included the chrome-lathered '58 Buick Limited, the bulbously awkward '58 Oldsmobile, and the infamous '59 Caddy.)

While it's entirely justified that the ostentatious '59 Cadillac has earned a reputation of "gross overstatement to the tenth power," the much simpler '60 version has proven to be a paradigm of timeless beauty. It's almost as if GM's stylists awoke from a three-year trance and quickly set about undoing all they had wrought between 1957-59. They took a hacksaw and cut a couple inches out of the tailfins, replacing the twin bullet lenses with a sleek daggerpiece of red plastic. With a pry bar, they removed the heavy horizontal bar in the grille, casting it aside into a pile along with the other excess ornamentation. And so the work went on until they arrived at a simpler, far cleaner visage that became the '60 model.

The mechanical makeup of the '60 Cadillac remained virtually unchanged from that of the previous year, which still made it a big, powerful road-going automobile. This is a machine Americans did best; a supertrain of the turnpike designed to carry passengers and their belongings

from coast to coast on the great new interstate highway system. No need to poke your way through every little town between Los Angeles and New York, just jump onto the superslab, set the cruise control at 75 mph, and head out. Hell, this is progress, boy, don't you know that?

Built on a mammoth 130-inch wheelbase chassis (with a rear body overhang of over 4 feet), the big Caddys tipped the scales at 5000-plus pounds of road-hugging weight. But these were no underpowered, wheezing hillhogs when the elevations be-

gan to climb. A big part of the Cadillac legacy is performance, and in 1960, that came from a 390-cubic-inch V-8 with 10.5:1 compression, four-barrel carb, dual exhaust, and 325 horsepower. The top-line Eldorado received a trio of two-barrel carbs for a total of 345 horsepower. With a 2.94-ratio ring-and-pinion, the big Caddy ragtop would spin the tires away from a stoplight and hustle to 60 mph in under 11 seconds. Give 'er enough rein, and the Eldorado would continue to pull past 120 mph (although approaching a turn at that

S P E C T

ELDORADO BIARRITZ

by C. Van Tune

PHOTOGRAPHY BY JIM BROWN

speed must have been a bit scary).

Everything about these cars was top quality, from the feel of the richly upholstered seats to the fit and finish of the body panels. Cadillacs were assembled on the slowest-moving of any of Detroit's assembly lines, and extra care was taken to ensure that each one met the required specs. Engines were built to close tolerances, and every motor was run-in on a dyno before installation. Cadillac General Manager (in 1960) Harold G. Warner felt he was competing with Rolls-Royce in terms of mechanical preci-

sion, and *Automotive Industries* magazine at the time reported that "Cadillac manufacturing methods on engine production equal virtual aircraft engine specification refinement."

These were the days before "platform engineering" became the law; back when Chevrolet, Pontiac, Oldsmobile, Buick, and Cadillac were separate and distinct divisions. As a result, the Cadillacs of that era were unique, sharing few if any components with their corporate siblings. In 1960, Cadillac sold a total of 142,184 vehicles—double the volume

of all competing luxury car sales combined, including Mercedes-Benz and Rolls-Royce.

Prices for the '60 Cadillacs ran the gamut from $4892 for the "62-series" two-door coupe to a Rockefeller-staggering $13,075 for the majestic Eldorado Brougham sedan. The Eldo Biarritz ragtop commanded the hefty sum of $7401, although it included items such as cruise control, Guide-Matic headlamp dimming, automatic-seek AM radio, power windows and door locks, and other top-drawer items as standard equipment. Essentially, on-

ly air conditioning remained as an option.

This was to be the final year of Cadillac's ill-fated "air ride" suspension, which had been giving dealer service managers fits since its introduction in '57. The system used conical rubber air bladders, which replaced the car's coil springs, and was designed to keep the vehicle perfectly level over road imperfections and during cornering. An engine-driven air compressor was used to inflate the air bladders, and an under-dash handle was fitted to allow the driver to raise the car to its highest setting if required to exit a particularly steep driveway (remember that 4-foot rear overhang).

Unfortunately, all did not work according to design. Not only did most of the air bladders leak, but the system was plagued by condensation problems in the lines, which had to be purged every week; not what the owner of a car that had cost as much as a small house wanted to have to do. As a result, most owners had their dealer remove the air-ride components completely, making any Cadillac with the system still functional an especially rare vehicle.

The Lucerne Blue Eldorado Biarritz in the photographs is

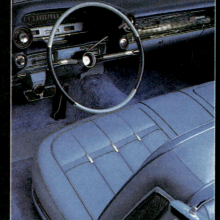

owned by television and radio personality Wayne Thomas. In addition to serving as the host of several Los An-geles-based shows during the late '50s, Thomas has produced a litany of programs including the popular "Your Choice for the Oscars." He bought the Eldorado in 1961 and sold it to a friend in 1969 for a mere $750. After a particularly disastrous engine fire in 1987 (those triple-deuce carburetors were notorious for flame ups),Thomas bought the injured Caddy back and began his restoration project.

Restoring a vintage Cadillac is not as easy as performing a similar project on something like a Corvette, for which there's no shortage of reproduction parts. To rebuild the Eldo into showroom-fresh condition required the dedicated effort of three SoCal firms: Briggs Automotive (mechanical), Coachcraft (paint and body-work), and Highland Plating (re-chroming). Not only was rebuilding the air-ride system a major project, but the 283-piece front grille required the patience of a monk to reassemble, according to Thomas.

This year marks the 30th anniversary of this beautiful Eldorado Biarritz—a car that was the grand finale to an era of sky-high dreams and open-road automotive aspirations. We'll never pass that way again. **MT**

The 1962 Cadillac Fleetwood Sixty Special retains its distinctive upper structure not shared by any other motorcar. The rear of the car presents a new deck lid with a beveled edge and a new cove molding that features a pattern similar to the front grille.

60th Anniversary Cadillacs

BEGINNING its sixtieth year in the automobile industry, Cadillac is now presenting for 1962 the most complete and competitive line of new models in the Division's history, according to Harold G. Warner, Cadillac general manager and vice president of General Motors.

"A dramatically new silhouette, outstanding engineering achievements and important safety features, new to any American motorcar, are combined in our anniversary automobile," Warner said.

"As the records show, safety always is of prime concern to Cadillac each year. This year is no exception. In fact, in 1962 there is even more emphasis on safety with a new dual braking system and significant lighting developments, both in the front and rear of the automobile," Warner points out.

In this anniversary year, Cadillac is offering 12 models, the same as last year. Five of the 12 will feature a classic new roof design giving an entirely new silhouette to the car and changing the over-all styling personality.

This sleek and low roof design which reflects the leadership of last year's Fleetwood Sixty Special Sedan appears on the Four-Window Sedan de Ville, the Coupe de Ville, Sixty-Two Coupe, Town Sedan and Park Avenue Sedan.

Wheelbase is unchanged: 129.5 inches on all models except the Series Seventy-Five Sedan and Limousine at 149.8 inches. Overall length remains at 222 inches on eight models, while the Series Seventy-Five Sedan and Limousine again are 242.3 inches in length. The new Park Avenue Sedan joins the Town Sedan at 215 inches. Overall width also is unchanged.

The two 215 inch sedan models have the exact interior dimensions as the new Four-Window de Ville. The seven inch difference in length comes out fo the rear deck and trunk. These two models will differ in interior trim and appointments. The Town Sedan has the Sixty-Two interior selections while the Park Avenue uses the de Ville interiors.

To create a more massive appearance, all 12 models have a new grille with the traditional Cadillac cross-hatch design which in profile is more vertical. Contributing to the broad shouldered look, the grille design also forms a background for the headlamps. A new Cadillac script appears on the grille.

The rear quarter styling is an excellent reflection of the 1962 design character. The fins are low and sleek. The new bumper end and taillight housing provides a solid visual anchor for the strong horizontal design lines of the body, and the use of chrome is held to a minimum.

The rear appearance of the car is enhanced by a new deck lid with a beveled edge in keeping with the crisp and angular styling motif of 1962.

Between the deck lid and rear bumper is a new ribbed cove molding of extruded aluminum which is painted the body color. On the Fleetwood Sixty Special and the Eldorado Biarritz this molding resembles the front grille.

Styling and engineering combine to bring exciting new lighting developments to the industry. At the side of the headlamps as an integral part of the front end appearance is a new cornering light, which illuminates the way into a turn at night. The taillight in the rear bumper also is completely new and houses a taillamp, stop lamp, turn signal light and back-up light. Yet under normal daytime operations the exterior lens appears white.

The dignified Sixty Special retains its distinctive upper structure not shared by any other motorcar.

The Eldorado Biarritz Convertible has a new body side molding which is painted to match the interior and bordered in chrome with Eldorado identification at the forward end.

The new deeply-drawn wheel disc is a finely tailored combination of chrome and matching body color.

There are 16 standard exterior colors available—one more than in 1961—plus five special Eldorado colors.

With tailoring and selection the finest ever offered, the exterior styling beauty of the 1962 Cadillac is fully complemented with new elegant and refined interiors. Wool broadcloths, natural grain leathers and the latest contemporary fabrics are featured in newly styled interiors.

A total of 92 interior options are available. Among the new highlights of interior styling are the inclusion of wool broadcloth trim for Series Sixty-Two models, handsome fabric options in the Biarritz Convertible and a greatly expanded selection of leathers and bucket seats in the de Ville models.

Interior elegance achieves new heights in the Fleetwood Sixty Special. The interior appointments of this motorcar are highlighted by large cherry veneer panels in all doors, an embroidered crest and laurel leaf design on the front and rear center arm rests and new reading lights on the upper rear quarter panels.

Unquestionably the major contribution to safer driving is the new three-way brake system on the 1962 Cadillac, the first of its kind in the automobile industry. Heart of the system is a dual-type power brake master cylinder with a separate piston and brake fluid reservoir for front and rear brakes. From a safety standpoint, this system is ideal because if one of the hydraulic lines is severed, only one pair of wheel brakes would be out of commission.

With the parking brake, which again this year can be employed as a true auxiliary brake, the 1962 Cadillac has three separate brake systems in an emergency. Faster braking also is achieved through a new suspended vacuum booster.

Another engineering first for the industry is a new cornering light which is introduced on all the 1962 Cadillacs. The steady beam angles out from the side of the headlamp, lighting the driver's way into a turn. It is activated by the turn signal lever when the headlights, parking lights, or fog lamps are on.

Also a Cadillac first is the unique new taillight, stoplight and turn signal—yet, it has a white lens in normal daylight operation. The lens shows white when backing up, but shines red when the taillight, stoplight, or turn signal are in operation.

Another safety innovation appearing on all 1962 Cadillacs is a vinyl-backed rear view mirror and vanity mirror, providing shatter proof construction in case of an accident. And seat belt anchors are provided as standard.

Changes in the front spring rate, new front and rear suspension bushings and re-valving of the shock absorbers give a silky smooth ride. Frame modifications and new bearings which reduce friction in the steering linkage provide sureness in ride and handling.

To give additional quietness, a new sound deadening material is used under the floor pan and in the cowl section between the front doors and front fenders. The roof is completely lined with a new sound deadening material for further noise isolation.

Significant chassis refinements include specially cut gears in the transmission, drive line improvements and new exhaust line mountings, all contributing to the quietness of operation.

New in 1962 is a 26-gallon gas tank which will be standard on all models except the Town Sedan and Park Avenue Sedan de Ville. They retain the 21-gallon tank.

The reliable 390 cubic inch V-8 engine remains unchanged in specifications with 325 horsepower and a 10.5 to 1 compression ratio. However, it is quieter in operation and has still better durability through selective fitting of all main bearings to develop closer fits.

For the first time, the heater will be standard equipment on all 1962 Cadillacs. Air conditioned cars will be quieter due to the use of a newly designed fan clutch and a smaller, lighter yet higher output six-cylinder Freon compressor.

Cadillac offers in 1962 a controlled differential while a new development in lubrication gives added life to the wheel bearings.

Other accessory changes in the new models include a cruise control that has been simplified for driver convenience. It is lighted and is of the wheel type, providing more accurate control.

The automatic trunk lock is now mechanical, rather than electric. The remotely controlled trunk release is now vacuum operated. ★

ELDORADO!

**No car could be more appropriate for The Land of Gold
than the Cadillac Eldorado of the fifties and sixties.
Mike McCarthy tells the tale . . .**

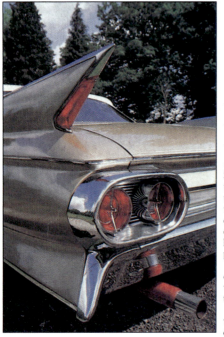

Say you were an enormously successful novelist of the Barbara Cartland genre, and you wanted to come up with a name for the cad's car. Said cad, naturally, would be insufferably foreign with a deep tan, dark curly hair and jewellery, for heaven's sake. On the other hand, if you were Harold Robbins, he'd be the hero. Either way, it doesn't matter: there's still the problem of the name.

Would you, in your wildest flights of fancy, *dare* to call it a Cadillac Eldorado Biarritz? I mean, if you were to try a roughly British equivalent it would be the Worsthorne Goldstreet Bournemouth. . .

Mind you, say you did come up with the name, would you once again in your wildest flights of fancy come up with the cars to match it? You would be

accused of gross excess, or too much imagination. But for once truth is stranger than fiction. The Cadillac Eldorado Biarritz in all its forms was a totally over the top machine, even judged by American standards.

'Twas not always thus. Up until the outbreak of the Second World War Cadillac were known for producing superbly engineered but restrained cars. Definitely subtle. Sober, even. The sort of car for which black was the only colour, anything else looking crass. The height of elegance, of good taste. This tradition continued into the first two years of post-war production, 1946 and 1947. And then in 1948 something happened, and Cadillac would never again be accused of being sober, or subtle, or

anything approaching restrained. No, never again.

What happened doesn't look very revolutionary now, but then – wow! The 1948 Cadillacs sprouted fins. Not FINS, but fins. Small, dumpy, right at the back of the rear wing, they were said to have been inspired by the tail of a Lockheed P38 fighter. They were aerodynamically laughable, but *there*. One small step for mankind, one giant leap for the stylists. In 1948 there were minor trim revisions and more chrome, while under the bonnet a brand new, potent ohv V8 engine appeared.

Come 1950 and zap, wham, kapow – Cadillac shed their sober image once and for all. The 1950 models were longer, lower, wider, much more massive and bulky. The grille looked like the mouth of a kid who'd eaten a chrome ice-cream with too much gusto. Along the side there was a dummy air intake just ahead of the rear wheel to mark the rear wing joint line which was nothing more than a vertical chrome strip. And the fin was there. For 1950 and 1951, Cadillac's half-centenary, the shapes were the same but the stylists as ever played around with the chrome-work.

The next year, 1953, saw another turning point in the Cadillac saga – the introduction of the Eldorado. This was a limited edition (532 made), ultra-luxurious (leather and cloth interior, wire wheels, white sidewalls, signal-seeking radio, a metal tonneau cover over the hood when down, and Hydramatic transmission were all standard), and expen-

Eldorado sales were doubled in 1955 – the year the famous Eldo fins and wrap-around screen appeared

The 1959 Cadillac had the highest fins of all – the model epitomised late fifties flamboyance in styling

sive (at $7750 it cost more than the Fleetwood limousine, and was the dearest American production car that year). It also had a unique styling feature: a wrap-around windscreen. One small step for mankind, one giant etc, etc. It was vulgar, gross, perhaps crass . . . or way-out, wild, stunning, depending on your viewpoint.

There was a revamp of the whole range in 1954, with longer, lower, sleeker bodies and wrap-around windscreens across the board. Alas, the 1954 Eldorado was no longer a limited edition super-luxury model but just a fancy version of the model 62. The price came down and sales went up. Cadillac know a thing or two about selling cars. . .

However, somebody at GM had second thoughts, because in 1955 the Eldorado was back as a speciality item, and with an additional name – Biarritz. Once again it was loaded, as the Yanks say: there was a 270bhp engine as against the standard product's 250bhp; an automatic radio aerial; power-assisted brakes (thankfully, you can hear many

For '57 the Cad was all new and had a 'shark' fin rear

Eleven years of fins, from the lowest to the highest

people murmur. . .); powered windows and even powered seats, not to mention 'sabre-spoke' wheels. Visually, the front two-thirds of the car were as the others, but the tail was something else again. Gone were the dumpy little fins, replaced by the *real thing*. These babies were loooong, and razor-thin, and pointed slightly upwards. They were finished off with a chrome tip beneath which there were a couple of bullet-shaped tail lights, and beneath *them* was a massive bumper whose flanks housed the exhaust pipes. Like the wrap-around screen, these fins would trickle down onto the lesser models, but not until 1957. Oh yes: the Eldorado Biarritz was once more at the top of the price league at $6286.

The big news for 1956 was an addition to the Eldorado sub-series – the Seville, a two-door pillarless coupe for those who eschewed open-air motoring. Following the usual two-year run, styling was much as before with but minor alterations here and there to the chromework – a finer textured grille, for example. Power, though, was up to 305bhp at 4700rpm, which sounds an *awful* lot but these were fairly tame ponies and by the time the oomph required to run the air conditioning, power steering and so on was used up there weren't all that many to provide the go for a car which weighed no less than 44.5cwt. . .

Come 1957 there was all-new engineering from the X-shaped chassis to the external bodywork. The Eldorado series soldiered on with new, distinctive rear end treatment: the wings were now rounded and the fins like those of a shark, sticking up from the rump of the beast.

However. . . The Seville and Biarritz were totally overshadowed by the sensation of the year – the Eldorado Brougham. This model, the absolute epitome of luxury in its day, was intended to out-do the beautiful Lincoln Continental Mk2 of 1956-57, and is really another sub-species of a sub-species, which deserves to be treated separately. Suffice to say that with the Eldorado Biarritz and Seville costing a healthy $7286, the Brougham came in at $13,074.

There was a carry-over year for Cadillac in 1958, and the major changes were cosmetic. There was a new, wide-grin grille and quad headlights across the board. Once again the standard Eldorados held second place to the Brougham in the prestige stakes, but now both shared the same 355bhp

engine. Intriguingly, five special Biarritz dropheads were made with humidity sensors which worked out that it was about to rain – and raised the hood automatically. Quite what happened if this occurred at speed isn't recorded. . .

Ah, but then came 1959, and the peak – or the trough, depending on how you look at it – of American (and Cadillac in particular) styling. This was all new from stem to stern, and at the stern were those FINS! Huge, enormous, graceful, long. Like nothing else, they epitomised late fifties flamboyance. And dammit, yes you can call the whole car graceful, especially from the side where for once sculpture, not chrome, dominated. The proportion of useable space to overall bulk would have made Sir Alec Issigonis cringe, but what the hell. The 1959 Caddies were not for the shrinking violets. . .

The proportion of usable space to overall bulk would have made Sir Alec Issigonis cringe, but what the hell

Actually, the 1959 Eldorados took a slight downswing in that they shared sheet metal work with other, more pedestrian, models, if *any* 1959 Cadillac can be called pedestrian. The Brougham, too, was brought back into the fold but with one essential difference: it was actually built by Pininfarina, part of the reason why it cost almost double the Biarritz or Seville. Looks-wise, though, it was not the unique machine that the earlier model had been. All featured six-way powered seats, and air suspension.

Like 1958, 1960 was a Cadillac body-shell carry-over year, but it seemed someone somewhere had cried 'Enough!'. For the first time in a decade the new cars were marginally more sober instead of more flamboyant: the grilles were tidied up, the fins cropped. Not much, but enough. The big news on the Eldorados was extensive chromework on the sill, running from front wheel arch to the tail. Big deal. . .

Come 1961 and matters were definitely sobering up. The Eldorado Seville and Brougham were dropped, leaving the Biarritz as the top model once again. In fact, all Cadillacs were restyled and re-engineered for this year. There were still long fins at the back, but shapes were becoming crisper and sharper, with more straight lines and knife edges. Part of this look came about through the use of a crease line in the side which ended in a set of *lower* fins. . . Like its predecessors, the Biarritz came fully loaded with all the goodies such as the six-way seat, remote boot lock, and almost everything that could be powered was, such as the hood. As Tex Smith and Tony Hossain say in their book on the marque, 'The series 62 was for bargain shoppers, the De Villes were the volume leaders and the Fleetwoods were prestige Cadillacs. The Eldorado Biarritz convertible was the sexy one'.

Huge, befinned, bechromed, smooth, opulent, wasteful, sluggish, ill-handling, thirsty – you can call the 1961 Eldorado Biarritz illustrated here all of these things. They were built for those who believe in the old axiom 'if you got it, flaunt it', for Hollywood stars in the ascendant who want them to be seen in, for Texas cowboy or oil millionaires, for Arab Sheikhs, for the gilded middle-aged youth on the Californian coast or the French Riviera, people to whom subtlety and restraint are anathema, larger than life characters. It's a car in which to be *seen*, and damn the dynamics.

The Eldorado soldiered on as the top-of-the-range convertible for some years, but somehow it became just a loaded Caddie. Until 1967, that is, when the name appeared on a brand-new model like no other Cadillac before. It had front-wheel drive. . .

But that, too, is another story. The Eldorados from 1953 to 1966 symbolised a way of life that by the middle and late sixties spilled over onto everything, so much so that by the end of the sixties all Yankee cars were big, and huge, and –

Well, just like the Eldorado.

CAR LIFE ROAD TEST

CADILLAC

COUPE DE VILLE

With a slogan like "Standard of the World" and a price tag to match, here's a car with a lot to live up to—the question is: Does it?

Our first acquaintance with the 1961 Cadillac Coupe DeVille was upon taking delivery at Cadillac's downtown Los Angeles headquarters. Gliding out onto the Harbor Freeway, we were surprised to find that the car accelerated into high-speed traffic lanes with a smartness that belied its great weight—we hadn't actually weighed the car at that time, but our guess was 5000 pounds. Check the data panel for an idea of how close an estimate that was—we were surprised ourselves.

Chalking up good acceleration for a car of its weight as No. 1 plus factor in favor of the Cadillac, we drove on, up the Harbor Freeway through the nightmare known as "the interchange" where the Hollywood, Harbor, Santa Ana, Pasadena and San Bernardino Freeways all link together. What better way to check out a car's ability to maneuver in close quarters than this, we reasoned. Into this maelstrom of traffic forged the Caddy—dodging and braking for all the world like a rodeo cowboy's roping pony.

So far, we'd found both acceleration and maneuverability to be surprisingly good for a car of this size and weight. Our next step was to explore the characteristics of the handling and brakes. We differentiate maneuverability from handling in these road tests by defining those terms as follows: Maneuverability is jockeying through traffic,

Starting up Angeles Crest Highway, we ran the Cad up and over the mountains down into the Mojave, across the desert floor, then back down through the foothills of the Santa Ana Mountains to San Bernardino; then we used that Freeway we mentioned earlier to return to the Los Angeles area. A round trip of some 200 miles, this course (covered at night) gave us ample opportunity to evaluate the handling and brakes of the Cadillac.

Summed up, the opinion thus formed is of necessity a relative one. In proportion to its size, this car handles very well. In relation to smaller, more agile vehicles, naturally it does not fare so well, of course—but if you're a potential small car buyer, that's one of the reasons you're not interested in Cadillacs!

Winging the Cad around mountain curves uncovers some good, some bad things about the car's engineering. On the good side of the ledger, there's the fact that as there are 2700 pounds of weight on the front wheels, both large cross section tires and power steering became a necessity. The tires were needed to support the weight and yet give reasonable tread life, and of course the combination of all that weight on those big fat tires made the power steering a must. You may wonder what's good about this? What's good is that since they felt a person couldn't steer this car without help anyway, they might just as well forget about the steering effort requirement and build a fast steering ratio into the car. As a result, it requires just 3⅔ turns of the wheel to crank the Caddy's front wheels from full left to full right, or vice-versa. This is considerably quicker than most other American cars currently being produced, and thus gives the Caddy an edge in handling, as well as maneuverability.

Although we may have a reputation of disliking power steering, it isn't true—we merely dislike it when it's overdone. The Cad needs power steering, for most people at any rate, and is furnished with an amount of power boost that we didn't find objectionable. We didn't require the usual 24 hours of acclimatization, and at no time did we sense a lack of road feel even while tooling through the mountains at a good clip. No, in this case the exception proves what the rule *should* be: "There's nothing wrong with power steering if the car is big enough to really need it and the amount of boost is calibrated so as to be innocuous at all times and not interfere with normal road feel."

making U-turns in narrow spaces, and in general, quickness of response in tight spots, including the old bugaboo of the novice driver, parallel parking.

By contrast, handling is the car's ability to make tracks in a situation where the lack of straight road causes average cruising speed to be determined by handling rather than by brute horsepower. We usually get our brake evaluation at the same time we're checking out the car's handling, since the type of road that puts a premium on handling qualities almost invariably gives the brakes a workout as well.

In the case of the sky-blue Cadillac, we explored the potentials of handling and brakes simultaneously by taking a tour of the mountains separating Los Angeles Basin from the Mojave Desert.

Speaking of innocuous, that same term could be applied to the Cad's brakes as well—these were among the very few power brakes we have encountered that didn't irritate us by their "all on or all off" proclivities. Just as the power steering did its job effectively but unobtrusively, so did the power brakes.

While attempting to see how much brake fade could be induced during mountain driving (in conjunction with our handling tests) we found out just how much the power boost was working for us. Although we pounded on the brakes often enough while running downhill to ensure that "fade" was in progress, the power boost's latitude merely made up for the increase in pedal pressure required, and we were completely unaware of anything untoward happening. Frankly, we do not like this, because if abuse of the brakes while running downhill continued long enough, certainly the point would be reached at which, power boost or no, there wouldn't be brakes at all. Due to the power boost keeping the driver in ignorance of the fact that his brakes were literally fading right out from beneath him, this could come apparently "without warning." To the novice, this could be disastrous.

To anticipate just what you could do should the brakes fade to a point of practical ineffectiveness, we tried slowing by downshifting the HydraMatic transmission. Although there was a retardant effect, automatic safety interlocks installed to prevent an inept operator from blowing the gearbox by selecting too low a gear at too high a road speed prevented the slow-down from being anywhere near dramatic—or effective, in the case of total loss of brakes. Our solution to this problem was to use the HydraMatic to control speed on descent through the mountains as much as possible, and rely on the brakes as little as possible. Under these circumstances, brake fade never became serious, which only goes to show that the best way to stay out of trouble in a modern, high performance car is to *know how to drive*.

Our acceleration runs were so good with the Cadillac that we checked the gear ratio to make sure it was standard. Cadillac lists 2.94:1 for all cars except those equipped with air conditioning, as was this one. Those with "air" have a 3.21:1 rear axle ratio, but this cannot be credited with the good acceleration times. Since the air conditioner is heavy, bigger tires are required, and they almost cancel

out the effect of the greater torque multiplication of the lower (numerically) gear ratio. The added weight disposes of the rest of the advantage, so we are convinced that the acceleration figures we recorded are representative of a typical '61 Cadillac.

An interesting phenomenon manifested itself during our acceleration runs. The automatic transmission's shift points seemed to be at a ridiculously low rpm. Subsequent slide rule drill showed that the shifts up to a higher (lower numerically) gear were being made with the engine turning as slow as 3300 rpm. Since it is rated to give its maximum output several hundred rpm higher up, we thought, "Here is a car that can have its acceleration bettered by manually overriding the automatic trans to make it shift at a higher rpm"—until we tried it. Try as we

might, no combination of finagling with different shift points gave figures any better than "George" could do it. We equaled the automaton's best times, but could not best them, so you might as well relax and just stand on it.

Actually, relaxation seems to be the keynote of this year's Cadillac—in fact, at first we found it rather danger- ous. This car is so quiet, so smooth, its hi-fi radio so sooth- ing, its heating-ventilating system so accommodating, that you forget you are in a car—and stop paying attention to your driving. After getting a good scare or two, we decided that perhaps a car could be *too* plush. But after a few days of familiarization the Cad became a car again, albeit a very special one. Once again we found our concentration on the road unwavering, but from a level of comfort we had

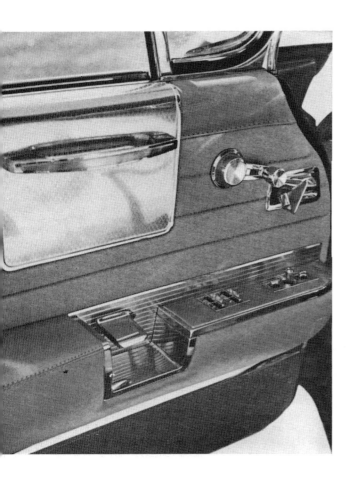

known only once before: while road testing the Lincoln Continental. Truly, if the happy predicament of having to choose between these two cars were *forced* upon us we'd really have to think it over. For longevity, and a little less wishy-washy handling, take the Lincoln—but for that living room on wheels—right now, Cadillac still has the franchise. ∎

CAR LIFE ROAD TEST

CADILLAC COUPE DEVILLE

SPECIFICATIONS

List price	$4810
Price, as tested	5457
Curb weight, lb	4780
Test weight	5080
distribution, %	53.5/46.5
Tire size	8.20-15
Tire capacity, lb	4900
Brake lining area	245
Engine type	V-8, ohv
Bore & stroke	4.00 x 3.87
Displacement, cc	6394
cu in	390
Compression ratio	10.5
Bhp @ rpm	325 @ 4800
equivalent mph	128
Torque, lb-ft	430 @ 3100
equivalent mph	82.8

GEAR RATIOS

4th (1.00), overall	3.21
3rd (1.55)	4.97
2nd (2.55)	8.18
1st (3.97)	12.75

DIMENSIONS

Wheelbase, in	129.5
Tread, f and r	61.0/61.0
Over-all length, in	222
width	79.8
height	55.9
equivalent vol, cu ft	574
Frontal area, sq ft	24.8
Ground clearance, in	5.28
Steering ratio, o/a	18.2
turns, lock to lock	3.7
turning circle, ft	43.1
Hip room, front	53.9
Hip room, rear	48.2
Pedal to seat back	40.6
Floor to ground	9.7
Luggage vol, cu ft	n.a.

PERFORMANCE

Top speed (est), mph	115
best timed run	
3rd (4120)	76
2nd (3980)	42
1st (3270)	22

FUEL CONSUMPTION

Normal range, mpg	12/14

ACCELERATION

0-30 mph, sec	3.5
0-40	4.6
0-50	6.8
0-60	9.5
0-70	13.2
0-80	17.8
0-100	
Standing ¼ mile	17.1
speed at end	78.7

PULLING POWER

4th, lb/ton @ mph	200 @ 60
3rd	360 @ 40
2nd	550 @ 35
Total drag at 60 mph, lb	

SPEEDOMETER ERROR

30 mph, actual	29.0
60 mph	57.3
90 mph	86.4

CALCULATED DATA

Lb/hp (test wt)	15.6
Cu ft/ton mile	100.0
Mph/1000 rpm	26.7
Engine revs/mile	2250
Piston travel, ft/mile	1450
Car Life wear index	32.6

ACCELERATION & COASTING

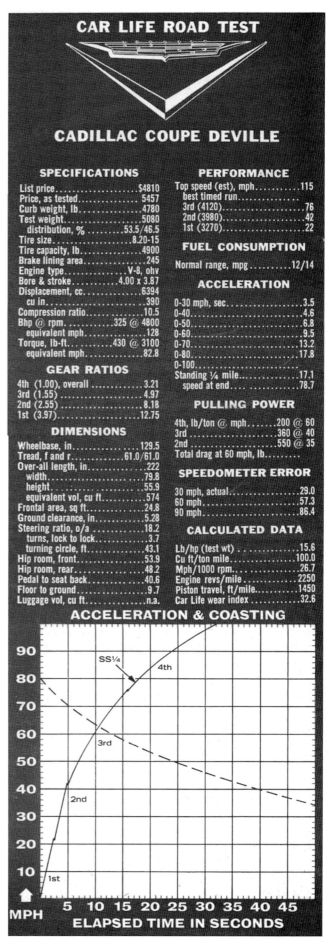

ELAPSED TIME IN SECONDS

Caddy Produces First New Engine in 14 Years

The casual eye will see little change for '63—but take another look

By Robert S. Ball Jr.

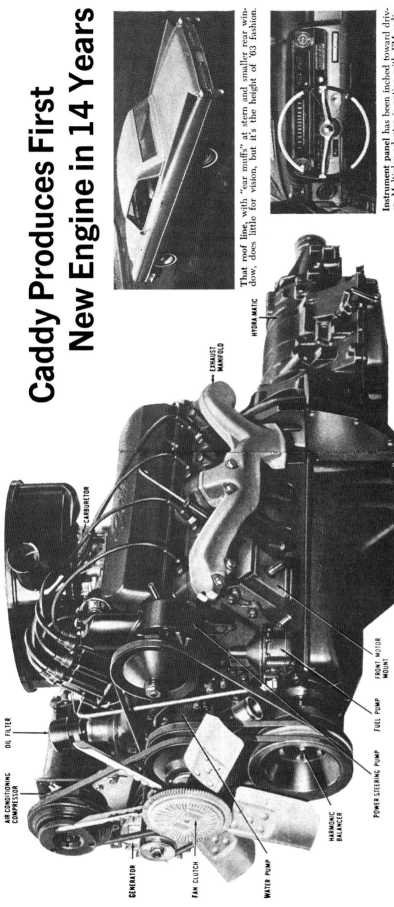

That roof line, with "ear muffs" at stern and smaller rear window, does little for vision, but it's the height of '63 fashion.

Instrument panel has been inched toward driver. Multiplex adapter is option with FM radio.

THE reigning monarch of U. S. luxury cars—the Cadillac, what else?—reached some sort of an anniversary last August. It turned out the last block, pistons, and accessories for an engine that it had used, with periodic modification, for 14 years. Total production in that time: a whopping 1,751,500.

When Caddy started up its factory machinery for the introduction of its 1963 models last month, it began producing a brand-new engine.

Member of the family. The new power plant was in keeping with the automobile's conservative traditions. It was still made of cast iron. It had the same displacement as its predecessor and even the same horsepower. Bore and stroke and compression ratio remained unchanged.

Then what was new in this engine, two years and more in gestation?

Two things stand out. It's lighter by several dozen pounds than last year's motor. (Cadillac engineers like to point out that the Rolls-Royce aluminum engine, seven cubic inches smaller, is actually heavier.) Second, most of the engine accessories have been regrouped in front for easier servicing.

Trimming off the fat. To lighten the engine, designers shaved nearly half an inch off the tops of the blocks, then shortened the connecting rods to keep the same compression. They cut down the length of the block by more than an inch. They hollow-cast the crankshaft,

which is 11 pounds lighter than its '62 counterpart.

A switch to a 42-amp alternator-rectifier system (52 amps in the Series 75 model) saved another 10 pounds. This new unit is about the size of a heater's blower motor.

The front engine cover, the only major aluminum casting under the hood, supports the generator, steering-gear pump, distributor, oil filter, and the water, oil, and fuel pumps.

Among the virtues this adds up to is easier timing. With last year's engine, one mechanic had to turn the distributor

CARBURETOR

EXHAUST MANIFOLD

HYDRAMATIC

FRONT MOTOR MOUNT

FUEL PUMP

POWER STEERING PUMP

HARMONIC BALANCER

WATER PUMP

FAN CLUTCH

GENERATOR

AIR CONDITIONING COMPRESSOR

OIL FILTER

LOOK ALIKES are '62 and '63 Cadillac (right) but new car has many changes including double U-joints, see inset

Cadillac Gets Lighter Engine, Double Universals

LONG LIVE THE FIN, at least the upper one which Cadillacs have worn since 1948. The 1963 car is at left

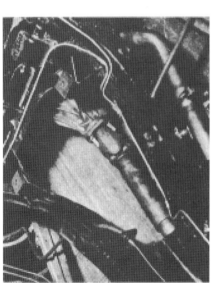

Constant-velocity joints are used at center and rear of drive shaft to reduce the slight vibration and noise set up by ordinary U joints. This is the rear one, at the differential.

(mounted toward the rear of the block) while another read the timing light.

Damping the noise. A more gimmicky innovation is the centrifugal viscous clutch on the five-bladed radiator fan used to pull air through both radiator and condenser on Cadillacs fitted with air conditioning.

Using a thermostat-controlled valve to measure out a silicone fluid between two clutch faces, the fan will barely turn at low engine speeds and low outside temperatures. It will speed up to 3,200 r.p.m. at high outside temperatures and highway speeds. The reason for keeping fan speed down: noise reduction. It also saves a bit of power.

There are other, minor modifications under the hood. The carburetor and positive crankcase-ventilation valve have been tinkered with.

In the light of today's horsepowers, Cadillac's engine of 1949 sounds, in the telling, almost like a caricature of yesteryear. It displaced 331 cubic inches, had a bore and stroke of 3.187 by 3.625 inches, a compression ratio of 7.5:1—and produced all of 160 horsepower.

That engine's immediate predecessor was called the "348" after its cubage. It had a bore and stroke of 3.5 by 4.5, a compression ratio of 7.25:1—and produced 150 horsepower.

With the passing years the cubage of the 1949 engine rose to 390. The bore and stroke became over-square—4 by 3.875. The compression ratio climbed to 10.5:1, the horsepower to 325.

With a disdain for Detroit's now-resumed "horsepower race" that only a car of Cadillac's breeding can exhibit, the power of the new engine remains exactly the same—325.

More sprightly in the joints. For '63, Cadillac also has made significant changes in the chassis for silence and durability. Throwing cost considerations out the window, the company put two constant-velocity universal joints in the propeller shaft as well as an ordinary U joint. The CV joints are in the middle and rear of the drive shaft, the U joint just aft of the transmission.

Constant-velocity joints, by eliminating the small variations in shaft speeds in each revolution, reduce vibration and, therefore, noise.

Cadillac held up use of the CV joint for several years until long-life operation could be assured. Buick, too, employs them. Some foreign cars have used them for many years.

There is more to the Caddy's chassis

CONTINUED ON PAGE 72

Cadillac stylists have an annual problem. Next year's Cadillac must look a lot like last year's, yet at the same time look brand new.

A glance at the '62 and '63 Cadillacs side by side should convince most people that the stylists have solved their problem for '63. The new car looks cleaner and crisper due principally to the removal of the "fin" that ran along the lower body of the '61 and '62, and to the switch to a straight windshield pillar.

What Cadillac calls a "modernized" engine for '63 has a new cast steel crankshaft with cored-out main bearings. The new engine is 1¼ inches shorter, but more important, 52 pounds lighter. The weight reduction is due to a new die cast aluminum front cover on which water pump, oil pump, fuel pump, distributor oil filter and steering gear pump are mounted. Bore and stroke remain 4 x 3.875 inches leaving displacement at 390 cubic inches, and horsepower at 325 is unchanged from '62.

To eliminate high speed vibration and quieten the prop shaft, Cadillac for '63 has gone to a two-piece drive shaft with double constant-velocity universal joints at the rear axle and between the two shafts, and a U-joint at the transmission. Delcotron alternators and extended life lubrication are on all models.

Cadillacs are little changed in size for 1963. Wheelbase remains at 129.5 inches on all but the series 75 limousines, while overall length generally is up an inch to 223,

Eleven pounds lighter than last year, crankshaft is hollow-cast of heat-treated iron alloy. Main bearings are cored out to take the thicker shaft. Shorter pistons help reduce weight, too.

Caddy Produces a New Engine
CONTINUED FROM PAGE 71

refinement for the new model year. Brake cylinders have been fitted with sintered-iron pistons to fight corrosion. A backing plate has been added to the front-wheel brakes to improve sealing in wet and dusty driving. Rear-wheel bearings have special seals to retain their own lubricant.

Cadillacs are about an inch longer than last year, a fraction of an inch narrower. Wheelbase is unchanged at 129.5 inches on 60-series models, 149.8 on the 75 series.

New models are cleaner in line. Fins,

Centrifugal viscous clutch, aluminum-cast, is mounted at end of concentric shafts to save space, eliminate bearing supports. Uneven spacing of fan blades cuts high-speed noise.

first introduced by Cadillac, have receded. For what it may mean, if anything, to a change of the Caddy "image," the word "massive" is missing from the press literature.

Hood and front fenders are split-leveled in a move away from the table-tennis-court design. On two models, the Coupe de Ville and 62-series coupe, the Cinemascope rear window is gone. It's smaller. Adds prestige, they say. The instrument panel is closer to the driver.

Most interesting among the new options is an AM-FM radio, with provision for a stereo-multiplex adapter, and a six-position steering wheel. ■ ■

Cadillac presents for 1962
the Masterwork of the
Motoring Age

1902–1962

Fleetwood Sixty Special, above; Sedan de Ville, below.

The most illustrious motor car in its distinguished sixty year history awaits
your most critical inspection at the Cadillac exhibit. By any standards of judgment,
you will find it the most luxurious, most superbly crafted automobile in all
of motordom. However, the real test of Cadillac superiority is a demonstration drive.
Your authorized dealer will arrange one at your convenience.

Cadillac Series 62 4-window sedan.

INTRODUCING THE '63 CARS

CADILLAC

Sixty, Sixty-Two & Seventy-Five

CADILLACS for 1963 will be slightly longer (about 1 in.) but slightly narrower, too (up to 0.7 in.), than they were in '62 and, like the '62s, have the same strong, solid styling. A straight, rather than curved, windshield post accentuates this feeling and the Coupe de Ville and Sixty-Two coupe have a new, shorter roofline. Padded vinyl tops also are offered, for the Coupe de Ville and Fleetwood Sixty Special. The tailfin, Cadillac says, is "tailored to present a lower profile."

Cadillac, which led the parade to overhead valve V-8s in 1949, has completely up-dated this famous engine with a complete redesign. The new engine, although the same displacement as before, is slightly smaller in overall size and 52 lb. lighter. It develops the same bhp as the '62 engine and is coupled to the same Hydra-Matic transmission. There are numerous other mechanical improvements, including an alternator, an aluminized muffler, a new drive-line with double constant-velocity joints and more safety features.

AM/FM radios are offered as optional equipment as are adjustable, tilting steering wheels. Power steering and power braking are standard equipment.

Series 62 Coupe de Ville.

MODELS & STYLES

Sixty Series	Sixty-Two
	coupe
Fleetwood	4-window sedan
	6-window sedan
Seventy-Five	convertible
limousine	Coupe de Ville
sedan	4-window Sedan de Ville
	6-window Sedan de Ville
	Park Avenue
	Eldorado Biarritz convertible

GENERAL SPECIFICATIONS
(SIXTY-TWO 4-DOOR SEDAN)

Wheelbase, in.........................(Seventy-Five, 149.8)....129.5
track, f & r...61.0
Overall length, in..223.0
    (Park Avenue, 215.0; Seventy-Five, 243.3)
width ....(Seventy-Five, 79.9)....79.7
height ....(Seventy-Five, 59.0)....56.4
box volume, cu. ft...................(Seventy-Five, 662).....580
Luggage capacity, cu. ft. ....n.a.
Fuel tank capacity, gal. 26
Brakes, swept area, sq. in...................................377.0
Tire size   (Seventy-Five, 8.20-15) 8.00-15
Curb weight, lb..n.a.

ENGINE

cu. in.	type	bhp/rpm	torque/rpm	carb.	comp.
390	V-8	325/4800	430/3100	1-4 bbl.	10.5

TRANSMISSION

	4th	3rd	2nd	1st	t.c.
Hydra-Matic (auto.)........	1.00	1.56	2.56	3.97	—

AXLE RATIOS

Automatic transmission—2.94, 3.36, 3.77

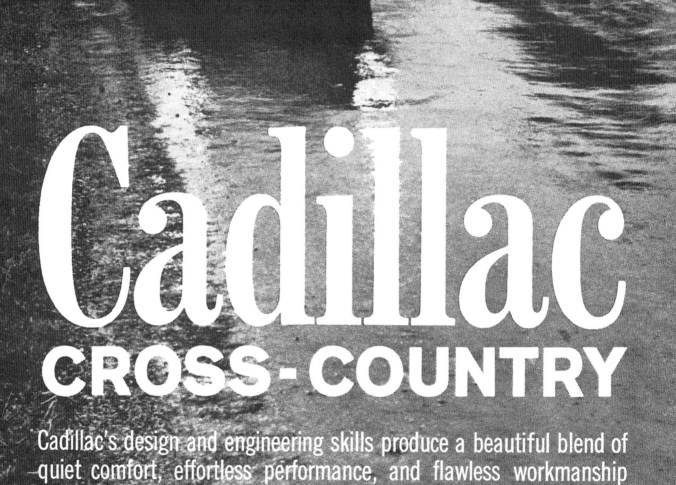

Cadillac
CROSS-COUNTRY

Cadillac's design and engineering skills produce a beautiful blend of quiet comfort, effortless performance, and flawless workmanship

MT Road Test

by Charles Nerpel, *Editor*

TAKE A CORNER of the most comfortable room in your house, add your best leather chair, float a steering wheel in your hands, imagine roadside scenery moving silently by — and you have the sensation of driving the new Cadillac.

Our 1963 Cadillac Coupe deVille test car had only 23 miles on it when we drove out of the Detroit plant, where a few days before this sporty, padded-top model had been just a series of parts numbers on a production-line chart. We did have a good chance to see MOTOR TREND's test car and others being put together on the most rigidly controlled assembly line in the United States. The pace is slower than other makers', allowing more individual attention to construction, with all major components pre-tested and adjusted before installation.

All engines, for example, have several hours of dynamometer time, running in, tuning under load, and inspection before they're put in a car. In addition, spot checks are made by grabbing engines ready for installation off the assembly line and running them again through a tear-down inspection, just to recheck previous procedures. Transmissions, brake systems, alternators — even the rear end, including differential, axles, bearings, and wheels — are also run in before assembly to the chassis.

As they leave the final production line, Cadillacs are ready to drive without a so-called break-in period. About all that's necessary for customer delivery is removal of the protective coating from the whitewall tires.

Simulated road conditions and test-running at the factory had prepared MOTOR TREND's test car, just like every Cadillac made, for regular driving immediately. We appreciated this because we drove out of the plant right smack into the thick of Detroit's metropolitan traffic. As if this baptism weren't enough for a sparkling new car, the weather was cold, and miserable rain loosened all the summer dirt into a dulling spray thrown up by passing cars. Instant heat, instant de-fogging, and a test of wipers were in order. All controls gave immediate action, with a ready flow of controllable heat, a good volume of warm, drying air over the inside windshield surface, and a wide, clean windshield pattern from the wiper blade arcs.

GM's Harrison Radiator Division, which designed the air-cooling and heating system for the Cadillac, had incorporated this unit into a complete climate control for car interiors. The refrigerated-air system and the air-heating system can be operated together, making it possible to heat refrigerated air. Unusual as this may sound, there's a noticeable difference between warm or hot air from heater control alone and warmed cooled air. Humidity under conditions of warming refrigerated air is more comfortable when outside

continued

MT'S SERIES 62 COUPE DEVILLE TEST CAR BRUSHED OFF THE RIGORS OF VARIED WEATHER AND ROAD CONDITIONS DURING 2600-MILE TRIP.

CADILLAC CROSS-COUNTRY

air is on the chilly (but not frigid) side. Of course, interior air outlets for cool and hot air are separate. When only the heater is on, warm air enters the car near the floor in the firewall area, but the regular air-conditioning outlets spew warmed cooled air when the two systems are blended. All controls for this combined interior temperature system, including high, low, and intermediate speeds for the nearly silent fan, are in one panel to the left of the steering column.

Much has been done to improve comfort in passenger cars generally, but Cadillac works at making the ultimate a reality. Seating and isolation of engine and road noises

Optional six-position steering wheel angle adjustment allows selection of desired stance while driving, ensures ample room for the stout drivers and good visibility for the short ones.

Handling ease and sure-footed stability are maintained on high-speed curves (RIGHT), without sacrificing the smooth ride and quiet comfort on the rough, gravel-covered detours (BOTTOM).

are only a part of this comfort engineering. Good temperature control and ventilation do much to lower wind noise. This plus general stability over bumps, dips, and around curves, coupled with the driver's ability to adjust himself in a position of complete ease behind the wheel, all contribute to the ultimate in comfort.

Cadillac doesn't believe in undercoating. Their engineers design for noise isolation instead of attempting to absorb or deaden existing noises inherent in a design. This isn't to say that there's *no* sound-deadening material in Cadillacs, but they do use a minimum compared to other luxury cars. Extra-size rubber bushings, designed for different cushioning rates at several impact angles, are used in all suspension pivot points. Freon-gas-filled shocks, introduced on Cadillac several years ago, are also great contributors to the car's quiet, stable operation. With this silent, non-swaying ride, devoid of the seasickening sensation once associated with such smoothness, the Series 62 has successfully combined living-room luxury with handling qualities compatible with the car's power and speed.

Power and speed are important, but the proper ratio of the power potential of the engine to performance demands is important for smooth and efficient motoring. Cadillac's new engine — lighter, smoother, and displacing 390 cubic inches — develops 325 hp at 4800 rpm. Like all engines for the full Cadillac line, this ohv, 90-degree V-8 has 10.5-to-1 (premium-fuel) compression ratio and a four-barrel carburetor. The torque output of 430 pounds-feet at 3100 rpm provides good acceleration at all speeds. Standard drive train includes the four-speed Hydra-Matic transmission and 2.94-to-1 rear-axle ratio.

Top gear gives 25 mph per 1000 rpm with 8.20 x 15 tires, but kick-down into third requires just a little extra throttle pressure even at 70 mph to provide that extra punch for shortened passing distances. The engine turns 4500 rpm in third (at 75 mph), and 4300 rpm produces 25 mph in first and 40 mph in second. Two settings for DRIVE allow quadrant selection to hold the Hydra-Matic in third for engine braking or to reduce automatic downshifting from fourth to third in heavy traffic.

The engine itself, all new for 1963, is one inch lower, four inches narrower, and 1¼ inches shorter than last year's powerplant. It adds up to a weight saving of nearly 52 pounds. Water pump, oil and fuel pumps, distributor, oil filter, and power steering pump are grouped together on a die-cast aluminum cover on the front of the engine — a great aid for easier servicing of these important components. Also helping performance and durability are the cast Armasteel crankshaft and cored-out main bearings of larger diameter for lighter weight and better wear characteristics — this plus shorter, lighter pistons.

Added weight reduction and improved electrical power output are provided by the Delcotron alternator, standard for '63. The normal unit has a 45-ampere output, but cars equipped with air-conditioning systems come with a 52-ampere unit. Even the five-bladed fan is alloy on air-conditioned cars, and it has a sensing device to maintain maximum efficiency for both speed and temperature.

Drive line noise, a big concern with most designers, has been virtually eliminated by using a split driveshaft, divided by a double, constant-velocity universal joint. Utilizing a

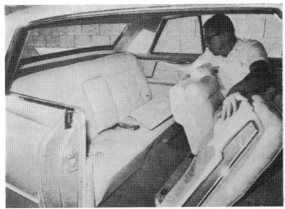

Rear seat has a folding center arm rest that doesn't interfere with the center seat back comfort when stowed.

Electric control console on driver's door groups all the switches for windows, windwings, seats, and door locks into one convenient location for fingertip operation.

Bench-type front seat (bucket seats are optional) has a center folding arm rest, well padded and wide enough for both driver and passenger. Both front seat backs can be tilted forward for easy rear seat access.

HEADING SOUTH IN THE CRISP, COLD DAWN, CADILLAC'S INTERIOR COMFORT FEATURES AND CLIMATE CONTROL MAKE DRIVING A PLEASURE.

front shaft anchored near the center, the relatively short rear section of this drive line is practically insensitive to heavy passenger or luggage loads.

Body design of the Coupe deVille is very interesting, especially the roof. Over the regular steel top is a layer of insulated padding, and covering this is cross-grain vinyl. The result is a smooth line, with the sporty look of a padded-top convertible. We believe that much of the silent ride and most of the air conditioning and heating efficiency are due to the pleasing roof material. It deadens noise and insulates against heat and cold.

Other styling changes for 1963 include a completely new front-end treatment, plus new hood sheet metal. A close look at this shape reveals a striking similarity to last year's rear deck lid, turned around of course, so that the lateral crease is forward. In addition, the ventral fins that ran along the lower rear fenders have been eliminated, smoothing the entire rear end and making the upper fins less conspicuous. Stop lights, combined with turn signals in the rear, are more noticeable when separated from the regular tail light system. Front lighting, using quad lamps, has been designed into the slight separate-fender-from-body style, and last year's curb light for illuminating the blind spot just outboard of the headlight beam has been retained and improved. This light, which comes on when the turn signal is actuated, is a valuable driving aid for maneuvering into dark, narrow areas.

On the road or in traffic, driving the Cadillac is a pleasure. Fingertip electric adjustment of the seat through a wide range of height, distance, and tilt, plus six different steering wheel settings, puts any driver in a near-perfect stance to handle this 129-inch-wheelbase car as if it were a compact.

Driving position probably has more to do with the feeling of the size of a car than anything else. Small cars with high steering wheels, low seats, and great seat-to-pedal distance can and do give smaller drivers the feeling they're driving a truck. Cadillac adjustments, on the other hand, provide

even the short driver with a position of visibility and ease not ordinarily associated with cars nearly 19 feet long.

This same lightness and sure-footed control are best noted on expressways and turnpikes, some of which now have legal speeds up to 75 or 80 mph. Route 66, under its present conditions of divided super-highway, stretches under construction, and about-to-be-abandoned parts of the "old" highway, gives just about every type of touring anyone's likely to find on a cross-country trip. Handling on curves and in the wet is firm, and the optional limited-slip differential shows its advantages in the loose gravel of detours.

Braking is superb, with a double system that still assures either forward or rear wheel braking, should one or the other half fail through line fracture or other mishap. All in all, cross-country touring in a Cadillac is like a conducted tour in your own private floating compartment.   /MT

All-new engine is smaller, lighter, smoother, and more rugged, with major serviceable components more accessible for repair or adjustment. New feature is the lightweight Delcotron alternator.

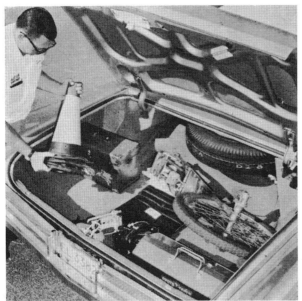

More usable luggage space is available through location of spare in seldom-used area over the rear axle body hump.

Cast iron drums with cooling fins house self-adjusting shoes. Hydraulic cylinders operated by dual master unit have new long-wearing, sintered-iron pistons.

The optional cruise control mounted on cowl can maintain constant speed on either level or hills. A touch of the brake pedal unlocks the system.

1963 CADILLAC SERIES 62 COUPE DE VILLE

2-door, 6-passenger sedan

OPTIONS ON CAR TESTED: Air conditioning, AM-FM radio, controlled differential, adjustable steering wheel, power headlight control, cruise control, power seat control

BASIC PRICE: $5386
ODOMETER READING AT START OF TEST: 23 miles
RECOMMENDED ENGINE RED LINE: 5000 rpm

PERFORMANCE

ACCELERATION (2 aboard)

0-30 mph	3.6 secs.
0-45 mph	6.4
0-60 mph	10.4

Standing start ¼-mile 19 secs. and 81 mph

Speeds in gears @ shift points
1st ......25 mph @ 4300 rpm
2nd ......40 mph @ 4300 rpm
3rd ......75 mph @ 4500 rpm

Speedometer Error on Test Car

Car's speedometer reading	30	45	50	60	71	81
Weston electric speedometer	30	45	50	60	70	80

Observed miles per hour per 1000 rpm in top gear ....25 mph
Stopping Distances — from 30 mph, 40 ft.; from 60 mph, 156 ft.

SPECIFICATIONS FROM MANUFACTURER

Engine
90-degree ohv V-8
Bore: 4.0 ins.
Stroke: 3.875 ins.
Displacement: 390 cubic inches
Compression ratio: 10.5:1
Horsepower: 325 @ 4800 rpm
Torque: 430 lbs.-ft. @ 3100 rpm
Horsepower per cubic inch: 0.83
Ignition: 12-volt coil

Gearbox
Hydra-Matic 4-speed automatic; quadrant selector

Driveshaft
Two-piece, open tube, with double constant-velocity joint

Differential
Ring and pinion — limited-slip
Standard ratio: 2.94:1

Suspension
Front: Independent, with coil springs, tubular shocks, stabilizer bar
Rear: Solid axle; 4-link stabilizer, coil springs, tubular shocks

Steering
Ball nut sector, with in-line hydraulic power
Turning diameter: 43 ft.
Turns: 3.7 lock to lock

Wheels and Tires
15-inch slotted steel disc wheels
8.20 x 15 tires

Brakes
Hydraulic drum; servo, self-adjusting
Front: 12-in. composite cast iron — finned
Rear: 12-in. composite cast iron — finned
Effective lining area: 221.8 sq. ins.

Body and Frame
Separate steel body on X-member frame
Wheelbase: 129.5 ins.
Track: front, 61 ins.; rear, 61 ins.
Overall length: 223.0 ins.
Shipping weight: 4750 lbs.

1963 CADILLAC

Power and smoothness characterize this truncated status symbol

CADILLAC'S brand-new engine, described elsewhere in this issue, prompted us to give one of the 1963 cars a full-scale road test. But which one should we try? The ultra-plush Sixty Special has always been considered one of the most desirable models, but for our test we finally selected a new model introduced in 1962—the Park Avenue sedan.

The Park Avenue is similar to other 4-window sedan models in all respects save one—the rear overhang and trunk area are 8 in. shorter. This brings the overall length down from 18½ ft. to slightly under 18 ft. and thus makes the Park Avenue just that much easier to park on Park Avenue. And it will fit into most pre-war garages, while the standard 223-in. models often will not. Although some local branch office personnel could not understand our selection of the "shorty," we think it looks much better without the extremely extended look of the others

and, of course, there is the additional advantage of less frequent tail end dragging on steep driveways, etc. Even so, the rear end overhang measures 52 in., quite some bit more than the 44 in. overhang of the first model with tail-fins (1948).

Frankly, the new engine surprised us in several important departments. First, though Cadillac justifiably claims the new powerplant makes the car smoother and quieter, we didn't expect the difference to be so noticeable. Our test car had 7 miles on the odometer when we took possession and, to our surprise, there is a difference. Maybe not much, but in 10 days of noiseless driving we came to realize that the car is even more refined, smoother and quieter than *Car Life*'s last Cadillac test car (June 1961). If the electric clock had worked, it would have been the loudest sound inside the car.

The noise level outside the car was a bit higher; for some reason this new

engine is more audible than its predecessors and a definite exhaust note is obvious at idle.

A second area of difference has more to do with the road feel of the car itself. Our 1961 test car had a slight tendency to shake when driving on the freeway at 60–65 mph. This manifested itself as an up and down bounce of the hood and occurred only when the road strips were spaced so as to coincide with the front wheel hop frequency. The 1963 car, with numerous small but important changes in the suspension, neither bounces nor shakes at any speed, on any type of surface.

The power steering is excellent but lacks in "feel." A steering booster is, of course, an absolute necessity on a car of this weight and we particularly liked the relatively quick steering, just under 4 turns lock to lock, which is employed. However, there isn't enough feel-of-the-road and little feel of the transition from no-power to power.

But there is some automatic return action after rounding a corner. Thus, our major criticism is that it seems to take a certain amount of skill at the wheel to keep the car in its own lane while traversing twisty multi-lane roads. The car will track and point exactly where you put it, but without a "feel" reference it takes considerably more visual attention from the driver to avoid crowding other cars under such conditions. Maybe it's just that we were overly conscious of our dollar responsibility—as well as being not too familiar with such a very large automobile.

The brake booster warrants high praise for not being too sensitive, yet retaining an action very light and properly progressive. The brakes, by the way, survived our two 80-mph crash stops, a feat all the more remarkable because of the 2.5 tons being slowed and the fact that less than half the cars we test can pass this test. (Some lighter cars we've tried will not pass even one crash stop from 80 mph without brake fade.)

"Step lightly, proud foot" is an old Cadillac slogan that might well be resurrected. When the foot gets heavy this car moves in impressive fashion. A 0-60 mph time of 10 sec. and 0-100 mph in half a minute suffice to categorize this facet of performance. On paper the Cadillac should be capable of even better performance but the

LOSS OF ventral fins from 1962 design, along with 8-in. shorter rear end, give improved sense of balance and proportion to styling of Park Avenue.

luxury car image has more or less forced the engineers to sacrifice a second or two by the design of the automatic transmission.

As before, the 4-speed Hydra-Matic transmission is used as standard equipment in all Cadillacs. The principal changes for 1963 are in heat-treating and materials to provide quieter gears with more durability. As is well-known, the Hydra-Matic uses a fluid coupling rather than the less efficient torque converter. In 1956 the unit was redesigned with higher (numerical) ratios to give converter-like breakaway from a dead stop (2nd gear is identical to the older 1st gear, 1st gear is even lower, or higher numerically). At the same time a second small fluid coupling was added in order to im-

prove shifting smoothness. Under full throttle the shifts can be felt, but in normal driving the 1-2 upshift is virtually impossible to detect and it requires concentrated attention to feel/hear the other shifts.

However, the shift points at wide open throttle are set at very low engine rpm—far below the peak power speed of 4800 rpm. This has been done to accentuate the luxury feel—the driver is never aware of the engine racing away and as the speed of the car goes up the shift-point rpm can also be raised because wind noise tends to cover up engine noise. Shifts from 1 to 2 are made automatically at 3600 rpm, but shifts 2-3 and 3-4 can be controlled by the column-mounted lever and we achieved our best accel-

Park Avenue

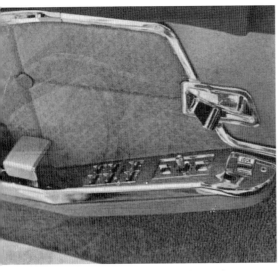

ARM REST console invites experimentation.

GROPE-FREE layout groups controls well for left-hand use.

STEERING WHEEL

CADILLAC

eration times by holding as high as 4800 rpm (49 mph in 2nd, 81 in 3rd). Even so, the time lag between gears is ferocious and these full-throttle up-shifts will consume as much as 1 sec. elapsed time.

We do think that "Super" range, which holds 3rd gear, might possibly be revised to give something similar to Chrysler's heavy-duty drag racing automatic which upshifts with a solid bite and at 5400 rpm. Then the owner could have the full potential perform-ance on demand and shift to "Drive" for traditional Cadillac luxury. At any rate the performance available is good and then, too, how many Cadillac owners go drag racing?

Many Cadillac drivers will swear they get 18, even 20 miles per gallon. Maybe such figures are attainable un-der favorable conditions and certainly the efficient Hydra-Matic transmission is an important factor in Cadillac's reputation for being easy on gas. We got an overall average of 13 mpg and when we used "Super" around town to avoid the too frequent 3-4 and 4-3 shifts, the mileage dropped below 12 mpg. Our best tank average was 14 mpg for 400 miles, driving at 65 mph most of the time. It takes fuel to pro-pel 5000 lb. of automobile (although a 2500-lb. car will not necessarily double the Cadillac's mpg rate).

Interior features are luxurious and complete, but not ostentatious. Electric seat adjustment and window lifts are

standard equipment and a majority of the cars built are ordered with air con-ditioning which costs $473 extra. Our test car had this option and it proved to be very effective as well as quieter than most. The instrument panel lay-out didn't appeal to any of our staff —no one could quite say why, other than that it just resembled those on all other GM products. It did have all the operating controls grouped on the left side (a convenience for right-handed drivers) and the six window buttons, three seat controls and power door lock button all on the left-door arm rest-cum-console. We found that we could learn the controls like a keyboard, moving windows up and down, changing the seat position and locking/unlocking the doors without averting our eyes from the road. The dash paneling also has good crash-padding along its top and front. The steering column had the new "swing-up" adjustment feature which we rec-

AIR CONDITIONER pump is above engine; battery has cool location.

SPARE TAKES much trunk space, but remaining room is impressive.

djustable for rake.   RIGHT HAND'S only duties are range selection and radio controls.   AN INVITATION to luxurious motoring.

ommend as an aid to more comfortable driving.

The trunk space was a little disappointing despite what we thought was considerable rear end overhang. The spare tire really takes up far too much space (it is moved up over the rear axle in the coupes) although there is still room for 3 or 4 good sized pieces of luggage.

In the final analysis, the Cadillac is as fine a car as you can find on the road today. It is a big car in size, surely, but big, too, in luxury, quality and durability. ∎

CAR LIFE ROAD TEST

1963 CADILLAC
Sixty-Two Park Avenue Sedan

SPECIFICATIONS

List price	$5633
Price, as tested	6652
Curb weight, lb	4855
Test weight	5190
distribution, %	54/46
Tire size	8.20-15
Tire capacity, lb @ 24 psi	5660
Brake lining area	377
Engine type	V-8, ohv
Bore & stroke	4.00 x 3.875
Displacement, cu in	390
Compression ratio	10.5
Bhp @ rpm	325 @ 4800
equivalent mph	126
Torque, lb-ft	430 @ 3100
equivalent mph	81
Carburetion	1 x 4

EXTRA-COST OPTIONS

AM/FM radio, power door locks, air condit., power seat, wsw tires, antifreeze, door guards, tinted glass, automatic dimmer, remote trunk release.

DIMENSIONS

Wheelbase, in	129.5
Tread, f and r	61.0/61.0
Over-all length, in	215.0
width	79.9
height	55.8
equivalent vol, cu ft	555
Frontal area, sq ft	24.8
Ground clearance, in	5.28
Steering ratio, o/a	18.2
turns, lock to lock	3.7
turning circle, ft	43.0
Hip room, front	63.3
Hip room, rear	63.4
Pedal to seat back, max	40.0
Floor to ground	14.0
Luggage vol, cu ft	n.a.
Fuel tank capacity, gal	21.0

GEAR RATIOS

4th (1.00), overall		3.21
3rd (1.55)		4.97
2nd (2.55)		8.18
1st (3.97)		12.7

PERFORMANCE

Top speed (4400), mph	114
Shifts, rpm-mph (forced)	
3rd (4800)	81
2nd (4800)	49
1st (3600)	24

ACCELERATION

0-30 mph, sec	3.6
0-40	5.1
0-50	7.4
0-60	10.0
0-70	12.8
0-80	16.1
0-100	28.5
Standing ¼ mile	17.7
speed at end	83

FUEL CONSUMPTION

Normal range, mpg	12-14

SPEEDOMETER ERROR

30 mph, actual	27.8
60 mph	59.1
90 mph	88.1

CALCULATED DATA

Lb/hp (test wt)	16.0
Cu ft/ton mile	99.5
Mph/1000 rpm	26.2
Engine revs/mile	2290
Piston travel, ft/mile	1480
Car Life wear index	33.9

PULLING POWER

70 mph, lb/ton	330
50	425
30	570
Total drag at 60 mph, lb	215

ACCELERATION & COASTING

4th

SS¼

3rd

2nd

1st

MPH — 5 10 15 20 25 30 35 40 45
ELAPSED TIME IN SECONDS

WHAT MILEAGE DO CADILLAC OWNERS GET?

AUTOMATIC TRANSMISSION
City Driving
Country Driving

MORE CITY DRIVERS got a fuel consumption rate of 10 miles per gallon than any other. On the open road, 15 miles per gallon was the most common figure

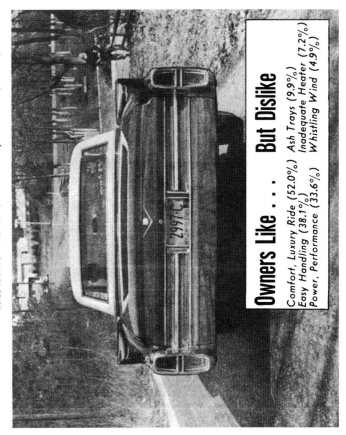

BEGINNING WITH THE P-38 LOOK right after World War II, Cadillac originated tail fins in the domestic market. They're lower now, but they won't die

ELEGANCE OF CADILLAC STYLING was mentioned by over half the owners surveyed as a major factor in their decision to buy the General Motors luxury car

---

Owners Like . . .

Comfort, Luxury Ride (52.0%)
Easy Handling (38.1%)
Power, Performance (33.6%)

But Dislike

Ash Trays (9.9%)
Inadequate Heater (7.2%)
Whistling Wind (4.9%)

Cadillac Owners Praise Handling Comfort, Find Ash Trays Distressing

A Nationwide Survey Based on 905,927 Owner-Driven Miles

Marginal and boldface comments by Jim Whipple, *PM's* Automotive Editor

CURIOSITY prompted *PM's* choice of Cadillac as a subject for an owners report. The car has been the unchallenged leader of its class for years and currently outsells its two domestic competitors *combined* by a three-to-one margin.

Although it is priced at less than half the cost of a Rolls Royce, Cadillac has become a world-wide symbol of a top-quality motor car. It is equally esteemed by Arabian sheiks, Argentine cattle barons and American bankers.

But why do these—and others—choose Cadillac? Although it sounds almost absurd, the reason that most people buy Cadillacs is simply because the car is a Cadillac. For example, 77.1 percent traded another Cadillac for this year's model, and 78 percent cited previous ownership as a primary reason for buying.

Of the entire group responding, a whopping 75.8 percent stated that they did not consider buying another luxury car. Of the 24.2 percent who did consider another car before buying their Cadillacs, 55.6 percent considered the Lincoln Continental, 16.7 percent looked at the big Buick, 11.1 percent considered the Imperial, while 5.6 percent each had looked into Oldsmobile and Thunderbird. And an overwhelming 98.7 percent stated that they

*Can you think of another car with a play on Broadway like the →
"Solid Gold Cadillac?"*

Cadillac management has shrewdly resisted temptation to over-→ produce for quick profits, thus they always have an order backlog and used models remain high in value

In no other owners report has reputation played so important a role in determining a purchase →

People seem to look for these qualities no matter what car they buy →

Cadillac owners are not fusspots. Those '63 ash trays are a comedy of errors →

That four-speed Hydra-Matic transmission and the 2.94 rear-axle ratio are what make the heavy Cad so surprisingly thrifty →

Note similar mileage at 30 and 50 m.p.h.; it's due to transmission characteristics making 50 a very economical cruising speed →

did *not* consider an imported luxury car which we assume would include such makes as Rolls Royce, Mercedes Benz and Jaguar.

In addition to previous ownership other important reasons given by owners for their purchases were comfort (62.3 percent), reputation (58.3 percent) and styling (54.3 percent). (Note that these are overlapping percentages.)

After driving their Cadillacs for an average of 4175 miles, the owners checked off as their Best Liked features, a list surprisingly similar to that of a group of low-priced car owners. The top four were Riding Comfort, Handling Ease, Performance and Styling in that order.

Some 46.2 percent of all owners reporting had no complaints whatsoever. Topping the list of what complaints there were was the location of ash trays. This is something of a left-handed compliment; a car must be pretty good if its major fault is misplaced ash trays.

Fuel economy would not seem to be important to owners of a luxury car costing over $6000, but Cadillac owners are aware of the degree of thirst of their cars.

A solid 69.1 percent felt that their Cadillacs were delivering about the mileage expected, which for most drivers ran between 10 and 14 miles per gallon in city traffic and from 12 to 17 miles per gallon on the open roads.

As a check, and for comparison with other cars, *PM* ran constant speed fuel mileages with a fuel meter on its test Cadillac. The car, a Coupe de Ville hardtop, had a full complement of power accessories including air conditioning. It delivered these fuel mileages:

19.83 miles per gallon at 30 m.p.h.
22.85 miles per gallon at 40 m.p.h.
19.18 miles per gallon at 50 m.p.h.
17.53 miles per gallon at 60 m.p.h.
15.65 miles per gallon at 70 m.p.h.

Over-all fuel consumption for approximately 850 miles of driving, about 40 percent of which was in city traffic, worked out to 14.9 miles per gallon.

The owners rated their Cadillacs high with 76.2 percent stating that the cars were excellent, while 20.6 percent felt that they were good. Only 1.4 percent of those reporting categorized their Cadillacs as fair, while 1.8 rated them as poor.

One sure proof of a car's worth is the inclination of its owners to buy another one of the same make. Cadillac owners made it almost unanimous with 91.4 percent of all the owners reporting that they would buy again.

Of the remaining 8.6 percent, 6.8 percent was undecided while 1.8 percent said that they would not buy another Cadillac.

What do the owners themselves say about their Cadillacs? Here, from the affirmative comments made, are the five that were mentioned most often:

"Rides well on both bumpy roads and smooth pavements."—New York restaurant owner.

"I like the driving comfort and lack of fatigue after a long drive."—Iowa surgeon.

"It's easy handling for its size."—New Jersey housewife.

"It's just like driving a cloud—practically effortless!"—New Jersey salesman.

"A nice running and easily handled automobile."—Illinois steamship agent.

"My Cadillac handles very well at all speeds."—Indiana doctor.

"Like its precision in handling."—New York clergyman.

"I like its smooth, quick acceleration."—Pennsylvania merchant.

"Has speed when needed."—New York sales engineer.

"I like the simplicity of styling; they've eliminated the

PM testers found Cadillac's ride generally superior, although on bad washboard surfaces there was some muffled vibration from the massive unsprung rear wheel and axle assembly →

Let's put it this way: If clouds were equipped with power steering, they'd handle like Cadillacs! →

Steering is precise and the car goes exactly where you point it. But some drivers may feel that the steering is a bit too light and easy →

SUMMARY OF OWNERS REPORT

EXCELLENT	76.2%	
GOOD	20.6%	
FAIR	1.4%	
POOR	1.8%	
PERCENTAGES	0 10 20 30 40 50 60 70 80 90 100	

Mileage experience
About as expected 69.1%
Better 14.5
Not as good 16.4

Best-liked features
Riding comfort 52.0
Handling ease 38.1
Power, performance 33.6
Styling 31.4
Smooth, quiet 10.3
Roominess 6.7
Adequate headroom 6.3

Specific complaints
Location of ash trays 9.9
Inadequate heater 7.2
Wind noise 4.9
Doors, windows fit poorly 4.0

Mechanical trouble if any
No mechanical trouble 76.7
Excessive oil consumption 3.1
Defective oil seal 1.8
Windshield wipers 1.8
Fast engine idle 1.8

Best-liked exterior style features
Clean, smooth look 10.8
Simple, plain, classic lines 9.0
Lower fins 6.3
Hood 6.3
Grille 4.0
Small rear window 4.0
Long, low lines 3.6
Front end 3.6

Least-liked exterior style features
Rear window 4.5%
Fins 4.0
Fenders 2.7
Length 1.8
Vulnerable front end 1.8
No protective molding 1.3
Plain, undistinguished 1.3

Best-liked interior style features
Dashboard 13.0
Upholstery 10.6
Comfortable seats 10.3
Adjustable seats 3.6
Arm rests 2.7
Legroom 2.2
Color harmony 2.2
Luxurious, quality look 2.2
Interior lighting 1.8

Least-liked interior style features
Ash trays 9.0
Transmission hump 5.4
Glove compartment 4.0
Upholstery 3.6
Uncomfortable seats 3.1
Dashboard 2.2
Interior lighting 2.2

Decision to buy Cadillac most influenced by:
Previous ownership 78.0
Comfort 62.3
Reputation 58.3

Consider buying another luxury car?
Did not consider 75.8%
Did consider 24.2

What make?
Lincoln Continental 55.6
Imperial 11.1
Buick 16.7

Consider An Imported Luxury Car?
Did not consider 98.7
Did consider 1.3

Make of family's other car, if any
No other car 41.7
Another Cadillac 6.3
Chevrolet 19.7
Other General Motors compacts 5.4
Other General Motors make 9.0
Ford 10.8
Other Ford Motor compacts 3.1
Other Ford Motor make 5.4
Chrysler Corp. compacts 0.9
Other Chrysler Corp. make 4.5
Other U.S. make 5.4

How is dealer service?
Excellent 60.5
Average 36.6
Poor 3.2

Would you buy from him again?
Yes, would buy again 68.1
No, would not 4.5

Would you buy another Cadillac?
Yes, would buy 91.4
No, would not buy 1.8

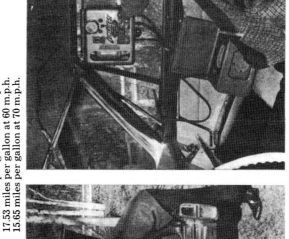

THE CAVERNOUS CADILLAC TRUNK is even equipped with a neatly painted wooden wedge to block a wheel in the unhappy event that you get a flat tire

PM'S FUEL METER REPORTED steady-speed economy up to 22.85 miles per gallon, but weight—nearly three tons—keeps owners' highway results under 20 m.p.g.

85

heavy, bulky appearance."—Connecticut labor union official.

Good general appearance — it's not ornate," Michigan sales manager.

"I like most its over-all length and streamlined appearance."—Ohio clerical worker.

A couple of years ago Cadillac offered a "compact" model with seven inches lopped off the trunk. It sold like a Valentine card on the 15th of February.

"Like the clean lines from front to rear."—New York investigator.

"The car has an all-around quality that makes for pleasant operation."—Washington retiree.

"It's the smoothest of the four different cars I've owned."—Ohio physician.

In normal driving Cadillac goes like a velvet canoe in a lake of pure cream.

Corresponding negative comments also were made, of course. Here, in the order of their frequency, are the five most often recorded:

"Do not like the dash ash tray; driver's side not illuminated."—Ohio executive.

"I wish the ash trays were better located and larger."—Arkansas investment counselor.

"Put the ash tray where it was in the '62 model."—Michigan executive.

"Ash trays difficult to open and midget-sized glove compartment, likewise."—California grain dealer.

On PM's test car the Auto Editor's wife broke a fingernail trying to get into flush-door right-hand tray.

"Heating system is too slow."—Illinois executive.

"On cars having air conditioning, there is no arrangement for getting fresh air into the car without having the air conditioner or heater on, or having a window open, and there are many times when neither of these is desirable."—Florida retiree.

Efforts to "simplify" Cadillac heater controls have gone awry, but completely! You cannot get either hot or cold air without using blower, and car is so tightly sealed that you need top blower speed to demist windshield.

"Heater fan and heater controls should be on right side of steering wheel."—Ohio retiree.

"Defrosters do not heat the bottom of the windshield, so snow sticks at the bottom."—New York restaurant owner.

"There's too much wind noise from wind wings—one cannot even hear the radio or talk."—California contractor.

One of the problems of making a truly quiet running car—little noises become big nuisances. Incidentally the radio (AM-FM) has great tonal quality. What this car needs most is a means of getting a large volume of fresh air into and out of the body quietly.

"Poorly fitting doors and windows which cause whistling noise."—Ohio executive. "It uses too much oil."—Tennessee pharmacist.

Returning to the bright side, here are numbers 6 through 10 of the praiseworthy points Cadillac owners mentioned. They're listed in the order of their frequency:

"Plenty of space for family travel."—Illinois factory representative.

"It's easy to get into, has good headroom."—New Jersey sales engineer.

Front and rear headroom dimensions are above average on '63 Cadillac.

"I like the higher top; it's easy for a tall person to ride without striking head."—Connecticut retiree.

"I like the convenience and dependability of the Cadillac."—Alabama accountant.

"Like the tip-up steering wheel."—New York physician.

It offers a worthwhile change of position, but the six-way power seat is much more important to driver comfort.

"I like the '63 model better than the '60. It has more headroom and better visibility when in traffic."—New York executive.

Large glass areas and sharply defined "corners" of the car make close-quarter driving less of a problem than you'd expect with a car this size.

"I like the performance, comfort and visibility."—New Jersey contractor.

For each bit of praise, some owner has a corresponding comment about something that disappointed him. Following are numbers six through 10 of the shortcomings noted:

"Very, very poor paint job over-all."—Michigan retiree.

"Poor paint job; they didn't tape up the white top when painting body."—Arizona doctor.

At $6000-plus, the paint job should be perfect on every single car.

"Selection of seat upholstery the worst in years. Cadillac buyers are entitled to much better."—Michigan retiree.

"It seems to me that the interiors are less attractive on each model I buy, and I have owned seven to date."—Nebraska retiree.

"Upholstery is not top quality."—South Carolina physician.

If you consider top quality equal to the grade of materials used in the $16,000 import whose initials are RR, you'd have to agree with the doctor.

"Body interior quality not as good as it should have been."—Michigan retiree. "'Ford' hardtop styling cuts down essential visibility toward rear of vehicle."—Indiana advertising executive.

He's right, of course, but this "blind rear quarter" styling originated on T-Bird, is the hottest thing in styling since fins went back to the fish.

"It should get better gas mileage compared to other Cadillacs I've had; I only get 12 to 14 m.p.g."—California businessman.

"It uses too much gas, but this was expected."—California housewife.

"It's too noisy for a luxury car."—Connecticut pharmacist.

"Elimination of dual exhaust makes motor exhaust much noisier. I miss the quietness of the 1960 Cadillac."—California court reporter.

To wind up the enthusiastic statements by Cadillac owners, here are comments number 11 through 16 on the good side:

"The workmanship is excellent."—Michigan self-employed man.

"I've had fewer rattles and squeaks than on any other car I have owned."—New York physician.

There are three reasons for this: 1) conservative engineering, 2) time, 3) money.

"No annoying mechanical adjustments required."—California food wholesaler.

"Cadillac has the reputation and "Fort Knox" association I enjoy and appreciate."—Ohio business speech teacher.

"What I consider very important is the trade-in value." New York banker.

Thousands of people have listed their names with Cadillac dealers waiting for carefully tended two or three-year old Cads to be traded.

"Holds the road better than previous year models."—Florida housewife.

"It drives well in snow because it's well-weighted."—New Jersey attorney.

"I like the adjustable brakes."—Colorado fire fighter.

"I also like the emergency brake release."—Texas executive.

This feature is great. When you move gear selector from Neutral to Drive, parking brake is automatically released.

"It's economical for a large car."—New Jersey physician.

It never ceases to surprise people, PM staff included, when they get 16 to 17 miles per gallon on the road in a Cadillac that weighs two and one-half tons.

Numbers 11 through 16 of the adverse owner comments wrap up negative reactions to the '63 Cadillac owners report:

"Inside rear view mirror is not in correct position for a tall person. I consider it dangerous."—Wisconsin dentist.

"The inside rear-view mirror is placed too low giving you a blind spot through the windshield."—Michigan plumber.

On a car in Cadillac's bracket, vertical adjustment of the mirror should be a matter of course.

"There are rattles indicating poor production supervision."—Illinois city mayor. "I don't believe the factory inspection at delivery time is thorough enough, for they have passed motor noises and final adjustments in general on to owner who has to appeal to dealer for correction easier said than done."—Ohio housewife.

"Had electrical failure of windshield wipers."—Colorado dentist.

"The roof is too low—hits my hat when I get in and out."—Minnesota traveling salesman.

"People continually scraping knees as ashtrays open by themselves and have sharp edges."—New York bakery owner.

This completes the roll call of owners' pros and cons on their 1963 Cadillacs based on a combined experience of 905,927 miles driven.

★ ★

'64 Cadillac Makes Its Own Weather

Some styling changes, a bigger engine, and a new drive for more zip in the passing ranges also make news in this luxury car

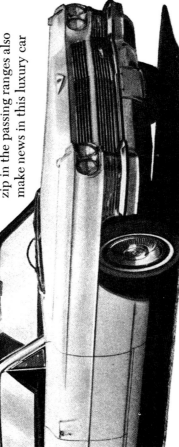

Styling changes include new grille, lower tail fins.

ONE day last June, Dan Adams, Cadillac's assistant chief engineer, fired up a test automobile on the streets of Denver, then moved a knob on his instrument panel until an arrow on it pointed at 72. That meant degrees of temperature.

Beside Adams was a fellow engineer. The day was bright, the outside air at 85 degrees. In a matter of minutes, with the windows rolled up, a thermometer in the car read exactly what Adams had asked for—72 degrees.

They started driving west. An hour and a half later they were in the middle of a snowstorm in the Rockies' Loveland Pass. The outside temperature had dropped 50 degrees to just above freezing. But the thermometer stayed right where it had been at the start, 72 degrees.

Last month, when Cadillac announced its 1964 models, a dial-your-weather system, called Comfort Control, was a prominent option. Comfort Control had been a long time in incubation. Cadillac started experimenting with dial-your-weather five years ago. The goal was complete freedom from adjustment of the heater and air-conditioner. When, last year, the engineers combined the heating-cooling systems, they were well on their way.

Giving Nature a hand. Comfort Control is based on the premise that the human body is the world's worst thermostat. It reacts slowly to small changes in temperature. The motorist, fiddling with his heater or air-conditioning controls, may overadjust, because he's let car temperature get way out of the comfort zone. Cadillac uses electric sensors to "read"

all car conditions affecting comfort. The result is the world's first wholly automatic inside-weather system for cars, or, for that matter, for anything else.

For an explanation of how Comfort Control works, see diagram on page 66. Cadillac has other things for '64. In only its third boost in engine displace-

ment in 14 years, the company has added 39 cubic inches for a total of 429. The bigger engine is combined in some of the new Cadillacs—about three out of every five coming off the assembly line—with a new transmission called the Turbo Hydra-Matic. And this is the first basic change in transmissions for Cadillac since 1940.

Zip and economy. In a car weighing almost 4,800 pounds, engine and transmission provide quite an improvement in performance. Zero to 60 miles an hour has been chopped from 12 to 10.2 seconds. The car has a third more torque for passing at 50 m.p.h., twice as much at 20 m.p.h. Astonishingly, Cadillac's gas economy hasn't been affected.

A couple of gadgets should please the absentminded: an electric eye that turns on the headlights at twilight and a time-delay switch that automatically turns the headlights *off* a couple of minutes after the car has been parked for the night.

But the big thing for the new model year is that Comfort Control. Any bragging that Cadillac does about it is characteristically conservative. "The inside temperature may vary plus or minus a degree or so from the setting," says Dan Adams with an engineer's preciseness. I say your home thermostat should be so good!—*Devon Francis.*

Electric eye for automatic headlight dimmer is moved from dash to tip of front fender. Horsepower is upped from 325 to 340. Fifteen years ago Cadillac boasted a whopping 160 hp.

Seat belt ends have a spring-loaded retracter. Tiltable steering wheel, introduced last year, now has seven instead of six positions. Leather seat trim is perforated for ventilation.

Cadillac's "ducks" aren't ducks

Those things that look like ducks on the famous Cadillac crest aren't. Part of the design since 1904, they are "merlettes"—birds that never existed—ancient heraldic symbols of knighthood. They are legless and beakless. Appearing in threes, and considered sacred to the Holy Trinity, they were granted by the School of Heralds to knights for valiant conduct in the Crusades.

The Exciting '64s!

REVISED parking lamp location marks the '64 Cadillac. New lamp is behind small grille.

CADILLAC, WHICH produced a new V-8 engine for last year's cars, has bored and stroked that engine to more competitively power its 1964s. Teaming this engine with a new automatic transmission, plus further automating various comfort and convenience accessories, makes the mechanical developments overshadow the styling refinements at this GM division.

With 0.125 in. added to the bore, and with a longer stroke (now 4.13 by 4.0 in.), displacement has been increased from 390 to 429 cu. in. The 10% increase in capacity, together with slightly altered cam configuration, increases output to 340 bhp at 4600 rpm and torque to 480 lb./ft. at 3000 rpm.

The new transmission, a combination of Hydra-Matic and torque converter called Turbo Hydra-Matic, is used in the de Ville series, the 60 Special Sedan and Eldorado (sans Biarritz) convertible. The 62 series and Fleetwood 75 sedan and limousine retain the older Hydra-Matic transmission, which also has undergone some engineering changes to increase cooling and, in commercial units, to beef up the reverse unit.

Shift lever pattern, in keeping with the trend, is PRNDL, which requires different shifting habits between series (H-M pattern is PNDDLR). To remind multi-Cadillac owners that reverse is engaged by pushing up on the lever rather than pulling down, a different shift lever knob is installed with the Turbo Hydra-Matic transmission. It can be downshifted to 2nd at speeds between 20-60 mph to provide engine braking on hills. Since the torque converter aids all gears, the transmission doesn't have "blank spots" where vehicle speed is too high for one gear and too low for another; it also performs with more agility in the city traffic range of 20-45 mph. The new unit weighs 30 lb. less than the old Hydra-Matic.

A new speedometer drive provision has four different worm gears and six different pinions available to more closely calibrate the speedometer to the vehicle weight, tire size and gearing. An iron spacer between engine and transmission to accommodate two different bolt hole patterns is the clue to this transmission's interchangeability with Buick.

Electronics have moved further into Cadillac's accessory field, with a thermostatically operated comfort control which combines the heater and air conditioner. This automatically warms,

Cadillac Series 60

FLEETWOOD ELDORADO convertible shows 1 in. lower fins for '64, plus slightly modified grille. New 429-cu.in. engine will power all Cadillac models.

cools, or blends air—all through a de-humidifier—on demand from a sensing valve to maintain a constant temperature within the car.

Another optional device is the Twilight Sentinel, operated by three photo cells, which automatically turns on headlights at dusk, turns them off at dawn, so long as the engine is running. The control is adjustable for sensitivity and has a delayed action which will keep headlights on for up to 90 sec. after the ignition is switched off. A de-activator switch has been added to the power window circuit, permitting the driver to cut off each individual window switch for safety reasons. The

automatic headlight dimming photo cell has been moved to the left head-light hood, where it is styled into the trim strip. A factory-installed rear window de-fogger is offered and the tilting steering wheel now adjusts to seven positions.

As befits a motor carriage considered the height of luxury by many Americans, there are 124 upholstery options available, including 4 standard and 15 optional leather colors (perforated or plain). The Eldorado and Fleetwoods have simulated wood veneer panels as part of the interior trim. Exterior restyling includes lowering the tail fin 1 in., flattening the deck lid between the tail fins, bringing the grille forward more on a single plane between front fenders and dividing it with a strip in body paint color. Relocating the spare tire above the rear axle results in a deeper trunk well and greater usable luggage space. ∎

POPULAR DE VILLE series will have two 4-door hardtops (4-window at left, 6-window above) and 2-door hardtop coupe (below). All will have new Turbo Hydra-Matic transmission as standard equipment.

Cadillac
SEDAN DE VILLE
⊙ᴹₜ ROAD TEST

by Jim Wright, *Technical Editor*

EVERY YEAR, Cadillac seems to turn out the standard for the luxury field – the car to beat. So far no one has beat it or even come close. Cadillac sales for 1963 will close out right at 160,000 units (probably more for '64). This means almost five times as many Cads will have been sold for the year as its two domestic competitors combined. After driving and evaluating all of them, including the choice European models, it isn't hard to understand why. On a straight dollar-value basis, none of the other luxury models offers quite what the Cadillac does in terms of quality, comfort, and overall performance. Most lack the interior roominess, too.

Some imported models have the quality by virtue of their hand fitting. But if these European manufacturers could find a way to *profitably* tool up for mass production, they'd do it. The comfort is there, too. But then, even the lowest-priced luxury imports cost at least twice as much as a Cadillac, and you'd have to beat us with a large club to convince us that they're that much better – if at all. When it comes to overall performance (including handling and roadability), the imports aren't equal, though some excel in individual aspects.

Of domestic luxury cars, the competition is in the same price range, and it's strictly a matter of opinion in judging their quality and comfort factors. When it comes to overall performance, we have to go by the results of our tests, and these tell us the Caddy is unequalled by anything at any price.

Our test car, a four-window, four-door Sedan de Ville, had a little over 800 miles on it when we picked it up. Even if the mileage had been zero, the test car would still have been ready for anything, because all Cads are run in at the factory and don't need a break-in. Our test car was loaded with every major accessory available. This is the way most of them are ordered (65 per cent with air conditioning), and in addition to checking out the car, we also wanted to check all the creature comforts. Standing at the curb with a full

Cadillac's famous fin, still very much in evidence, was lowered an inch this year.

Just above headlights, in chrome decoration, stands sensor for automatic dimmer.

Tail lights, bumpers, and grille are massive, but otherwise trim use is minimal.

CADILLAC SEDAN DE VILLE *continued* ▬▬▬▬▬▬▬▬▬▬▬▬▬▬▬▬▬▬

tank of gas (26 gallons), our test car weighed in at a not-so-modest 5050 pounds. And if there's ever been anything this big that'll move as fast, we haven't heard of it.

As you can see from the acceleration tables, it's going to take a hot-option model of anything else to stay with this one from a standing start. Our '64 times are also quite a bit faster than the '63 times. This is due to the redesigned and enlarged engine *and* the new torque-converter transmission.

The bigger engine is the result of both bore and stroke increases. With displacement now at 429 cubic inches, the '64 Cadillac engine is one of the two biggest in the industry. Horsepower has been increased from 325 to 340 (at 4600

Large, plush interior sports arm rests in both front and rear seats. Grouped controls add to convenience, are balanced and pleasing. Sturdy, padded vinyl top has become de Ville hallmark.

rpm), and the torque rating is now 480 pounds-feet at 3000 rpm. Incidentally, this torque figure is equal to what the big Super/Stock engines are putting out and does a lot to explain the rapid acceleration and pulling power of the Cadillac.

The new Turbo Hydra-Matic transmission installed in the test car comes as standard equipment in the de Ville, Sixty Special sedan, and Eldorado convertible. The old Hydra-Matic is still being used in the Sixty-Two series and the Seventy-Five sedan and limousine. We covered the details of the Turbo Hydra-Matic pretty thoroughly in our December issue, so we won't go into that again here. We will add, though, that the torque multiplication makes the Cad a real bear off the line and that the shifts are extremely smooth and positive. We rate the new automatic right on a level with Chrysler's TorqueFlite, which we've always considered the best. (This isn't too surprising since GM's automatic is for all practical purposes identical to Chrysler's — they even pay royalties to the same inventor.) All air-conditioned cars are equipped with a 3.21 rear axle, while the others use a 2.94. The lower ratio helped acceleration in our case.

This isn't the whole performance story, though. Our test car not only had a boulevard ride that was the match of *any*, it also handled like no other big car we've ever tested. The MT crew took the test car on one extended road trip over to Phoenix, then back to Los Angeles by way of Las Vegas. During the trip, we had occasion to run on straight, smooth, high-speed freeways as well as mile after mile of up-and-

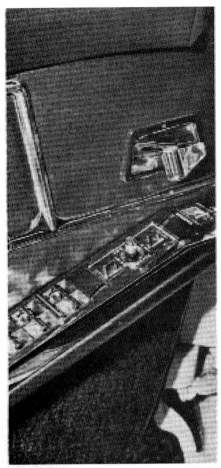

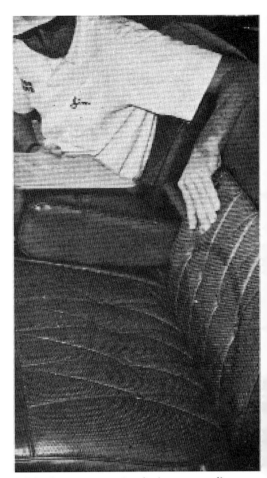

Switches for doors, windows, and seat are all grouped where driver can get at them.

Simplicity of operation of new Comfort Control air conditioner is evident here.

All-leather seats, optional, feature small perforations for better air circulation.

down, roundabout mountain roads. On the straight stretches in Nevada (where there's no speed limit), we rolled along at 110 without any concern. The big Cad is extremely stable at these high speeds, and even though some moderate crosswinds were blowing, we didn't notice them.

Over the mountain stretches, we still maintained a high average speed. We got this mostly by hard acceleration between corners, hard braking for turns, and by limit-of-adhesion cornering. We wanted to wring the car out and find its faults, if any, as well as its limitations. The faults are few (even the understeer characteristics aren't so excessive as you'd expect in a car of this size and weight — this opinion is based not only on how the car felt to us but by close inspection of the front tires after the run; they were feathered from hard cornering but weren't showing excessive wear from scrubbing), and the limitations are so far up the scale that even the worst driver will be hard-pressed to get into trouble with this car. The Cadillac may be big as a tank, but it's well balanced. Its suspension has a high degree of roll stiffness, and as the photos show, it corners very level.

The brakes held up very well during the hard use they got in the mountains. There was one stretch where we came down from 7900 feet almost to sea level — they did fade noticeably then, but we just stood on them harder and they did what was asked of them. During our test stops at Riverside, they behaved well — even survived two maximum stops from 115 mph before fading completely. The cast-iron drums

are finned and cool quickly. An added feature here is the split master cylinder that Cadillac adopted several years ago. If the front brakes go out, the rears will keep right on working — and vice versa.

We put in over 2000 miles with the test car and averaged slightly better than 13 mpg. The air conditioner was never off, and this cut mileage by 1-1½ mpg. Around town, the average was 12.5 mpg, and out on the road it was up to 14.7. This could've been better if we'd stayed around 65 mph, but we were usually up to about 75 or 85.

Much has been said about the real (and sometimes imagined) quietness of various makes of luxury cars. From past

Considering sheer size and bulk of Cadillac, handling characteristics proved outstanding. This photograph was taken on a loose, rough surface while Cad was pushing better than 70 mph.

experience, we can only say that none is quieter than our test car was. At any speed and under any condition, the air flow over and around the car was barely more than a gentle hiss. Engine and transmission noises were hardly discernible, and never did we have to turn up the radio or raise our voices because of any ambient noise.

At the risk of sounding soft, we think the most significant advance offered by Cadillac is their new air-conditioning system. This is really the unit to end all units and will no doubt be widely copied by the rest of the industry. It's called Comfort Control, and it does everything, including think for the driver. The first thing you notice is that the controls have been reduced to complete simplicity. Where there used to be as many as two or three levers *each* for both the heater and air conditioner, there are now just two. One is a control dial that incorporates temperature settings from 65° to 85° on it, and the other is a sliding lever with four settings.

Now all the driver has to do is dial the desired temperature setting, move the lever to AUTOMATIC, and forget it. From then on the system will thermostatically keep the desired temperature inside the car, regardless of outside changes. For example, we set it at 75° one morning in Phoenix and set out through the desert, where we ran into high 90° weather. Later that afternoon and evening we were in the higher regions, where the temperature dropped to 30°. The original setting hadn't been touched, yet the interior temperature was constant and completely comfortable. No more fiddling around. Theoretically, you could set it once when you buy the car and then forget about it.

The system goes on and off automatically according to demand. To do this, it uses several electronic gadgets. These include three thermistors that sense temperature changes (from outside the car, inside the car, and at the outlet of the heater/air conditioner), a potentiometer (the control dial where the driver sets the desired temperature), an amplifier, a transducer, and a power servo. A signal from any of these four sources (three thermistors and the potentiometer) is fed into the amplifier (a two-transistor unit), where it's multiplied. The amplified voltage is then fed into the transducer, which is a 10-inch steel tube with one strand of fine wire running through it. The wire is sensitive to heat, and since the amplified voltage is giving off varying amounts of heat, the wire reacts to it by either expanding or contracting slightly. This action causes a needle valve at one end of the transducer to open or close. The needle valve controls the amount of engine vacuum that will be applied to the power servo, which in turn opens or closes the air door of the heater/air conditioner. The greater the vacuum, the wider the door opens.

The servo unit also controls blower speed and at which point in the car the incoming air will be discharged. The power servo shuts off the water flow to the heater coil when maximum coolness is needed. There's another position under AUTOMATIC that gives a higher blower speed. Also controlled by the lever is the defrost action, which has a HIGH and LOW position.

As always, the Cadillac offers plenty of room on the inside — enough to allow six full-sized adults plenty of comfort on long trips. Our test car had optional leather seats — very comfortable. They were perforated with lots of tiny holes, which makes them much cooler to sit on. The six-way power seat and the adjustable steering wheel allowed us to find just the right seating position for our particular frame.

There's no need to go into any great detail about how the test car was put together. Cadillac has always had an excellent reputation for quality, and while styling and engineering might change over the years, that hasn't. /MT

1

2

3

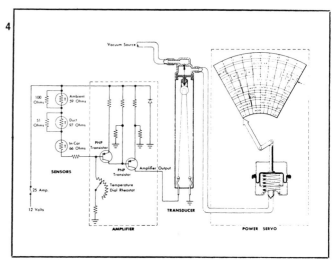

4

(1 THROUGH 4) *New Comfort Control heater/air conditioner is probably the most important single development that this field will ever see. Theoretically, buyer can dial desired temperature when he first gets his car, then never touch it again. The unit actually has automatic controls to keep temperature constant, even though the car may be going through hot, arid deserts or low-temperature, high-altitude mountain passes. We kept constant check on both outside and inside air temperature during our extensive road test. Regardless of outside conditions, the inside was always right where we wanted it — all without touching the simple dial after its initial setting. Also shown, for you technically inclined readers, is the schematic diagram of the entire system. Complete explanation is found in text.*

5) *Extra inches of this year's engine plus the more efficient torque converter transmission have added quite a bit to the Cadillac's performance, combine for outstanding acceleration.*

6) *Stopping power proved equal to all situations. Brake fade, always present with drums, turned out to be below average — a fact attributable to the cooling fins in constant air stream.*

7) *Cadillac engine's basic design dates back to 1949, when it was introduced as one of the first modern, high-compression V-8s. Since then, it's been refined and enlarged somewhat.*

8) *No scarcity of room here. Spare location is out of the way but also a bit awkward should it have to be used. Best way to remove tire is to climb in trunk, as shown in photograph.*

CADILLAC DE VILLE

4-door, 6-passenger sedan

OPTIONS ON CAR TESTED: Air conditioning, vinyl roof, leather seats, adjustable steering wheel, electric seat and vent windows, AM-FM radio, remote-control trunk, automatic dimmer, twilight sentinel, Cruise Control, controlled differential, rear defrost, seat belts

BASIC PRICE: $5633
PRICE AS TESTED: $7527 (plus tax and license)
ODOMETER READING AT START OF TEST: 837 miles
RECOMMENDED ENGINE RED LINE: 5200 rpm

PERFORMANCE

ACCELERATION (2 aboard)

0-30 mph	3.4 secs.
0-45 mph	5.7
0-60 mph	8.5

Standing start ¼-mile 16.8 secs. and 85 mph
Speeds in gears @ 4400 rpm (shift point)
1st . . . . 45 mph   3rd . . . . 115 mph (actual
2nd . . . . 80 mph   top speed)
Speedometer Error on Test Car

Car's speedometer reading	30	46	52	63	73	84
Weston electric speedometer	30	45	50	60	70	80

Observed miles per hour per 1000 rpm in top gear . . . . 25.5 mph
Stopping Distances — from 30 mph, 38 ft.; from 60 mph, 153 ft.

SPECIFICATIONS FROM MANUFACTURER

Engine
Ohv V-8
Bore: 4.13 ins.
Stroke: 4.0 ins.
Displacement: 429.0 cu. ins.
Compression ratio: 10.5:1
Horsepower: 340 @ 4600 rpm
Torque: 480 lbs.-ft. @ 3000 rpm
Horsepower per cubic inch: 0.79
Carburetion: 1 4-bbl.
Ignition: 12-volt coil

Gearbox
Turbo Hydra-Matic (3-speed automatic with torque converter)

Driveshaft
2-piece, open tube, with 2 constant-velocity U-joints

Differential
Hypoid, semi-floating
Standard ratio: 3.21:1

Suspension
Front: Independent, with coil springs, upper A-arm, single lower arm with strut, direct-acting tubular shocks, anti-roll bar
Rear: Rigid axle, with coil springs, 4-link stabilizer, and direct-acting tubular shocks

Steering
Ball nut sector, with integral power
Turning diameter: 43.0 ft.
Turns lock to lock: 3.7

Wheels and Tires
5-lug, steel disc wheels
8.20 x 15 4-ply nylon tubeless tires

Brakes
Hydraulic, duo-servo, self-adjusting, with split master cylinder
Front and rear: 12-in. composite cast-iron finned drums
Effective lining area: 221.8 sq. ins.

Body and Frame
Separate steel body on X-member frame
Wheelbase: 129.5 ins.
Track: front and rear, 61.0 ins.
Overall length: 223.5 ins.
Overall width: 79.7 ins.
Curb weight: 5050 lbs.

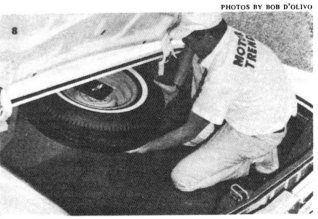

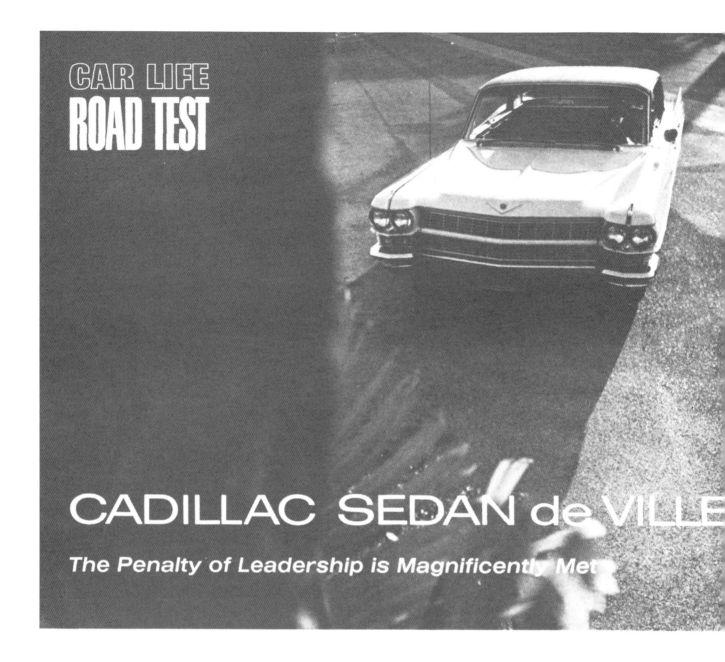

CADILLAC SEDAN de VILLE

The Penalty of Leadership is Magnificently Met

I N GENERAL, people tend to view the Cadillac from one of two vantage points: Either the individual is completely attuned to this motor car or he is actively uninterested to the point of blunt skepticism. It's possible there are some who have no feelings when the name is mentioned, but the vast bulk of Americans are either like that legendary million Chevrolet owners who aspire to Cadillac ownership or are like the equally large throng that believes the car is nothing more than a vastly overrated status symbol.

Our approach to the test Cadillac Sedan de Ville was admittedly tinged with the latter outlook, from a news-journalist's heritage of cynical objectivity. This despite the fact that the two previous Cadillacs which have undergone our scrutiny (CL, June '61 and February '63) proved thoroughly excellent vehicles. The latest test car up-

held that tradition in most respects.

Cadillacs for 1964 seem little changed in appearance from the previous year, yet their styling has been refined. The now-traditional tail fins have been shaved down an inch in their inexorable march toward oblivion. The indentions separating grille and front fender have been smoothed into a massively integrated frontal aspect. Though such refinements are enough to identify the latest model, they do not significantly outdate the 1963 models. A design continuity therefore is maintained, which in turn promotes a higher resale value for "pre-owned" models.

Underneath the broad-shouldered hood, however, more than mere refinement has taken place. Cadillac had introduced a new V-8 engine for 1963, but enlarged it this year and teamed it (in the de Ville series) with a new auto-

matic transmission. Such engineering innovations two years in a row are not exactly commonplace in the industry and bear testimony to Cadillac's determination to maintain leadership in its increasingly competitive field.

Interestingly enough, when the new engine appeared for '63 it had the same bore and stroke, and the same power rating, as the 14-year-old design it replaced. The new design, differing from the earlier in many significant ways (among which were shorter block and crankshaft length, moving all accessories except starter to the front, and a redesigned lower end), was produced for two reasons: Engine tooling had to be replaced with more modern equipment and engineers wanted a new design as a basis for future development.

As the first step in that development, the engine has been increased 10% in displacement for '64, from 390 to 429

cu. in., and the power rating boosted from 325 to 340 bhp at 4600 rpm. Bores (on 4.625-in. centers) have been widened from 4.00 in. to 4.13 in. and the stroke has been lengthened from 3.875 in. to 4.00 in. Peak torque, increased from 430 to 480 lb.-ft., is now achieved at 3000 rpm, slightly lower than before for improved city speed performance.

Pistons, though of larger diameter, are still the shorter and lighter type utilized in the '63 design and compression ratio remains at 10.5:1. A single Carter AFB carburetor with barrels of 1.438 and 1.688 in. is used. The camshaft, operating hydraulic lifters, has timing altered to 34-102-89-63° (including ramps), although the valve sizes remain at 1.875 in. intakes, 1.50 in. exhausts. Though only a single exhaust system is used, it has been increased in capacity with larger diameter piping.

The transmission in the test car (which is also used in the 60 Special sedan and Eldorado convertible of the Fleetwood series) is the GM-developed torque converter with two geared speeds and direct. Cadillac calls it the Turbo Hydra-Matic and in the near future it quite probably will (and should) be used throughout the rest of the Cadillac line still utilizing the venerable Hydra-Matic. The 3-element converter has a multiplication of 2.10:1 at stall; geared ratios are 2.48:1 first and 1.48:1 second, with Drive direct. Somewhat smoother than Hydra-Matic, the new transmission has the added advantages of providing more flexible, effective gearing, on demand, with less variation because of atmospheric pressure, and of being less complex.

With this power train, our relatively light (for Cadillac) 4-window sedan turned in some spirited—if not startling—performances. Acceleration figures show a full second is sliced off the standing ¼-mile and some 2 sec. off the 0-60 times compared with the

MARVIN LYONS PHOTO

SPARE TIRE over rear axle hump leaves more room within trunk for luggage.

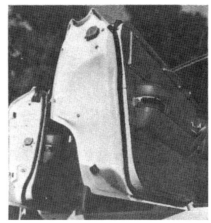

DOORS HAVE safety lights built into armrests, swing out wide for easy entrance.

POWER CONSOLE is nicely arranged to give control over seats, locks, windows.

INCREASED BORE and stroke of Cadillac V-8 gives 10% boost in displacement.

REAR DOOR armrest incorporates lighter, ash tray and window control.

CADILLAC SEDAN de VILLE

barely heavier 1963 Cadillac tested. Since shifts are made automatically at 4400 rpm (at w.o.t.), there was only a slight improvement through the forced shifts our testers used for the data panel figures. The greater torque of the engine combined with the effect of the transmission's torque multiplication launched the Cadillac off the line in truly impressive fashion, particularly when compared with earlier models and present competition.

Once at speed, the car's ride and handling proved to be a yardstick for cars in this class. It was possible to go slamming along the roughest roads with abandon, carrying the passengers along with only the mildest of nudges. One tester commented that the Cadillac had "all the feeling of a supple bridge girder."

The softness of the suspension, however, causes momentary panic during brisk cornering—until the driver accustoms himself to it. Once the car reaches full side tilt, it tenaciously plows its way around a corner; but the transition from full level to full lean is apt to be traumatic for the unwary driver.

The generous tread patch area of the huge 8.20-15 low-pressure, low-profile tires accounts for a great deal

of cornering stick-to-itiveness. And the pleasantly quick power steering, though betraying only minimal road feel, is an important factor in the car's handling ease and maneuverability.

The latter attribute provided one of our most pleasant surprises about the Cadillac. Despite the car's bulk and overhanging extremities, it could easily be jockeyed about to take advantage of tight parking and turning situations, once a driver was attuned to the vehicle. The first few hours behind the wheel, however, explains why some Cadillac drivers have been accused of being road-hogs: They just don't know how much pavement the car is occupying. Once this is realized, the problem vanishes.

With the new power train well launched, Cadillac engineers might turn their attention to the brakes. The 377 sq. in. of swept lining area would seem to be none too generous, since even in our relatively light test car they faded completely during our all-on stops from 80 mph. Deceleration rates were hardly spectacular, at 20 and 18 ft./sec./sec., and even around town their effectiveness seemed hardly in keeping with the car's character.

Character the Cadillac does have— in vast amounts. From the optional

vinyl-covered roof to the nostalgic fender skirts at the rear wheel openings, the car can be summed up in one word: Polish. What other automobile can boast of hard gold contact points in its voltage regulator?

The momentary confusion of a first glance at the control panel (it hardly can be called an instrument panel any longer) quickly gives way to admiration for the logical layout. Our testers, at least, found that all controls are well-placed at the exact location where one unconsciously reaches for them. Only the trip odometer reset knob evaded us for awhile, but later was discovered hiding 'way back under the lower lip of the dashboard.

The cruise control, which was the most consistent and responsive of all such devices we've tried so far, was conveniently spotted on the dashboard to the left of the wheel. Once locked on, it was possible to fly the freeways by merely rolling on or off a notch or so of speed trim (providing the traffic wasn't too heavy). A similar control, rolling horizontally, operates the electronic thermostat for the combined heater/air conditioner "Comfort Control." This device had a tendency to be somewhat noisy, but then that probably was because of the high degree of sound deadening and silence engineered into the rest of the car.

Another item which added to the fun and games when driving the Cadillac was the "Twilight Sentinel," an automatic headlight switch operated by a photocell in the lip of the dashboard hood. This switched on the lights at dusk (or when driving into a garage) and then turned them off automatically —after a variable interval of up to 90 sec.—once the key was turned off. A conventional headlight switch is also fitted for those who find it difficult to accept such automation. There were many other items over which to exclaim: But most of all, there was the pure sensual pleasure of turning the key, setting the speed and climate dials to 70, and settling back to effortlessly guide the Cadillac into the gathering dusk with only the squeak of the perforated leather cushions, as you move to a comfortable position, to annoy you. With all that power-assisted automation, Cadillac probably needed the larger engine as much to drive the accessories as to be powered somewhere near its competitors.

There is an old and very famous Cadillac advertisement which had, as an opening line, "The Penalty of Leadership . . ." And no other statement could better sum up our own impressions of the 1964 Cadillac. Being a leader presents problems, invites hypercritical examination and encourages adverse comments. Yet our test crew, after 10 days with the new Cadillac, came away marveling at the magnificent manner in which that "penalty" is being paid. ∎

CAR LIFE ROAD TEST

1964 CADILLAC
Sedan de Ville Hardtop

SPECIFICATIONS

List price	$5655
Price, as tested	6932
Curb weight, lb	4900
Test weight	5230
distribution, %	53/47
Tire size	8.20-15
Tire capacity, lb	5660
Brake swept area	377
Engine type	V-8, ohv
Bore & stroke	4.13 x 4.00
Displacement, cu. in	429
Compression ratio	10.5
Carburetion	1 x 4
Bhp @ rpm	340 @ 4600
equivalent mph	120
Torque, lb-ft	480 @ 3000
equivalent mph	77.8

DIMENSIONS

Wheelbase, in	129.5
Tread, f & r	61.0
Overall length, in	223.5
width	79.7
height	54.8
equivalent vol, cu. ft	581
Frontal area, sq. ft.	25.0
Ground clearance, in	5.28
Steering ratio, o/a	18.2
turns, lock to lock	3.7
turning circle, ft.	43.0
Hip room, front	63.4
Hip room, rear	63.6
Pedal to seat back, max	43.0
Floor to ground	13.0
Luggage vol, cu. ft	15.8
Fuel tank capacity, gal	26

CALCULATED DATA

Lb/bhp (test wt)	15.1
Cu. ft/ton mile	112
Mph/1000 rpm	26.0
Engine revs/mile	2310
Piston travel, ft/mile	1540
Car Life wear index	35.6

PERFORMANCE

Top speed (4650), mph	121
Shifts, @ mph (auto., forced)	
3rd ( )	
2nd (4400)	77
1st (4400)	46
Total drag at 60 mph, lb	160

EXTRA-COST OPTIONS

Leather upholstery, vinyl roof cover, power windows, Twilight Sentinel, comfort control, cruise control, tinted glass, AM/FM radio, tilting wheel.

GEAR RATIOS

3rd (1.00) overall	3.21
2nd (1.48)	4.75
1st (2.48)	7.96
1st (2.10 x 2.48)	16.7

SPEEDOMETER ERROR

30 mph, actual	29.8
60 mph	57.0
90 mph	86.5

FUEL CONSUMPTION

Normal range, mpg	9-12

ACCELERATION

0-30 mph, sec	3.4
0-40	4.8
0-50	6.5
0-60	8.5
0-70	11.0
0-80	14.1
0-100	23.5
Standing ¼ mile, sec	16.4
speed at end, mph	86

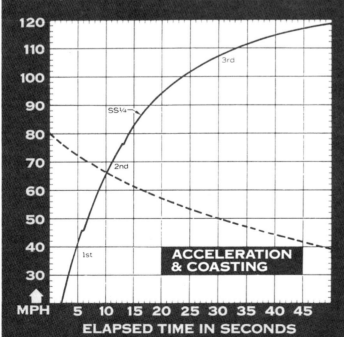

ACCELERATION & COASTING

ELAPSED TIME IN SECONDS

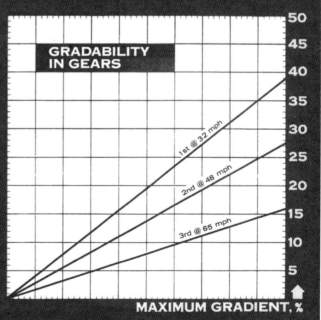

GRADABILITY IN GEARS

1st @ 32 mph
2nd @ 48 mph
3rd @ 65 mph

MAXIMUM GRADIENT, %

Cadillac Coupé de Ville 7,030 c.c.

IT'S just over three years since *Autocar* last tested a Cadillac—a long-wheelbase limousine with seating for nine and an astonishing performance. This week our subject is the current Coupé de Ville on the standard wheelbase, and once again we are indebted to J. C. Bamford, the renowned manufacturer of earth-moving machinery from Rocester, Staffordshire, for the loan of his car. It had covered less than 2,000 miles when handed over, but every Cadillac's engine and transmission are run-in at the Detroit factory before assembly.

Still generally acknowledged to be the U.S. industry's top luxury product, the Cadillac has the fundamental difference, as compared with European "prestige" vehicles, that it is mass-produced. Last year, for instance, some 165,000 were made, an average of over 630 per day for a five-day working week. Although there is a wide variety of standard body styles, the mechanical side is thoroughly rational; there is only one type of Cadillac engine, with no tuning options, and only two transmissions are listed, both automatic.

While the detail body finish, inside and out, is not so meticulous as one expects of European equivalents, and under its bonnet the Cadillac really looks no neater nor better arranged than less pretentious American cars with big vee-8 engines, this must be related to its retail price which, in this country and with a stiff import duty included, is still far below what must be paid for the classiest home produce. Moreover, as a dynamic object it represents the highest

standards attainable today in most important respects, as well as having several luxuries incorporated, or available as extras, that cannot yet be had at any price on European cars.

For example, the steering-wheel is instantly adjustable to any of six angular positions in the vertical plane—although not for reach; at night, with the town or parking lamps lit, an extra lamp set in each front bumper end lights the kerbside when the appropriate direction signaller is flashing. One can specify a time switch that provides a 90sec grace after turning off the headlamps, allowing one to close the garage doors, or to find and insert the front door key before they are extinguished. Another option is a constant-speed governor for the throttles for motorway cruising, overridden by a touch on the brake pedal.

Both inside door locks can be engaged or released by

PRICES		£	s	d
Two-door saloon Coupé de Ville		3,062	0	0
Purchase Tax		638	7	1
	Total in (U.K.)	3,700	7	1
Extras (including P.T.)				
Air conditioning		253	15	0
Rear-window de-froster		14	5	0
Padded roof covering		48	6	8
Radio		82	3	4
Power door locks		24	0	10

How the Cadillac Coupé de Ville Compares:

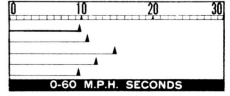

Manufacturer : *Cadillac Motor Division, General Motors Corp., 2860 Clarke Avenue, Detroit 32, Michigan, U.S.A.*
U.K. Concessionaires : Lendrum & Hartman Ltd., 26b, Albemarle St., London, W.1.

Test Conditions
Weather .... Fine, dry, with 8-12 m.p.h. wind
Temperature .... 13 deg. C. (55 deg. F.)
Barometer .... 29·4in. Hg.
Dry concrete and asphalt surfaces.

Weight
Kerb weight (with oil, water and half-full fuel tank)
44·7cwt (5,006lb-2,271kg)
Front-rear distribution, per cent F, 53; R, 47.
Laden as tested .... 47·7cwt (5,342lb-2,423kg)

Turning Circles
Between kerbs .... L, 43ft 4in.; R, 44ft 2in.
Between walls .... L, 46ft 2in.; R, 47ft. 1in.
Turns of steering wheel lock to lock .... 3·8

FUEL AND OIL CONSUMPTION

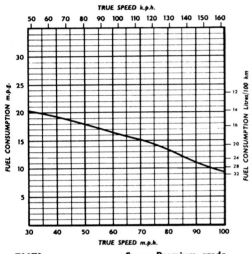

FUEL .... Super Premium grade
(100-102 Octane RM)

Test Distance .... 929 miles

Overall Consumption ...... 10·9 m.p.g.
(25·9 litres/100km)

Estimated Consumption (DIN)13·8 m.p.g.
(20·5 litres/100km)

Normal Range.................. 10-15 m.p.g.
(28·3-18·8 litres/100km)

OIL: SAE 20 Consumption 8,000 m.p.g.

HILL CLIMBING AT STEADY SPEEDS

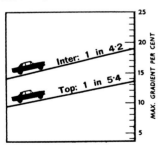

GEAR	Top	Inter
TAPLEY READING (lb per ton)	410	520

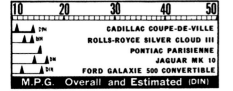

DIN /	CADILLAC COUPE-DE-VILLE
DIN /	ROLLS-ROYCE SILVER CLOUD III
	PONTIAC PARISIENNE
DIN	JAGUAR MK 10
DIN /	FORD GALAXIE 500 CONVERTIBLE

M.P.G. Overall and Estimated (DIN)

MAXIMUM SPEED AND ACCELERATION TIMES

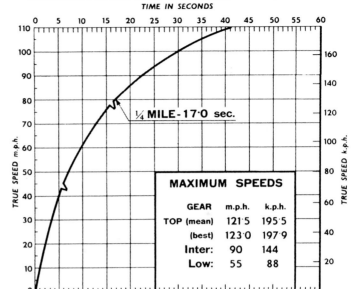

¼ MILE - 17·0 sec.

MAXIMUM SPEEDS		
GEAR	m.p.h.	k.p.h.
TOP (mean)	121·5	195·5
(best)	123·0	197·9
Inter:	90	144
Low:	55	88

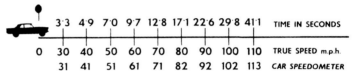

Speed range, gear ratios and time in seconds

m.p.h.	Top (6·42-3·21)	Inter (9·50-4·75)	Low (13·29-6·64)
10—30	—	—	2·5
20—40	—	3·9	3·1
30—50	7·0	5·0	4·1
40—60	8·0	5·0	—
50—70	9·3	5·7	—
60—80	9·9	7·4	—
70—90	10·0	—	—
80—100.........	12·7	—	—
90—110.........	18·5	—	—

BRAKES

	Pedal Load	Retardation	Equiv. distance
(from 30 m.p.h. in neutral)	25lb	0·57g	53ft
	45lb	0·86g	35ft
	50lb	0·92g	32·8ft
Parking brake		0·40g	75ft

All Cadillacs have left-hand drive. Seat trim here is in buttoned cloth and leather, moulded rubber mats over the soft carpets are extras. Electric switches for windows, seat adjustment and door locks are concentrated on the driver's door. Circular air-conditioning outlets are seen at each end of the facia, and there's a third in the middle

Cadillac Coupé de Ville ...

the driver at the touch of a switch, and the boot-lid (which also secures the hinged number plate covering the fuel filler cap) can be unlatched by another. Selecting forward or reverse from Neutral or Park automatically releases the parking brake, which is applied by a foot pedal. There is also a manual device for this. There are red safety lamps in the door trailing edges, lit as they are opened, and tiny repeaters above the front wings for the direction flashers.

But of all the Cadillac's contributions to motoring ease and well-being, the latest form of air-conditioning is surely the most outstanding. Called *Comfort Control*, it demands only that the driver selects an appropriate temperature on a small dial and slides a quadrant lever to Automatic, and a sensitive, all-electronic thermostatic device maintains that temperature, whatever the conditions outside. Indeed, one could set this where required on taking delivery of the car, and never need to fiddle with it thereafter.

Since our last Cadillac test there have been two major engine developments. For the 1963 season a much more compact vee-8 was introduced, 4in. narrower as well as shorter and lower, but with the same bore, stroke and hence cylinder capacity as previously—6,384 c.c. This year's version has an enlarged bore and longer stroke, and is up to 7,030 c.c. Gross power is raised from 325 to 340 b.h.p. at lower revs (4,600 instead of 4,800 r.p.m.), and torque, too, is up from 430 to 480 lb ft.

Although the four-speed HydraMatic transmission, with a two-stage fluid coupling giving a little torque multiplication, is still fitted to some models, the de Villes have G.M.'s latest turbo Hydra-Matic, combining a torque convertor with three speeds. A divided propeller shaft incorporates a double, constant-velocity universal joint, and the final drive unit includes a limited-slip differential. The car is coil-sprung at both ends, the back axle being live. Heavily ribbed cast-iron brake drums contain self-adjusting shoes,

and the servo-assisted hydraulic system has separate front and rear circuits. Powered steering is standard.

While some of the larger American cars are still somewhat unwieldy and not much fun to drive on British roads, memory of the giant Cadillac limousine tested in 1961 was still sufficiently fresh to remove any qualms about handling this considerably smaller 1964 coupé. Of course, it felt enormous at first, after stepping straight from a small British saloon, but the outward visibility is practically panoramic through the deep windows and over the boot and bonnet, which are so low that the road surface can be seen within a yard or two of the car.

Electric controls shift the bench front seat (with divided backrest) to and fro, and raise, lower or tilt it. These ready adjustments, together with the variable steering-wheel rake, should enable almost any driver to combine an easy, relaxed posture with a proper field of vision. On a long run the ability to change one's driving position slightly from time to time helps combat fatigue and cramp; ideally, the Cadillac

Even with the huge luggage boot otherwise empty, removing the spare wheel from it would represent quite a problem. The lid can be unlocked pneumatically from within the car, or with a key; it is lit automatically

Since 1959 the famous fins have been clipped down year by year. Direction signals are concealed in them. Cornering lamps are set in the wrap-around ends of the front bumpers. This Coupé de Ville has the optional padded roof trimmed with plastic-coated fabric

could do with one more adjustment—for varying the back-rest angle relative to the cushion, to exercise the spine. The seats are very comfortably shaped and sprung, trimmed in an attractive cloth weave with leather panels, and provided with centre folding armrests front and rear. There is plenty of legroom behind, and easy room for three abreast.

One cannot buy a Cadillac with right-hand drive, and the difficulties of driving from the left in this country are inevitably accentuated by the car's width and low build. However, the driver's task is made extremely easy in other respects. He can adjust the external mirror from inside the car, and set in the door beside him are electric controls for the side windows (including swivelling quarter-vents), seat position and door locks. As already stated, the parking brake is released automatically, steering and brakes are power-assisted, the wipers function when the screenwash button is pressed, and the radio has a self-seeking tuner.

Power to Spare

From cold start to hot stop the big vee-8 engine is a paragon of unobtrusiveness, with a surge of instant power always in reserve. One comes to regard it as an almost silent source of energy, like electricity, that one can switch on or off and regulate at will. It seems scarcely conceivable that some 340 b.h.p. are being developed beneath the bonnet by such violent means as internal combustion.

Although inertia pulls one back firmly into the seat when the accelerator is pressed flat for a rapid getaway, this is the main evidence that one is being rushed from a standstill to 60 m.p.h. in under 10sec or to 100 m.p.h. in less than 30sec. Progressive torque multiplication holds engine revs down as the car gathers speed and upward changes are particularly smooth. With so much power on call it seems superfluous to override the automatic transmission, except sometimes to supplement the wheel brakes by a downward change to intermediate before a corner.

Normal full-throttle change-up points from low to intermediate and thence to top occur at about 45 and 77 m.p.h. respectively, but by selecting the appropriate holds with the steering column lever one can stretch these to 55 and 90 m.p.h.

On the move, the highest speeds from which it is possible to kick down are 70 m.p.h. for top to intermediate, and 21 from that to low. In top this car can exceed 120 m.p.h., still with very little mechanical fuss or other disturbance. Being

Beneath the bonnet is a somewhat intimidating spectacle with no aesthetic appeal. The Fridgidaire air-conditioning compressor is above the right bank of the cylinders, a tiny alternator beneath it. Air horns beside the cross-flow radiator are not standard

fitted with air conditioning, the test car had the lower of alternative final drive ratios, 3·21 to 1 instead of 2·94, to balance the power absorbed by its compressor. Naturally the higher-geared car without the air-conditioning plant would use less petrol.

At our overall figure of 10·9 m.p.g. on super premium fuel the Cadillac de Ville covers only 40 miles or so per pound sterling in this country, which is somewhat costly motoring one-upmanship; it becomes much more logical when the car's capacity is fully employed. With a 21½-gallon tank capacity the safe touring range is, say, 200 miles when the car is driven hard. Some discretion with the throttle pedal, resisting the temptation to display the car's accelerative powers at every opportunity, naturally extends this range considerably.

It has been said often before that when it comes to driving them the best big cars feel much smaller than they appear. This is certainly true of the Cadillac, a major contributor being the power-assisted steering. This combines the virtue of requiring very little physical effort despite relatively high gearing by American standards (3·8 turns of the wheel lock to lock), with outstanding precision and sensitivity. There is no perceptible lag in response, particularly for self-centring, and the car is extremely stable at high speeds, being scarcely affected by side gusts. It is

much less of an embarrassment than one might expect in average country lanes; if they are very narrow, however, one must be prepared to stop instantly, due to the car's width. On normal roads the low-rate suspension is very soft and comfortable, while providing excellent stability for rapid cornering, without heeling over much. It provides the essentially "boulevard ride" expected of this type of car, which is not at its best over rough stuff. Once or twice it was "caught out" by a succession of waves or bumps on a public road, bad ones causing quite a build-up of pitch and wallow. Nor was it any too happy over the washboard and *pavé* surfaces at the MIRA proving grounds, but these are special circumstances that cannot take precedence over the car's usual habitat, where it would be difficult to better for restful motoring.

If the U.S. manufacturers were faced with our road conditions, coupled with the general freedom from speed limits outside built-up areas, no doubt they would provide their cars with brakes to suit. As it is, these are still the weakest feature and the Cadillac can be acknowledged only as better than most of its compatriots in this respect. One quick stop from maximum speed stretches their capacity to the limit, and fast driving over give-and-take roads can fade them out quickly until one learns to use them as little as possible, holding them ready to meet any sudden emergency. This is where the transmission selector comes into its own, a flick into intermediate from top pulling the speed down quite quickly and unobtrusively. The brakes were scarcely affected by several runs through a deep water splash, and the parking brake held the car safely on 1-in-3. It was powerful enough to lock the rear wheels if pulled on hard with the car travelling at 30 m.p.h.

Although the screenwipers have three speed settings to deal with varying conditions, they begin to lose effect from 80-85 m.p.h. onwards due to the long blades lifting. Up to that point they clear generous arcs. Penetrating wind horns are sounded by press-bars set in the two steering-wheel spokes, perhaps the best arrangement of any. Although of small diameter, the paired headlamps project powerful beams on the open road, but the contrast between these and the dipped range is rather severe. The Cadillac falls in line with the current trend in requiring the very minimum of routine servicing.

Things have progressed somewhat since those first single-cylinder Cadillacs of the early 1900s, but one has the impression that, behind all the sophisticated gadgets for gracious motoring and the flashing performance of this great car, the hardware's just as good as ever.

Specification: Cadillac Coupé de Ville

PERFORMANCE DATA

Top gear m.p.h. per 1,000 r.p.m.	25·5
Mean piston speed at max. power	3,066 ft/min
Engine revs. at mean max. speed	4,770 r.p.m.
B.h.p. per ton laden	143

ENGINE

Cylinders ...	8 in 90 deg vee
Bore ...	104·9mm (4·13in.)
Stroke ...	101·6mm (4·00in.)
Displacement ...	7,030 c.c. (429 cu. in.)

▼ *Scale: 0·3in. to 1ft. Cushions uncompressed.*

Valve gear ...	Overhead, pushrods and rockers, hydraulic tappets
Compression ratio	10·5-to-1
Carburettor ...	Carter, four-barrel
Fuel pump ...	Mechanical
Oil filter ...	Full-flow, renewable element
Max. power ...	340 b.h.p. (gross) at 4,600 r.p.m.
Max. torque ...	480 lb. ft. at 3,000 r.p.m.

TRANSMISSION

Gearbox ...	Turbo-Hydra-Matic three-speed with torque converter
Gear ratios...	Top 1·00-2·00, Inter 1·48-2·96, Low 2·40-4·80, Reverse 2·07-4·14
Final drive ...	Hypoid-bevel 3·21-to-1

CHASSIS

Construction ...	Separate cruciform frame and steel body

SUSPENSION

Front ...	Independent, wishbones, trailing links, coil springs, telescopic dampers, anti-roll bar
Rear ...	Live axle, radius arms, coil springs, telescopic dampers
Steering ...	Power-assisted, re-circulating ball
Wheel dia.	16in.

BRAKES

Type ...	Servo-assisted drums (self-adjusting), separate hydraulic circuits front and rear
Dimensions ...	F, 12in. dia., 2·5in. wide shoes; R, 12in. dia., 2·5in. wide shoes
Swept area ...	F, 189 sq. in.; R, 189 sq. in. Total: 378 sq. in. (159 sq. in. per ton laden)

WHEELS

Type ...	Slotted steel disc, 5 studs, 6in. wide rim
Tyres ...	8.00—15in. Dunlop Fort

EQUIPMENT

Battery ...	12-volt 73-amp. hr.
Headlamps ...	37·5–50-watt
Reversing lamp ...	Two standard
Electric fuses ...	13
Screen wipers ...	Two-bladed, three-speed, self-parking
Screen washers ...	Standard, electric
Interior heater ...	Extra
Safety belts ...	Standard for front seats
Interior trim ...	Cloth and leather
Floor covering ...	Carpet
Starting handle ...	No provision
Jack ...	Screw type
Jacking points ...	Under bumpers
Other bodies ...	Saloon, convertible, limousine

MAINTENANCE

Fuel tank ...	21·5 Imp. gal. (no reserve)
Cooling system ...	30 pints (including heater)
Engine sump ...	8·3 pints SAE20 Change oil every 6,000 miles; change filter element every 6,000 miles
Transmission ...	23 pints ATF type A suffix A. Change oil every 24,000 miles
Final drive ...	4·2 pints SAE90. Change oil every 24,000 miles
Grease points ...	None
Tyre pressures ...	F and R, 24 p.s.i. (normal driving)

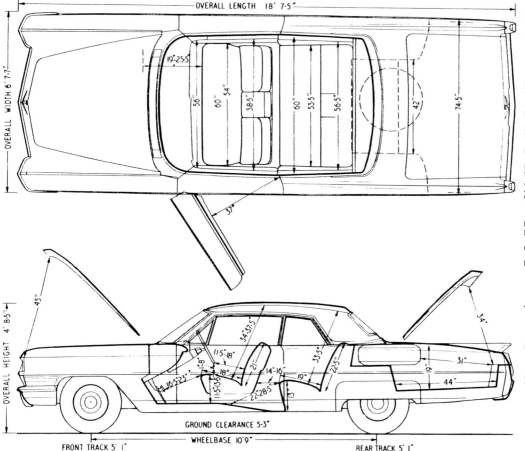

OVERALL LENGTH 18' 7·5"
OVERALL WIDTH 6' 7·7"
OVERALL HEIGHT 4' 85"
GROUND CLEARANCE 5·3"
WHEELBASE 10'9"
FRONT TRACK 5' 1"
REAR TRACK 5' 1"

TULIP-TAIL styling let Cadillac dispose of traditional, 14-year-old tail fins gracefully by continuing the hint of fins. Side sheet metal styling is a distinctive 3-plane design and roof lines have been softened.

Cadillac Calais

CADILLAC MOTOR Division is calling its 1965 line-up "the most extensive model change in the history of Cadillac —in both styling and engineering." Prominent in this change is the model name "Calais," which will designate what used to be the Sixty-Two series and will remain as the lowest-priced models in the Cadillac book.

The Calais will be available in hardtop coupe and sedan, and regular sedan body styles, on a 129.5-in. wheelbase. Overall length will be just a half-inch more than the Sixty-Two, at 224 in. (18.7 ft.), while width is increased and height decreased, both slightly. New

styling, top to bottom and fore and aft, readily identify all the '65 Cadillacs.

Fins have given way to bevel-edge blades at the rear, where the massive bumper makes up virtually the whole rear panel. At the front, projecting dual headlights are arranged vertically, flanking the traditionally massive Cadillac grille. The profile view is of clean, sweeping lines, running uninterrupted from headlight to taillight. Stylists like to point out that it can be readily identified as a Cadillac, even when all nameplates and identification are removed.

Although power steering and brakes, and automatic transmissions are stand-

ard features, the Cadillac list of options grows longer each year. In '65 there will be a tilt-and-telescope steering wheel, which tilts through six positions and telescopes in-and-out through 3 in., a 6-way power seat, an automatic leveling device for the car's rear suspension, power door locks, automatic headlight dimmer and 150 upholstery combinations ranging from perforated leather to nylon broadcloth.

A new chassis and widened front track should further improve Cadillac's soft ride and highway stability, and a new engine mounting system isolates that unit's inherent vibrations. Turbo-Hydra-Matic transmissions, the 3-speed plus variable stator vane torque converter unit, will be used on all Cadillacs but the Seventy-Five series; that will have the similar transmission with fixed vanes.

CALAIS LINE was formerly known as Sixty-Two series but picked up new name with new body and chassis. Coupe is a half-inch longer than '64.

DE VILLE SERIES convertible illustrates frontal styling, with headlights set in scalloped housings at the end of lengthy front fender extensions.

Cadillac Cruiser

Richard Worrall marvels at a car built like an aircraft carrier

The old adage that bigger is better has always been held close to the hearts of America's car makers but even by Uncle Sam's own standards Don Campbell's '65 Cadillac Coupe de Ville convertible is a whopper of a rag top. No matter how you measure it, Don's car doesn't do things by half.

Detroit's grandest convertible occupies near 125 square feet of road space, courtesy of its near-seven foot width and 18'8" of flat-top body bumper-to-bumper, which gives the huge Caddie the appearance of an aircraft carrier on wheels.

Under the bonnet, which alone appears bigger than some cars, lurks a lazy 429 cubic-inch or 7-litre overhead valve pushrod V8 and that wasn't even the biggest engine option with 489 and 501 cubic inch alternatives also available.

Don is quick to point out his car's engine is the original Cadillac factory-fitted unit, not a Chevy engine which some Caddie owners resort to installing when the original gives up the ghost. Customers in the free-wheeling cheap petrol days of the 1960s apparently didn't think too much of the 'small' engine, as the 429 was only fitted to the Coupe de Ville between 1965 and 1967. Keeping the gargantuan engine supplied with petrol is a 26(US) gallon fuel tank which empties Don's bank account of $140 each time the fuel gauge heads down to 'E' – which, surprisingly for such a large machine, is not as often as you might think with 16 to 18mpg possible on the open road.

Don, who lives in Timaru, bought the sky blue Coupe De Ville in 1993 from well-known classic car importer Lex Emslie, who lives at Lake Hayes near Queenstown.

Side lights are activated by the indicators when the park lights are switched on to provide extra illumination when turning at night

Long-held dream

The day he parted with $15,000 of his hard-earned cash for the big boulevard cruiser marked the fulfilment of a long-held dream for Don, who says he had always wanted to own a Cadillac.

He opted for the '65 rather than the more flamboyant big-finned '59 because he prefers the later model's more subtle styling.

Subtle in Cadillac terms is of course relative as no car this big could ever be described as anonymous. The car thumbs its nose at aerodynamic efficiency with its proud angular lines softened only at the corners.

Nevertheless the Caddie still manages to look sleek thanks to its partially covered rear wheels and the light blue body is offset nicely by the 15-inch whitewall tyres.

Don's 116,000 mile example was one of only 800 to leave Cadillac's Motown factory that model year (though total produced is listed as 19,200) and he says the car may possibly have been languishing in a Los Angeles wrecker's yard before Lex rescued it.

"There were quite a few missing parts such as the hood, air conditioning pump and hub caps and the wheels were not original."

The news was even worse under the bonnet as the motor was completely wrecked with five of the eight pistons broken.

"Someone had played with the engine and butchered the valve timing."

The news was much better for the body which, thanks to the dry Southern Californian climate, was in good shape apart from a small patch of rust in the bottom of the right-hand door.

Restoration began in earnest in late 1993 and took just over a year to complete.

Don carried out most of the engine rebuild himself which, he says, helped keep the cost down to about $3500, less than half what it could have set him back if he had farmed out the work.

The engine block was rebored and new pistons fitted using parts imported from the US and six months later the engine was back in tip-top condition. Some work had to be done on the suspension and brakes with all the bearings and the brake shoes having been stripped and rebuilt.

The body needed little in the way of panel work aside from removing small patches of rust and taking out the panel dents.

The body has, however, been completely repainted while inside the dashboard has been refurbished and a new hood pocket and carpets fitted.

Original chromework

All the chrome work is original and Don saw no reason to touch the synthetic leather seats as they have weathered the ultraviolet onslaught of the past three decades remarkably well.

Don has by his own admission limited his restoration efforts and, although the car still has plenty of minor blemishes that would annoy some classic car buffs, he says he is not interested in bringing the car up to concours standard.

With the roof up, the convertible is transformed into a sleek, pillar-less coupe

Vertically stacked headlights divided by a full width grille typify the car's sense of grandeur

Sharp edges rather than gentle curves are the order of the day yet the '65 Caddie still looks sleek aided by partially enclosed rear wheels. The flamboyant finned styling excesses of the '59 models are nowhere to be seen

Big is beautiful. The enormous size of Don's '65 Coupe de Ville convertible is readily apparent in this bird's eye view. The trunk is still huge despite the space taken by the folding roof

Stateside number plate adds a touch of realism

Room to spare up front. Flat bench seats provide little lateral support but are comfortable. The synthetic leather upholstery is original and the retractable seat belts were ahead of their time

"I'm a car user and not a displayer. I want a car I can get in and motor around in and enjoy."

To see exactly what the Cadillac experience is all about Don invited me to take the wheel. The view forward is quite intimidating with the huge expanse of bonnet almost completely obliterating the country road we are driving along.

The car seems almost twice the width of the road and one-lane bridges have never looked so narrow.

There's certainly no shortage of interior space with the lanky frames of an entire basketball team easily able to be swallowed up with elbow room to spare.

Floor the accelerator and the big V8 rumbles into life although never obtrusively. Gear changes are as smooth as silk with the three-speed automatic gearbox (passing power to the driveshaft via four cv joints) swapping cogs seamlessly, not that changing gears was overly necessary with the huge reserves of torque on tap.

Steering is feather light thanks to hefty power assistance. Tight corners can be negotiated with little more than finger pressure applied to the wheel which is a real bonus when parking.

The downside is that feel is almost totally absent and the suspension is definitely set up for long inter-states short of demanding corners.

Suspension comprises wishbones and coil springs up front, with coils and live axle at the rear and telescopic shock absorbers all round. Tuned for maximum comfort and combined with the de Ville's hefty weight, the car pummels any road irregularities into oblivion to provide

The Cadillac emblem is emblazoned on almost every last detail of the car including the seat-belt buckles

outstanding ride comfort. Sharp handling is not a strong point but as any Cadillac salesman would have pointed out in '65, if you are looking for sporting thrills your local Chevy dealer might have another convertible that may be more to your tastes.

Heavyweight

Stopping the monster is entrusted to huge 12-inch drum brakes, which is just as well as Don reckons the car weighs close to 2.1 tonnes!

Plenty of space and leg room for at least three back-seat passengers despite thick front seats. Access is easy. An unusual feature is the centrally mounted back speaker for the car radio

Driving at night is well catered for with four vertically stacked headlights.

The car also features side marker lights mounted just ahead of the front wheels. These are switched on when the car's indicators are activated, while the park lights are turned on to provide improved visibility when cornering and help light the ground when getting out at night to avoid stepping into unforeseen puddles or other hazards.

When the weather turns cold or wet, it's simply a matter of activating the powered hood which consists of a main outer fabric roof and a smaller secondary inner skin containing the rear window and secured with clips to the windscreen.

By modern standards, the car's interior does not look particularly luxurious with the chrome-laden dash home to relatively few embellishments aside from a centrally mounted glove box and simple radio and air-con heater controls.

Instrumentation is similarly quite spartan comprising a wide horizontal strip speedo flanked by a circular binnacle for the headlight controls to the left and a clock to the right while beneath the speedo are temperature and fuel gauges.

The big soft button-style leatherette seats add an air of upmarket ambiance, however, and the car is loaded with luxury goodies and thoughtful design touches designed to pamper its occupants.

The backs of the front seats turn inwards towards the centre of the car as well as tipping forward to help ease getting in and out of the back seat – presumably to cater for Americans who may have had one hamburger too many.

Electricity is put to good use too. Tick off air conditioning, heater, power steering, factory fitted Selectomatic push button radio with matching electric aerial, electric windows front and back, electric front seat adjustment, courtesy lights under the front

Giant chromed buttresses encapsulating the tail lights bring the de Ville to an abrupt end

armrests and a quartet of cigarette lighters. Other nice touches include the Cadillac name and badge embossed on the retractable seat-belt buckles and kick plates.

Don's completed 8000 cruisy relaxed miles in his Coupe De Ville since bringing it back to life and, road pricing and petrol tax reform permitting, his head-turning flagship of the American freeways and boulevards will be wafting down the byways and highways of South Canterbury on sunny afternoons for a good many years to come.

RICHARD WORRALL

The de Ville's proud owner – Don Campbell

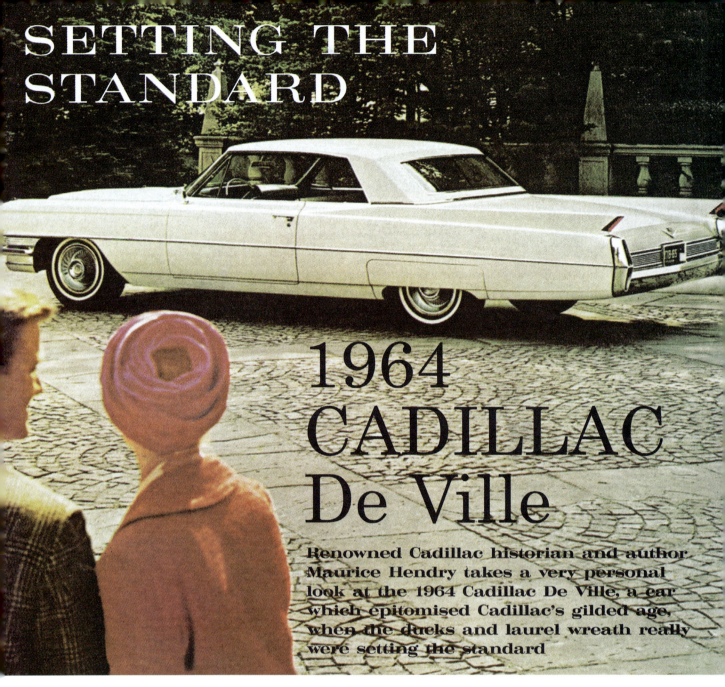

SETTING THE STANDARD

1964 CADILLAC De Ville

Renowned Cadillac historian and author Maurice Hendry takes a very personal look at the 1964 Cadillac De Ville, a car which epitomised Cadillac's gilded age, when the ducks and laurel wreath really were setting the standard

In 1964, after a 10-make comparison with the finest cars in Europe, the venerable *Autocar* magazine stated that the Cadillac not only incorporated features unobtainable in European cars 'at any price', it also 'set the highest standards attainable in most important respects'. The same year, *Motor Trend* magazine – likewise referring to both domestic and imported models – commented that 'Cadillac seems to set the standard for the luxury car industry; it's the car to beat.'

Cadillac sales for 1963 exceeded 163,000 units, nearly five times the combined volume of Lincoln and Imperial. Cadillac could have rested on their laurels for a year or two, but instead they introduced two major advances in 1964, both of which were sure to be noticed by customers. These were the three-stage Turbo-Hydramatic transmission, and the fully automatic 'Comfort Control' air conditioning system, later called 'Climate Control'.

The all-new 390cu.in. V8 of 1963 was bored out 10-percent to 429 cubes. 1964 also saw two noticeable 'lasts'; the massive X-frame chassis introduced for 1957 (although it was retained on the series 75 for 1965) and, most 'Cadillac' of all, the famous tail-fins, were shaved down an inch from their 1963 height,

bowing out all together in 1965. Styling was facelifted for '64, with a vertical 'V' motif front and rear replacing the straight-line 1963 treatment. The 'arrow' taillight surrounds were abandoned in 1965, but reappeared in later years.

Engineering of the '64s was under the direction of Fred Arnold, who succeeded Ed Cole in 1950. Arnold, who retired in 1965, was a quietly competent director whose 15 years saw many important changes at Cadillac. None was more important than the Turbo-Hydramatic and Comfort Control introduced in '64. Turbo-Hydramatic came as standard on the de Ville, Sixty Special sedan and Eldorado convertible. The old four-speed Hydramatic was continued on the Sixty-Two and Seventy-Five series.

The old Hydramatic featured a simple fluid coupling and four fixed planetary ratios. It continued to be used at Rolls-Royce (under licence) and by Mercedes-Benz (their own version) for some years, but was rendered obsolete by the Turbo-Hydramatic with its simpler three-stage, torque converter combination. This was really GM's answer to the earlier and similar Lincoln Turbo-Drive and Imperial Torqueflite. Rolls later also adopted this transmission, as did Jaguar, whilst Mercedes' later designs were similar.

'Comfort Control,' said *Autocar*, 'is surely Cadillac's most outstanding contribution to motoring ease.' Comfort Control thinks for itself and for the driver. The first thing you notice is that there is only one control lever instead of several and, in effect, it is little more than an on-off switch. The only other control - rarely used at all - is the little wheel for setting the required ambient temperature between 65 and 85 degrees. All you have to do is dial the desired temperature, move the lever to 'Automatic' and forget about it. It really was the first ever 'set 'n' forget' automatic climate control system 'This really is the unit to end all units,' commented *Motor Trend*, 'and will no doubt be widely copied by the rest of the industry.' And indeed it was.

Other features and options were a six-position steering wheel, Twilight Sentinel, cruise control, power windows, seats, door locks, vacuum trunk lock release, three-speed windscreen wipers with automatic wash, automatic headlamp dipping, auto-release parking brake and a two-speaker signal-seeking radio with power aerial. It would have been impossible in 1964 to find a more comprehensively equipped automobile.

The cruise control unit mounted on the carburettor was governed directly by car speed and acted as a speed warning device as well as an automatic speed control. The desired cruising speed is selected by a calibrated wheel in the dash. Actually, this is simply a very sophisticated engine governor, a principle known in the earliest days of motoring. Cadillac had one – though not quite so advanced or refined – on its four-cylinder models 60 years previously.

The Twilight Sentinel automatically turns on the headlights and taillights at dusk, the timing controlled by an adjustable photo-electric cell. It only operates with the ignition switch on, but a variable time delay allows the headlamps to stay on after the ignition is switched off. This permits about 90 seconds of light for the driver and passengers to reach their doorway - a common feature today, but pretty revolutionary back in '64. Whilst most drivers feel quite capable of switching on their headlights at dusk, the car will even do it when entering dark tunnels or other areas.

The Coupe de Ville, one of the most popular Cadillac models, originated back in 1949 and was intended to capture the style of a convertible with the practicality of a hardtop. The interior of the Coupe de Ville is roomy, even for 5 adults. A sixth person can ride in the centre of the front seat, but the transmission hump limits this to children, for comfort. There is an abundance of lamps, cigar lighters and ashtrays, but only one glove compartment (small) and only one vanity mirror (on the sunvisor). There is a rear window defogger, switched from the dash, which is a two-speed electric blower with a heater element, and while it does its job, is no match for the buried-wire unit fitted on Rolls-Royces of the time. Upholstery is an attractive combination of leather and vinyl, with perforated panels for seat ventilation. Good quality nylon carpet covers the floor.

DRIVING IMPRESSIONS

So, let's slip back 37 years, to the reception centre at 2860 Clark Avenue, Detroit, Michigan. Your new Cadillac is ready. Slide behind the instantly set, six-position steering wheel. Close the door with a crisp, solid 'thunk'. Adjust your seat perfectly with the tiny joystick. Close the windows to the hum of electrics. All

outside noise ceases, and you're in an insulated world of your own. Flip the starter on the V8 with the longest pedigree of all, and more than 300 horses come to life and quietly await your command. At your fingertip is the finest automatic in the world, select 'low' and you can burn off all but a super-sports car. Not very Cadillac-like behaviour, but reassuring to know.

It's interesting to compare this car with a 1934 12-cylinder Pierce Arrow I once owned. Both cars have a legendary reputation and represent the finest the American car industry could offer during their respective eras. The Pierce did have a much greater degree of hand-craftsmanship and fine finish, but in practically every other respect the Cadillac wins hands-down. In terms of honest, utilitarian workmanship, the Cadillac is at least the equal of the Thirties classic, despite what they say about 'not building 'em like they used to'. Chrome is plated over nickel, over copper - the best there is.

Trim strips are bolted, not snapped on. The trunk is carefully lined and carpeted. In some areas - the fuel tank, for example - the 1964 car is built better than the 1934 vehicle, and the overall standards of construction are just as rugged. Eight cylinders in 1964 gave almost the double what 12 did in '34, and even more smoothly and quietly. Acceleration, cruising speeds and maximum speeds are far higher, braking, steering and road-holding are superior, and fuel economy is about 50 percent better!

First, however, a few criticisms. The car is, frankly, too big for parking ease. A foot shaved off its length and a proportionate four inches shaved off its width would have detracted little from its appearance and would have made for less worrying about scraping walls or other cars.

Up to 1963, Cadillac did in fact market a bob-tailed version, the Park Avenue. This was 215-inches long and also had a smaller 21 gallon fuel tank versus the standard 26 gallon tank. Whether this was a penalty of the shorter rear deck, or whether Cadillac really meant it when they called it a town car, isn't clear; however Cadillac claimed it was 'specially designed with a shorter rear deck and less overall length, but with full interior Cadillac roominess - the Park Avenue manoeuvres to the envy of smaller cars. It is a motor car with particular appeal to the ladies'.

Sales charts show why Cadillac abandoned this model (and the Town Sedan); they sold only 2000 or 3000 units a year, sometimes less. Don't blame Cadillac for building bigger cars; obviously the public wanted them that way!

The only other criticism is that on tight bends, this car does

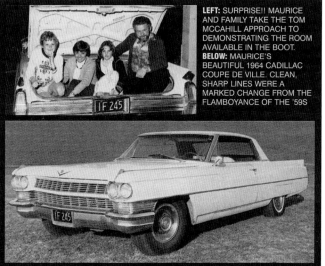

LEFT: SURPRISE!! MAURICE AND FAMILY TAKE THE TOM MCCAHILL APPROACH TO DEMONSTRATING THE ROOM AVAILABLE IN THE BOOT.
BELOW: MAURICE'S BEAUTIFUL 1964 CADILLAC COUPE DE VILLE. CLEAN, SHARP LINES WERE A MARKED CHANGE FROM THE FLAMBOYANCE OF THE '59S

SETTING THE STANDARD

1964 CADILLAC de Ville

'The car is a pleasure to drive in traffic. All corners are clearly visible, three-and-a-half turns take the steering from lock to lock, and the power brakes are smooth and predictable'

IT'S EASY TO BE A WEATHERMAN IN A NEW CADILLAC!

Or weatherwoman, as the case may be. For with the exclusive new Comfort Control, which combines heating and air conditioning in a single unit, the interior weather never changes. Even humidity is under perfect control. This system, now available as an extra-cost option, actually anticipates outside conditions and adjusts for them before they

occur. All in all, the Cadillac for 1964 is more than a hundred ways new. It has amazing new agility and responsiveness in traffic. Its ride is smooth and quiet as never before. And its luxury and styling are the finest of all time. Arrange a date with this new Cadillac motor car someday soon. *It's more tempting than ever—and just wait till you drive it!*

Cadillac Motor Car Division · General Motors Corporation

feel a real handful and begs to be driven gently. Under all other circumstances, its handling is good. In a recent car club slalom I posted better times than a rival with a Rolls-Royce Silver Cloud II, despite his 10-inch overall shorter wheelbase and 12-inch overall shorter length. Since he is a lifetime car enthusiast and expert driver, and keeps his car immaculate, I put the Cadillac's victory down to superior matching of power steering and front suspension linkages, better located rear axle and lower centre of gravity.

The steering on this car ranks at the very top. It has a silken, 'quality' feel, power assistance that is virtually perfect, and that hallmark of the top-quality car; it feels smaller than it is. The car responds immediately. As *Autocar* said, it has 'outstanding precision and sensitivity ... no perceptible lag in response, particularly for self-centring, and the car is extremely stable at

112

CLOCKWISE FROM TOP: '61, '62,'64 AND '63 CADILLACS

high speeds, being scarcely affected by side-gusts'.

The car is a pleasure to drive in traffic. All corners are clearly visible, three-and-a-half turns take the steering from lock to lock, and the power brakes are smooth and predictable. Either foot can be used on the double-width pedal, and in case of power failure, both feet together restore the equivalent braking power. Safety is enhanced by the separate front and rear hydraulic circuits, and the foot-operated emergency brake/parking brake.

Performance was more than adequate: 'Tremendous performance,' said *Autocar*, 'a surge of instant power is always in reserve. Exceeds 120mph with contemptuous ease.' *Motor Trend*, recording 0-60mph times of 8.5 seconds, and the standing quarter-mile in 16.8, commented of the '64 de Ville that it was 'a real bear off the line. It's going to take a hot-option model of anything else to stay with this one from a standing start'. Both magazines found that even when cruising at 110mph, the Caddy was effortless.

But if the Cadillac's straight line performance was unquestionable, the subject of braking was somewhat more controversial. Of four published road-tests of the time, two rate the brakes as satisfactory, whilst two claim them to be inadequate. From my own experiance, the car's brakes are completely adequate for its designed purpose as a fast, luxury car. *Motor Trend* found that the brakes survived several consecutive stops from 115mph before fading. Fuel consumption is satisfactory, averaging about 16mpg. Using the air conditioning makes about a one mpg difference, while in the cut and thrust of city driving the average fuel consumption comes down to 10 or 12mpg.

Of course, the perennial question is: 'What'll she do wide-open?' Here I'd like to sidetrack a bit, to a letter written to the factory a bit more than 50 years ago, asking what was the true top speed of the then-new 1949 model. The factory's rather disdainful reply was that

'we do not have official figures on the maximum speeds of any of the models.' They did allow that many owners had reported speeds 'in excess of 100mph with the 1949 valve-in-head engine', but continued 'as of today, Cadillac is not anxious to publicise the speed of its cars. It feels that owner satisfaction and excellence of performance at ordinary speeds are far more important factors'.

This reply was of particular interest to me, since I had written the original letter of enquiry. Of course, with all the resources of GM's gigantic proving grounds at their disposal, Cadillac knew better than all the auto journals in the world exactly what their cars could do down to the last fraction of one mph. Cadillac's contempt for top speed figures show in a speedometer that stops at 120mph, but the car will deliver more than that. *Car Life* recorded 121mph, and *Autocar* made one best run at 123mph and, on another occasion, published a figure of 125. As a mean, *Autocar* listed 121.5, which agrees very closely with *Car Life*. *Motor Trend* clocked 115, but it seems that their top speed runs may have been done

in Nevada, where altitude robs a car of several mph. Speedo error, incidentally, was very low. *Autocar* found that at an indicated 113mph, the car was doing an honest 110mph.

Because of her age, I never drive my car above 110mph today - and that only when I can find a cop-free motorway. Only two references to high speeds appear in the driver's handbook; 'for sustained speeds above 75mph, tire pressures should be increased to 28lbs cold,' and 'Break-in procedure unnecessary. Your Cadillac is ready for driving just as you receive it. Precision manufacturing techniques have prepared it for the road.'

How does the 1964 Cadillac measure up to its contemporaries? To put it bluntly, the question should be the other way around. The only marque that can challenge an all-round comparison with the '64 Cadillac is the Lincoln Continental, for reasons which will be obvious to anyone who studies their respective specifications.

The '64 Rolls-Royce Silver Cloud III cannot by any stretch of the imagination be regarded as a modern car, and the '64 Mercedes 300 series are likewise not really in the same league. The only Mercedes model standing comparison is the 600, which had been newly introduced around that time to counter dissatisfaction with the 300s.

Interestingly the 600 was quite unlike any previous Mercedes model. It was clearly aimed at the American market, and Mercedes historian Kenneth Ulyett wrote that 'in designing the Grand Mercedes, Daimler Benz AG adopted certain guiding principles exemplified in the Cadillac'. Moreover, the 600 was never a viable economic proposition, it was merely a prestige excercise and a loss leader.

This car is expensive and you won't win any economy runs or parking contests, but for engineering advances, style and luxury in 1964, you were driving the 'Standard of the World.' ★

GM's crown jewel

Cadillac's casual car, the De Ville convertible, provides the last word in carefree driving

by John Ethridge
Technical Editor

CADILLAC OCCUPIES an enviable position in its field. Not only does it outsell all domestic cars in its class combined, but it's often considered in the same league with foreign luxury cars costing over three times as much.

When you look into the underlying reasons, you find it isn't quality alone that accounts for Cadillac's enormous prestige. The car's quality is undeniably good — it compares favorably with that of any automobile at any price. But the makers realize that, by itself, quality won't guarantee continued leadership in the luxury field. They've long known that things bordering on the abstract, such as association (fine jewelry) and distinctiveness (even with all insignia removed, it's instantly recognizable as a Cadillac), help assure concrete benefits like high resale value and owner loyalty. These two things are mutually regenerating and are what really account for the unassailable position Cadillac has enjoyed for quite some time. The Cadillac people have carefully nurtured these things in their advertising and by such devices as affixing the original purchaser's signature to the car.

For the sake of identification, the current model has to look like those of past years. In fact, if you go back a decade, you'll find today's car bears a marked resemblance to the 1955 model. Yet there's nothing antiquated about it. From both styling and engineering stand-

114

points, it's as contemporary as anything on the road. The most significant styling change for 1965 is that the famous fins, which have adorned Cadillacs for 17 years, have receded into the rear fender line.

A new frame, the first in nine years, heads the list of engineering changes. Like those of other GM cars, the frame is a perimeter type, and it gives a weight saving of about 300 pounds over the old one. For the past several years, most Cadillacs have been sold with several hundred pounds of accessories. Weight was getting out of hand. The tires, brakes, and suspension will welcome the relief. Those of you who feel a Cadillac *should* be heavy shouldn't worry. It still weighs plenty and has one of the most favorable sprung/unsprung weight ratios (for good ride) of any car.

The engine's been moved farther for-ward in the new frame, reducing the size of the transmission hump. The bulk of the Comfort Control heating/air-conditioning unit now occupies under-hood space instead of being in the passenger compartment. This results in far more knee room for the front-seat passengers and simplifies servicing the unit.

The history of Cadillac is to a large extent the story of a list of well engineered accessories available as extras on the car. Foremost is the Comfort Control unit. The heating and air-conditioning systems are combined and are controlled by a "brain" on the instrument panel. In engineering language, it's a *servo-mechanism*. It senses the difference between the temperature you've dialed and that of the passenger compartment, then gives the necessary commands to appropriate parts of the system

to adjust the temperature. In addition to turning the compressor and hot water on and off, the system also opens and closes various ducts. At one phase, both the heater and air conditioner go on simultaneously to de-humidify the air.

We approached the Comfort Control with a certain amount of skepticism at first, because we appreciate the problems involved in making a system like this — that sells for less than $500 and still does all the things it's supposed to do. We were pleasantly surprised to find it worked perfectly under all tests we devised. It did tend to hunt (alternately blew hot and cold) when ambient temperature reached that set on the dial. This, though, isn't a real complaint. Changing the set temperature slightly cured it if we didn't want to shut it off and open the windows.

Besides the automatic headlight-

Numerous power-consuming accessories call for very busy engine compartment. Extra capacity of cross-flow radiator and condenser stops overheating.

Smooth, powerful "429" V-8 comes already broken in, uses Carter AFB or Rochester four-barrel carb.

GLASS REAR WINDOW CURES MAJOR CONVERTIBLE BUGABOO. TOP'S TAUTLY ATTACHED TO EACH BOW TO PREVENT BALLOONING AT HIGH SPEEDS.

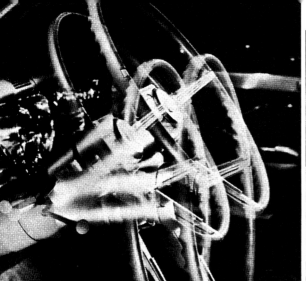

Just a few positions possible with the Saginaw swiveler. There ought to be at least one to suit every driver.

New layout of engine and accessories adds to roominess and comfort inside. All manually operated controls can be reached with seat belt fastened.

dimmer control, our test car had the Twilight Sentinel. This automatically turns on the headlights when sunlight falls below a certain level. It incorporates a variable delay so you can park the car, turn off the ignition, and the lights will stay on until you, say, find the keyhole and are safely inside your house.

Between the four-way bucket seat in our test car and the tilting and telescoping steering wheel, most everyone can find a comfortable driving position. The bucket seats are perforated for ventilation and are among the most comfortable we've sat on. They cost $187.85, including a console with locking compartment.

We almost forgot to mention one optional extra ($80.65) our test car had, so unobtrusively did it do its job. The Automatic Level Control, which works with gas pressure on the rear shocks, quickly restores the status quo when a change in loading causes the rear end to sag.

Cadillac continues with its powerful and — for its size — economical 429-cubic-inch V-8. Overall average for our 888-mile test was 12.1 mpg, which covered mostly city driving. A freeway trip at steady legal speed gave 14.2 mpg. This was, of course, with the air conditioning and 3.21 axle. The standard 2.94 axle should yield phenomenal fuel economy. Performance runs dropped mileage to 10.5 — our low for the test.

Although stopping distances weren't unusually short, the big 12-inch brakes showed no signs of fade during turn-arounds after our acceleration runs. About seven out of 10 cars we test won't get through these turn-arounds without some degree of fade.

As for the rest of the Cadillac line, all models except the Series 75 are pretty much as we've described the De Ville. The nine-passenger 75s continue with last year's X-braced tubular frame and horizontal headlamps. Also, the 75s retain the two-piece driveshaft, while other models have gone to a single shaft. What was formerly called the Series 62 is now more euphoniously referred to as the Calais.

You always get that extra that comes with every Cadillac at no extra cost: It's an unmistakable status symbol in the eyes of the well-to-do as well as the man in the street. With this on top of good engineering and distinctive styling, what more could you ask for in a luxury car? /MT

CADILLAC DE VILLE
2-door, 5-passenger convertible

OPTIONS ON TEST CAR: Comfort Control, bucket seats, AM-FM radio, automatic level control, electric seats, electric windows, power door locks, adjustable steering wheel, controlled differential.
BASE PRICE: $5639
PRICE AS TESTED: $7494.60 (plus tax and license)
ODOMETER READING AT START OF TEST: 4785 miles
RECOMMENDED ENGINE RED LINE: 5200 rpm

PERFORMANCE

ACCELERATION (2 aboard)
```
0-30  mph  ..........................................3.3  secs
0-45  mph  ..........................................6.0
0-60  mph  ..........................................9.5
```
PASSING TIMES AND DISTANCES
```
40-60 mph  ...............................5.2 secs., 382 ft.
50-70 mph  ...............................6.0 secs., 528 ft.
```
Standing start ¼-mile 17.2 secs. and 82 mph
Speeds in gears @ 4400 rpm (shift point)
```
1st ...............  45 mph      3rd ...............113 mph
2nd ...............  76 mph                      (observed)
```
Speedometer Error on Test Car
```
Car's speedometer reading .................32  48  54  64  74  85
Weston electric speedometer ..............30  45  50  60  70  80
```
Observed mph per 1000 rpm in top gear ....25.2 mph
Stopping Distances — from 30 mph, 37 ft.; from 60 mph, 184 ft.

SPECIFICATIONS FROM MANUFACTURER

Engine
Ohv V-8
Bore: 4.13 ins.
Stroke: 4.0 ins.
Displacement: 429 cu. ins.
Compression ratio: 10.5:1
Horsepower: 340 @ 4600 rpm
Horsepower per cubic inch: 0.79
Torque: 480 lbs.-ft. @ 3000 rpm
Carburetion: 1 4-bbl.
Ignition: 12-volt coil

Gearbox
Turbo Hydra-Matic 3-speed automatic with variable-vane torque converter; column-mounted lever

Driveshaft
1-piece, open tube

Differential
Hypoid, limited slip
Standard ratio: 3.21:1

Suspension
Front: Independent, with coil springs, upper A-arm, SLA with strut, tubular shocks, anti-roll bar
Rear: Rigid axle, coil springs, 4-link arms, tubular shocks

Steering
Ball nut sector with coaxial power assist
Turning diameter: 44.7 ft.
Turns lock to lock: 3.7

Wheels and Tires
15 x 6JK 5-lug, slotted steel disc wheels
9.00 x 15 4-ply tubeless whitewall tires

Brakes
Hydraulic, duo-servo, self-adjusting, dual master cylinder
Front: 12-in. dia. x 2.5 ins. wide
Rear: 12-in. dia. x 2.5 ins. wide
Effective lining area: 203.6 sq. ins.
Swept drum area: 377.0 sq. ins.

Body and Frame
Separate steel body on perimeter frame
Wheelbase: 129.5 ins.
Track: front, 62.5 ins.; rear, 62.5 ins.
Overall length: 224.0 ins.
Overall width: 79.9 ins.
Overall height: 54.6 ins.
Curb weight: 4820 lbs.

WIDENED TREAD AND LOW-PROFILE 9.00 X 15 TIRES IMPROVE CORNERING STABILITY, ALREADY RELATIVELY GOOD FOR A 4800-POUND CAR.

De Ville convertible stows top within body outline, without sacrificing any trunk room.

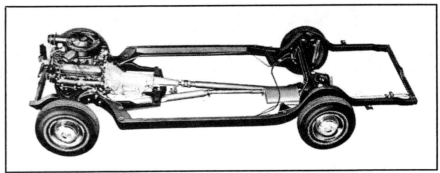

New weight-saving perimeter frame mounts engine farther forward. Four-link rear suspension's been redesigned. Two-piece driveshaft's been abandoned for one-piece unit.

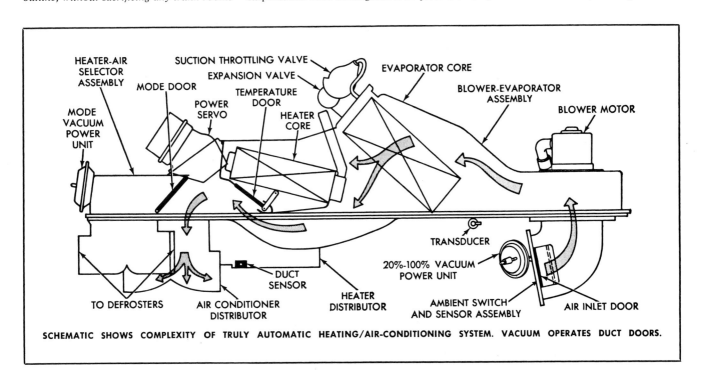

SCHEMATIC SHOWS COMPLEXITY OF TRULY AUTOMATIC HEATING/AIR-CONDITIONING SYSTEM. VACUUM OPERATES DUCT DOORS.

GO WEST YOUNG MAN...

IN A 1966 CADILLAC !

CADILLAC BRAKES ARE BRAWNY STOPPERS, GOOD ENOUGH TO PRECLUDE A SWITCH TO DISCS IN FUTURE. DUAL MASTER CYLINDERS STANDARD.

3,000 MILES OF ELEGANCE, LUXURY, AND ADJUSTABILITY
IS ENOUGH TO CONVERT ALMOST ANYBODY

by Robert E. McVay,
Associate Editor

GO EAST, young man," our editor instructed, "and head back West with a 1966 Cadillac." That's how it all started. Some 3,000 miles later, we returned with this top luxury machine, very much impressed with the car and with the way it's put together.

Our personal tour of Cadillac's vastly expanded facilities (they've increased working space by 50% and have added tons of new testing equipment) impressed on us the fact that this is a thoroughly tested automobile, probably far more refined than certain other top luxury cars from across the pond whose makers couldn't begin to afford the facilities Cadillac has.

Take for instance their one-of-a-kind Road Simulator. It holds a car on four hydraulic pistons and can be programed to simulate any road surface, anywhere in the world. It finds out in 30 seconds what it took hours to find out on the old mechanical shakers. Cost of this device was $250,000. In addition, we saw a vast array of dynamometers, hot and cold rooms, wind tunnels, and component-testing setups.

Watching the assembly line was another surprise. At maximum pace, 50 cars a day is tops, with two shifts. Care is taken in the building, and a high degree of personalization goes into each Cadillac. Workers are allowed more time to do their respective jobs right.

Already the top luxury car on our market (sales were over 181,000 in 1965), Cadillacs are more refined this year. Technical improvements of major importance include a Saginaw-built variable-ratio power steering with 2.4 turns between locks. In normal road

118

driving, there is a new preciseness of control and, as the wheel nears full lock, the ratio quickens, adding control in parking and accident-avoiding maneuvers. Steel strut-type autothermic pistons with slotted rail top rings are used for better oil control, a common problem with big-inch engines.

Rear brakes are all cast-iron, instead of composite iron and steel, for more uniform quality. Effective lining area is greater too, and big 9.00 x 15-inch tubeless 2-ply tires are standard. They give better temperature control at high speeds and add seven miles per hour to the car's capabilities.

Now, let's look inside. In addition to 171 different interiors, from full perforated or unperforated leather to beautiful gold brocades, there are some very nice 1966 improvements.

Harold Warner is a hi-fi and stereo enthusiast, in addition to being general manager of Cadillac. So, it was no surprise to find one of the finest AM-FM stereo radios available in "his" car. Four speakers, arranged in "crossfire" fashion, are 180 degrees out of phase in every direction. It's like taking the Boston Philharmonic along to the corner drugstore.

Cadillac's new "hot seat" — they call it a seat warmer — shoots 150 watts of electricity through carbon yarn woven into pads under seats and seat backs of the front seats, giving instant heat when the key is turned on. This is tops for bottoms on those below-zero mornings, and it shuts off automatically when water temperature reaches 160°.

Cadillacs come in three passenger series, Calais, DeVille, and Fleetwood, plus the extra-luxurious limousines. Our test car was the middle-series DeVille four-door hardtop with a normal (for Cadillac owners) complement of accessories.

Our 3,000-mile road test covered all those states west of Detroit along famous Route 66. Weather varied from deluge to sunshine, from 35° to 100°, with day and night miles covered. We had an excellent chance to sample the luxuries of America's top-selling high-priced automobile and in the process, found out why there's an extra charge for first-class travel.

Comfort means many things to many people, and people with money come in as many different sizes and shapes as those without it. Cadillac's ride is pillowy soft, yet like a good pillow, is firm enough (a bit more so than the 1965 models) for good balance at cruising speeds. There's lots of stretch-out room inside and a huge trunk that'll hold all the suitcases any family should need.

"Adjustability" is big at Cadillac. Six-way power front seat, tilt-and-telescope steering wheel, full power (right down to the vent windows), Climate-Control, and Cruise-Control enable the driver to

Whisper-quiet at speed with good balance and control, car was an excellent tourer.

Adjustability of wheel, seats, speed, and temperature means top comfort on long trips.

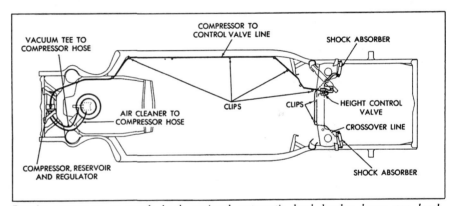

Despite passenger or trunk load, optional automatic load leveler keeps car level.

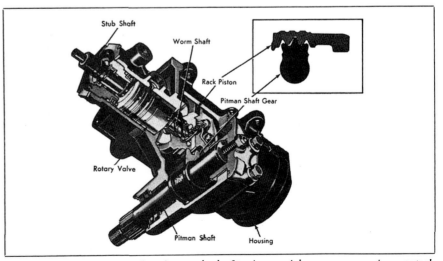

Variable-ratio power steering is standard. It gives quicker, more precise control.

More paint and less chrome make car look longer — but it's only an optical illusion.

"set it and forget it." In the wide-open areas, all we had to do was steer, try to keep the speedometer from nibbling at 80 and listen to stereo, of course. Mileage ranged from 13 to 14.5 mpg at highway speeds.

We found, too, that adjustability can have its drawbacks. We now understand why too many Cadillac owners settle down in air-conditioned isolation, aim their machines down the fast lane on a turnpike, and become oblivious to the presence of folks in lesser cars.

The "hot seat" should contain an automatic pin to remind one that the car really doesn't drive itself. The stereo should have another ear to pick up the horn blast of the fellow who wants to pass. The Cruise-Control should occasionally reach out and tickle the driver's foot. The automatic windows should lower at random to let in a bit of road noise. And, it should be mandatory that every Cadillac passenger have a grating voice and use it constantly. In essence, our complaint — or compliment, as you will — is that Cadillac has carried refinement to a degree that is soporific. /MT

CADILLAC

PHOTOS BY MC VAY, NORENBERG

Tangle of accessories and connections is a mechanic's nightmare, but underneath it all lies a smooth, powerful, 429-inch V-8.

CADILLAC ACCESSORY PRICE LIST

Padded roof	$136.85
Leather upholstery	137.90
AM-FM stereo radio	287.90
6-way adjustable front seat	83.15
Climate-Control air conditioning	484.15
Tilt-and-telescope steering wheel	89.50
Power door locks (4 doors)	68.45
Twilight Sentinel	28.45
Remote-control trunk lock	52.10
Rear window defogger	26.35
Cruise-Control	94.75
Power vent windows	71.60
Closed crankcase vent system	50.00
Seat warmer (front only)	78.95
Bucket seats	184.20
Bucket seats with 4-way driver power, 2-way passenger power, 2 head rests, and reclining passenger seat back	321.04
Automatic level control	78.95
Controlled differential	52.65
Headrests (for bench seats)	52.65

CADILLAC SEDAN DE VILLE
4-door, 6-passenger hardtop

OPTIONS ON TEST CAR: Air conditioning, 6-way power seat, tilt/telescope steering wheel, power vents and door locks, AM-FM stereo radio, padded roof, leather upholstery, Twilight Sentinel, Cruise-Control, whitewalls, misc. access.

BASE PRICE: $5581
PRICE AS TESTED: $7306.25 (plus tax and license)
ODOMETER READING AT START OF TEST: 2723 miles
RECOMMENDED ENGINE RED LINE: 5000 rpm

PERFORMANCE

ACCELERATION (2 aboard)

0-30 mph	3.5 secs.
0-45 mph	6.8
0-60 mph	11.1

PASSING TIMES AND DISTANCES

40-60 mph	5.9 secs., 431 ft.
50-70 mph	7.0 secs., 616 ft.

Standing start ¼-mile 17.7 secs. and 74 mph
Speeds in gears @ shift points

1st	42 mph @ 4200 rpm	3rd	100 mph @ 3700 rpm
2nd	74 mph @ 4200 rpm		

Speedometer Error on Test Car

Car's speedometer reading	31	46	52	63	75	86
Weston electric speedometer	30	45	50	60	70	80

Observed mph per 1000 rpm in top gear .... 25 mph
Stopping Distances — from 30 mph, 35 ft.; from 60 mph, 170 ft.

SPECIFICATIONS FROM MANUFACTURER

Engine
Ohv V-8
Bore: 4.130 ins.
Stroke: 4.00 ins.
Displacement: 429 cu. ins.
Compression ratio: 10.5:1
Horsepower: 340 @ 4600 rpm
Horsepower per cubic inch: 0.79
Torque: 480 lbs.-ft. @ 3000 rpm
Carburetion: 1 4-bbl.
Ignition: 12-volt coil

Gearbox
3-speed automatic (Turbo Hydra-Matic); column-mounted lever

Driveshaft
1-piece, open tube

Differential
Hypoid, semi-floating
Ratio with air-conditioning: 3.21:1

Suspension
Front: Independent, with coil springs, upper A-arm, SLA with strut, tubular shocks, anti-roll bar
Rear: Rigid axle, coil springs, 4-link arms, tubular shocks

Steering
Variable-ratio ball nut sector with coaxial power assist
Turning diameter: 44.7 ft.
Turns lock to lock: 2.4

Wheels and Tires
15 x 6JK, 5-lug slotted steel disc wheels
9.00 x 15 tubeless, 2-ply (4-ply rated) tires

Brakes
Hydraulic, duo-servo, self-adjusting, with dual master cylinders
Front: 12-in. dia. x 2.5 ins. wide
Rear: 12-in. dia. x 2.5 ins. wide
Effective lining area: 221.8 sq. ins.
Swept drum area: 377.0 sq. ins.

Body and Frame
Separate steel body on perimeter frame
Wheelbase: 129.5 ins.
Track: front, 62.5 ins.; rear, 62.5 ins.
Overall length: 224.0 ins.
Overall width: 79.9 ins.
Overall height: 55.6 ins.
Curb weight: 4860 lbs.

ECONOMY CADILLAC

Image Incarnate With Climate Control

FABLED IN SONG and story, surrounded by the golden aura of excellence, desirability and success, Cadillac is at once the admiration, the outrage and the despair of its luxurious competitors. Cadillac is reputation rampant, image incarnate, mystique multifold—a promoter's dream—a product so overwhelmingly accepted that its popularity is now self-sustaining in what amounts to a psychological chain reaction. Everyone knows that it is one of the most expensive cars built in the United States—or is it? No, actually it is not; not necessarily. A Cadillac can become quite a bargain when compared with semi-prestige cars from the next-lower price stratum.

The bottom-of-the-line Calais model, Cadillac's nod to the increasingly affluent middle and working classes, retails for just $4955 (f.o.b factory). This is no more than a 1-carat stone's throw, or a few monthly payments, away from the upper echelons of Buick, Oldsmobile, Chrysler and Thunderbird, and is well below the price of Cadillac's direct competitors, Continental and Imperial.

For an accurate cost comparison, however, it is necessary to pile the scales high with the wealth of accessories Cadillac supplies without additional charge, but which are extra-cost options on many cars. Even on the Calais this includes such attractive and

useful devices as a heater and defroster, electric clock, Hydra-Matic transmission, center-front armrest, power brakes, power steering, extra lights for every conceivable purpose from cornering to trunk loading, remote-control side mirror, retractable seat belts both front and rear, 429-cu. in. V-8 engine, and variable-speed windshield wipers and washer, to name only the more substantial items. And all at no additional cost. Installation of this cornucopia of creature comforts in a lesser car would cost at least $1200. Without doubt, membership in the prestigious Cadillac club has its benefits.

Each of the above mechanical ameni-

CADILLAC

ties adds its mite to the overall impression of silky-smooth, utterly obedient power and luxury that has become as much a Cadillac trademark as the name itself. It is a road tester's cliché by now to describe in dazzled awe the Splendid Sensations of Driving a Cadillac—and yet the car's silence, responsiveness and sheer comfort exist and must be recognized. The goal of its designers obviously is to create the grand and ultimate expression of mobile luxury, and every year they come closer to doing it.

At steady freeway speeds of 70–75 mph, the overriding sensations for both driver and passengers are ease, quiet and safety. The car never seems

taxed or even extended—for example, while running at 75 mph for several hours on a hot day, and with the air conditioner on, the engine-temperature needle never left the bottom third of its range. The Calais simply never lost its cool.

When engaged in a car-brag, one of the Cadillac owner's most satisfying ploys is a sort of rich man's poormouth, earnestly maintaining that he buys his cars only for their economy. His usual evidence ranges from the extraordinary gas mileage he gets with that great big engine to the incredible distance those good, big 9.00-15s will go before the nibs wear off. Oddly enough, although his examples are un-

sound, he does have a point, a very good point.

The real economies in Cadillac ownership lie in mechanical reliability and sustained resale value. Initial cost is substantial, but the dependability, the promise of luxury and consequent high trade-in diminish very slowly, giving their final glow of consumer satisfaction at trade-in time—consequently predisposing the buyer toward purchasing another Cadillac, of course.

Prominent among the niceties of driving the 1966 Calais is a benefit poetically referred to in the descriptive brochures as "a subtle feel at the steering wheel." It turned out that this romantic phrase referred to a very practical and effective development by GM's Saginaw Steering Gear Division called "variable-ratio power steering," which is standard this year in all Cadillacs.

Simply stated, in this system the steering ratio changes to either side of center, with road-wheel lateral direction changing more rapidly as the steering wheel moves toward its rotational limits. This is accomplished through modifications to the shape of the Pitman shaft gear teeth: Shortening the side teeth gives a faster turning rate to right or left of center.

The variable-ratio steering system has two big advantages. First, the engineer can use a ratio which will give the driver desirable "road feel" in the middle of the steering range, where nearly all highway driving is done, without worrying about the effect this choice of ratio may have on the rest of the steering. Second, more rapid steering change may be given to the extremes of the range, used mainly for parking and slow cornering, where drivers of large cars like the Cadillac have always gone through their awkward exercise of endlessly winding and rewinding the steering wheel. Variable-ratio steering has reduced the number of steering wheel turns lock-to-lock from 3.6 turns in 1965 to 2.4 in 1966.

THE GREAT range of adjustments allowed by the "tilt and telescope" steering wheel and the 6-way power seat, two optional accessories, permit almost any driver to find a relaxed but authoritative driving position. The wheel can be tilted up and down through six stops, and can be slid in and out over a 3-in. span, even while the car is in motion (hardly to be recommended in traffic), and the seat can be raised, lowered, moved fore or aft and tilted forward or backward, all at the touch of the appropriate lever.

Basic engineering changes in the 1966 Cadillacs are as conservative as usual, consisting primarily of a new perimeter frame and revisions in front and

SET IT and forget it. The Cadillac Climate Control maintains a pre-set temperature, dialed in with the knob, left, and with lever at automatic.

TEMPERATURE SENSOR inside car transmits signals which open vents, valves, switches and ducts that regulate compressor, vacuum system and blower.

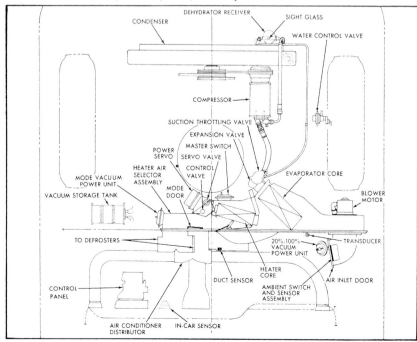

rear suspension components for ride and handling improvements. Silence and smoothness are refined by modified engine and body mounts, and a 2-piece propeller shaft with constant-velocity joints.

Cadillac's Moraine & Bendix vacuum-boosted hydraulic brakes have a dual-reservoir master cylinder which actuates the front and rear brakes separately, making it most unlikely the car will ever be entirely without brakes. Neither freeways nor mountains brought any signs of fade under normal driving. However, during the consecutive 80–0 brake-life tests, there was definite evidence of fade during the second all-out stop. Admittedly, it will take a set of remarkable brakes to bring the over-5000-lb. Cadillacs to repeated smooth and safe halts, but such systems are available, and on Cadillac's competitors.

One of the most impressive accessories on today's automotive market, both in cost ($484.15) and operation,

is Cadillac's automatic Climate Control (formerly called Comfort Control), which combines heating and air conditioning functions into a single system. The appearance of the control panel for the unit is deceptively simple, with just two settings necessary: A thermostat dial that reads from 65° to 85° and a lever that can be positioned at either "automatic" or "defrost."

To PUT Climate Control into action, one sets the desired temperature on the thermostat, then selects the mode of operation with the lever: That is all. The system then supplies dehydrated air, either warmed or cooled, to bring the interior of the car's air into the specified temperature range. Everything is automatic—individual temperature sensors located about the car transmit their messages back to the power-servo mode and selector centers, which in turn open and close the vents, valves, switches and ducts which control the operation of the compressor,

vacuum system, blower motor and air distribution chambers.

In addition, the Climate Control system almost seems to have a degree of free choice. If turned on when the car is started up on a cold morning, it simply waits until heat is available to it from the engine coolant before going into operation. And, too, when interior temperatures are completely out of line with its instructions, it attacks them with impatient vigor, supplying extra-hot or icy air under full blast from the blower until matters are under control, then throttles itself back to a silent, contented and masterful maintenance of the status quo.

Among the many optional accessories which naturally are provided for the gilding of Cadillacs are various am/fm and stereo radio combinations, bucket seats with headrests and a reclining mechanism, a rear-window defogger, power door locks, power window vents and the like. Within the long list, however, are several items

CHAN BUSH PHOTOS

CRISP, CLEAN and finless, the Cadillac Calais' lines lead in unbroken sweep from vertical front to vertical rear. The smooth side expanse is broken only by the rectangular cornering light on the front fender and the slimmest of chromium accent stripes.

which have that certain touch of devil-may-care elegance and flair. One of these is the seat warmer, a device which makes use of an electrically conductive carbon yarn developed by Union Carbide Corporation. The yarn is woven with insulating glass yarn into a high-strength, high-electrical-resistance cloth, which is installed in the seat backs and cushions. The activating current is disconnected by a

thermal switch when heater water reaches a temperature of 150° F, allowing use of the regular heating system.

Another accessory of special interest is the automatic level control, which brings the car back to an even keel with up to 500 lb. in the trunk or rear seat. Trailer buffs will covet this feature on their own cars, recognizing its ability to compensate for tongue weight.

And, approaching drivers at night will pass more safely when low beams have not been cocked up by a trunkful into the high-beam position.

Blanking out old memories of lacquered dorsal fins cavorting in a frothy sea of chrome, the present-day simplicity, good taste and permanence of Cadillac styling are prominent among the factors that make its cars a good buy. In the 1966 models this relative

1966 CADILLAC
CALAIS COUPE

DIMENSIONS
Wheelbase, in.	129.5
Track, f/r, in.	62.5/62.5
Overall length, in.	224.0
width	80.0
height	54.6
Front seat hip room, in.	62.0
shoulder room	59.7
head room	38.5
pedal-seatback, max.	43.0
Rear seat hip room, in.	55.0
shoulder room	60.6
leg room	38.2
head room	37.6
Door opening width, in.	43.5
Floor to ground height, in.	14.0
Ground clearance, in.	6.0

PRICES
List, fob factory	$4955
Equipped as tested	6077
Options included: Air conditioning, door-edge guards, emission control, tinted glass, am radio with power antenna and rear speakers, 6-way power seat, tilt and telescope steering wheel, whitewalls, power windows.	

CAPACITIES
No. of passengers	6
Luggage space, cu. ft.	17.1
Fuel tank, gal.	26.0
Crankcase, qt.	5.0
Transmission/diff., pt.	6.0/5.0
Radiator coolant, qt.	18.2

CHASSIS/SUSPENSION
Frame type	perimeter
Front suspension type: Independent by short and long control arms, coil springs, telescopic shock absorbers, link-type stabilizer.	
ride rate at wheel, lb./in.	86
anti-roll bar dia., in.	0.815
Rear suspension type: Live axle with 4-link location, coil springs, telescopic shock absorbers.	
ride rate at wheel, lb./in.	115
Steering system: Concentric gear, variable-ratio power steering with parallel drag-link and spherical spindle joints.	
gear ratio	variable
overall ratio	n.a.
turns, lock to lock	2.4
turning circle, ft. curb-curb	44.7
Curb weight, lb.	4760
Test weight	5150
Weight distribution, % f/r	52/48

BRAKES
Type: Dual-line hydraulic, duo-servo shoes in composite drums.	
Front drum, dia. x width, in.	12 x 2.5
Rear drum, dia. x width	12 x 2.5
total swept area, sq. in.	377.0
Power assist	vacuum, integral
line psi @ 100 lb. pedal	930

WHEELS/TIRES
Wheel size	15 x 6JK
optional size available	none
bolt no./circle dia., in.	5/5.5
Tires: UniRoyal Laredo	
size	9.00-15
recommended inflation, psi	24
capacity rating, total lb.	5680

ENGINE
Type, no. cyl.	V-8, ohv
Bore x stroke, in.	4.13 x 4.00
Displacement, cu. in.	429
Compression ratio	10.5
Rated bhp @ rpm	340 @ 4600
equivalent mph	120
Rated torque @ rpm	480 @ 3000
equivalent mph	78
Carburetion	Carter AFB, 1x4
barrel dia., pri./sec.	1.4375/1.6875
Valve operation: Hydraulic lifters, pushrods and overhead rockers.	
valve dia., int./exh.	1.875/1.50
lift, int./exh.	0.427/0.466
timing, deg.	34-102, 89-63
duration, int./exh.	290/332
opening overlap	97
Exhaust system: Single, co-axial resonator.	
pipe dia., exh./tail.	2.5/2.25
Lubrication pump type	spur gear
normal press. @ rpm	30 @ 1300
Electrical supply	alternator
ampere rating	55
Battery, plates/amp. rating	13/73

DRIVE-TRAIN
Transmission type: Variable vane torque converter, planetary gearbox.	
Gear ratio 4th ( ) overall	
3rd (1.00)	3.21
2nd (1.48)	4.76
1st (2.48)	7.64
1st x t. c. stall (2.00)	15.28
synchronous meshing	planetary
Shift lever location	column
Differential type: Hypoid with cone clutch limited slip.	
axle ratio	3.21

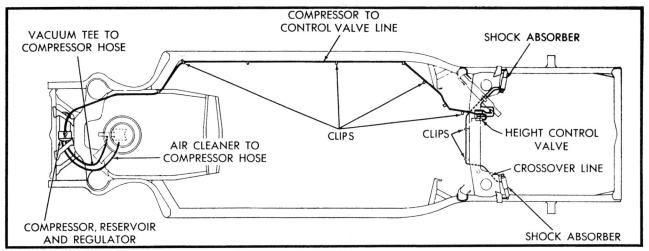

VACUUM TEE TO COMPRESSOR HOSE

COMPRESSOR TO CONTROL VALVE LINE

SHOCK ABSORBER

AIR CLEANER TO COMPRESSOR HOSE

CLIPS

CLIPS

HEIGHT CONTROL VALVE

CROSSOVER LINE

COMPRESSOR, RESERVOIR AND REGULATOR

SHOCK ABSORBER

OPTIONAL WITH Cadillac cars is this automatic leveling control which maintains the car on an even keel with up to 500 lb. in the luggage compartment. Motor-driven compressor supplies regulated air pressure to special rear shock absorbers.

understatement extends all the way from the front grille through the instrument panel and back to the rear bumper. The front and rear ends profit both from design simplification and the omission of chrome from around the headlights and the side-fender cornering lights, from the tops of the fenders, and even from painting the lower half of the rear bumper in the car's body color.

The instruments are few, obvious in purpose and natural to use. As on the Climate Control panel, functions have been combined wherever possible, a welcome relief from unnecessarily proliferating knobs, handles, levers, switches and buttons. Careful, effective design like this is difficult, but highly rewarding to the customer.

In discussing the possibility that a Cadillac, particularly the Calais model,

may under some circumstances be considered a bargain, we have deliberately omitted Cadillac's greatest stock in trade: Pride of ownership. Each buyer must weigh for himself the intangible value of seeing a Cadillac each morning when he opens the garage. But pride aside, pound for pound and function for function, the Calais is good value in any automotive marketplace. ∎

CAR LIFE ROAD TEST

ACCELERATION & COASTING

(Graph: MPH vs ELAPSED TIME IN SECONDS — curves labeled 1st, 2nd, 3rd, SS ¼)

CALCULATED DATA

Lb./bhp (test weight)	15.1
Cu. ft./ton mile	112
Mph/1000 rpm (high gear)	26.0
Engine revs/mile (60 mph)	2310
Piston travel, ft./mile	1540
Car Life wear index	35.5
Frontal area, sq. ft.	24.3
Box volume, cu. ft.	567

SPEEDOMETER ERROR

30 mph, actual	29.3
40 mph	38.9
50 mph	47.8
60 mph	57.1
70 mph	66.7
80 mph	76.2
90 mph	86.4

MAINTENANCE INTERVALS

Oil change, engine, mo.	2
transmission/diff., miles	24,000
Oil filter change	6000
Air cleaner service, mo.	6
Chassis lubrication	as req.
Wheelbearing re-packing	as req.
Universal joint service	as req.
Coolant change, mo.	24

TUNE-UP DATA

Spark plugs	AC-44
gap, in.	0.035
Spark setting, deg./idle rpm.	5/400
cent. max. adv., deg./rpm.	9/2000
vac. max. adv., deg./in. Hg.	12/20
Breaker gap, in.	0.016
cam dwell angle	28-32
arm tension, oz.	19-23
Tappet clearance, int./exh.	0/0
Fuel pump pressure, psi.	5.3-6.5
Rad. cap relief press., psi.	13.5-16.5

PERFORMANCE

Top speed (4400), mph	115
Shifts (rpm) @ mph	
3rd to 4th ( )	
2nd to 3rd (4400)	77
1st to 2nd (4200)	44

ACCELERATION

0-30 mph, sec.	4.0
0-40 mph	5.4
0-50 mph	7.3
0-60 mph	9.4
0-70 mph	12.3
0-80 mph	15.6
0-90 mph	19.8
0-100 mph	26.2
Standing ¼-mile, sec.	17.0
speed at end, mph	83
Passing, 30-70 mph, sec.	8.3

BRAKING

(Maximum deceleration rate achieved from 80 mph)

1st stop, ft./sec./sec.	23
fade evident?	none
2nd stop, ft./sec./sec.	21
fade evident?	definite

FUEL CONSUMPTION

Test conditions, mpg.	11.6
Normal cond., mpg.	12-15
Cruising range, miles	312-390

GRADABILITY

4th, @ grade @ mph.	
3rd	12 @ 65
2nd	19 @ 55
1st	28 @ 35

DRAG FACTOR

Total drag @ 60 mph, lb.	155

Cadillac owners claim you get a lot to like

By BILL KILPATRICK,
PM's New York Automotive Editor

THE PAPER IS OLD, its edges yellowed and brittle to the touch. Yet the print is clear, the message as modern as a moonshot:

"Smooth-riding, powerful, absolutely dependable, the Cadillac is a car surprising alike in performance and cost."

This quote from a 1904 advertisement for the car that once billed itself as the "standard of the world" accurately summarizes the opinions of most 1966 Cadillac owners surveyed by *PM*. Even as the copywriter of over 60 years ago claimed, Cadillac owners still find today's car "smooth-riding, powerful . . . dependable" and they like its performance.

But many owners—based on what they feel they got for their money—think "surprising" is hardly the word to describe the $5000-plus cost of the car.

"It's time the makers of all cars start producing a car worth what they ask for it," wrote an Illinois businessman.

A Massachusetts claims investigator, however, said of her 1966 two-door Cadillac, "It's an excellent car from the front to rear bumper and in my opinion has no equal."

What has no equal, owners surveyed by *PM* feel, is the way the car handles, an attribute to which they accorded an FMR (frequency-of-mention rating) of 36.8

percent. Next in order, Cadillac owners praised comfort (34.4 percent), ride (29.4 percent) and styling (22.7 percent).

But owning a new Cadillac apparently isn't all roses, either. Even owners generally pleased with their cars added to the complaints listed by those who regard their comparatively expensive invest-

ments as a waste of money.

Owners didn't like, for example, wind noise, a gripe to which they accorded an FMR of 9.8 percent. Also at this rating level were complaints of various rattles and noises, hardly the sort of thing one expects from the "standard of the world." Tied with FMRs of 8.9 percent were as-

sorted knocks about Cadillac's automatic climate control airconditioning and heater system (it either doesn't work or it works too well) and overall workmanship. Most emphatic, despite an FMR of only 7.3 percent, were owner complaints about location and size of the glove compartment. All by itself, surprisingly, was an old

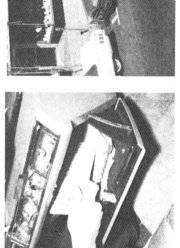

AWKWARD AND SMALL glove compartment drew owner ire. Contents tend to spill when it's opened

CADILLAC PARKS EASILY, many owners claim, citing handling as a big plus. Power steering is standard

Cadillac gas mileage chart

— City driving
--- Long trips

Percentages

25
20
15
10
5

MPG 7 8 9 10 11 12 13 14 15 16 17

CADILLAC AND THRIFT aren't synonymous, owners say. Engine is 429-cubic-incher, puts out big 340 hp

The affluent folk like:

Handling	36.8%
Comfort	34.4
Ride	29.4

But don't like:

Wind noise	9.8%
Rattles/noise	9.8
Climate control system	8.9

lament traditionally expressed by Cadillac owners. An Iowa sales executive wrote, "My biggest complaint is that just because you drive a Cadillac, motels, garages, gas stations and any other place of service will try to take you. Why, just this year a (brand) station tried to tell me I needed new shocks when I had only 5000 miles on my car."

So, accolades aside, realize that wearing a Cadillac crown apparently can be a heavy, expensive responsibility at times.

Cadillac owners responding to *PM*'s survey rolled up an aggregate of 1,011,746 miles of both around-town and long-trip driving during which they averaged overall 12.4 mpg. But discussing Cadillacs and mileage is like J.P. Morgan's commentary on yachting—if you're concerned about cost, you can't afford it. Anyway, here's what the surveyed owners of 1966 Cadillacs had to say for and against. Their comments are listed in order of frequency mentioned. The boldface comments are the author's.

"I like the way the car drives and handles. It's smooth, quiet, and I like the secure feeling of driving a car such as a Cadillac."—Michigan engineer.

"Very easy to handle during parking."—Indiana, retired.

"It's solid, quick steering and precise."—Massachusetts druggist.

"The car holds the road and performs more like a Cadillac than any model of the past 13 years."—California, retired.

"Although it's a large, heavy car, it handles well."—California supervisor.

Next on the praise list was plain ol' down-home comfort, an undeniable attribute of just about any Cadillac extant. That people often buy a certain car for a specific reason is verified by a Nebraska attorney, who wrote:

"I bought my Cadillac because it was the most comfortable car I could buy."

"Extremely smooth to ride in and tireless on long trips."—Iowa, retired.

"We find our Cadillac spacious, with ample, luxurious room for others."—Ohio housewife.

Listed almost on a par with comfort was ride.

"Excellent ride. No tendency to bottom-out when going over dips in the road."—Michigan tool engineer.

"The car has outstanding riding qualities in both city and mountain driving."—California, retired.

"It's like a cruiser going over small swells in the ocean."—Missouri contractor.

▶ In Missouri?

One thing most Cadillac owners feel they get for their money is one of the best looking cars on the road. Part of this, I'm sure, stems from the car's prestige mystique—at these prices it better be good looking. Actually, however, from a styling point of view, Cadillacs aren't too different from similar Detroit products. Yet a

CADILLAC OWNERS' REPORT

Michigan engineer feels: "Overall style is far ahead of other so-called luxury cars."

"I appreciate the simple, uncluttered lines and lack of gingerbread."—Florida engineer.

"Tops for beauty and luxury, inside and out."—Virginia salesman.

Another thing Cadillac owners feel they obtain with their bill-of-sale is reliability.

"I have found the Cadillac to be the most dependable car I have ever owned."—New Mexico, retired.

"I can drive it a full year with little or no service."—New York optometrist.

"Car offers good all-'round dependability."—New Jersey technician.

Despite the positive note struck by owner praises, however, America's Motoring Majesty has some loyal (generally) opposition, most of it like communists in the French Assembly—small in percentage, but loud.

"There's a lot of noise around the windows and door frames."—District of Columbia showman.

"We have a wind whistle with our '66 that we didn't have with our '64."—South Dakota housewife.

"I get a lot of noise through and around the front windows."—Wisconsin educator.

Added to wind noise are complaints about rattles and road noise.

"It rattles like a truck."—Michigan broker.

"Body isn't as tight as in previous Cadillacs I've owned."—California executive.

"Rumbling noise from the road seems to come right up into the car."—New Hampshire clergyman.

In theory the automatic climate control system sounds peachy, but in practice a number of owners think it's a dud, or at least something less than its billing.

"The climate control does not operate fully automatically, as the salesman said it did. I think the thermostat is too sensitive and the warm air suddenly changes to cold before a comfortable temperature is reached."—Connecticut physician.

▶ I found this to be true in **PM's** test car, too.

"Climate control has no manual override; when on freeways or behind buses and trucks, fumes fill the car."—Mississippi, USAF.

"It's hard to control the heater part of the climate control."—Michigan engineer.

Next on the complaint list is a category one hardly expects to find when it comes to a Cadillac: workmanship. As pointed out in previous owners reports, poor and/

or indifferent workmanship seemingly dogs the entire auto industry. Still, with the "little" Caddy selling for just under $5000, it's more than out of place, particularly with the "standard of the world."
A Maryland businessman makes the point:

"A car in this price field shouldn't have as many faults in workmanship as does mine. For example, there were several loose bolts, the rubber window molding was twisted, and so on. The car has several signs of negligent workmanship."

"More attention should be paid to small details of workmanship. There were loose thread ends hanging all over my new car's upholstery."—New Jersey businessman.

"The doors have never fit properly and the rear speaker rattles."—Virginia executive.

"They ought to do a better job of assembly. With my last ten Cadillacs it has taken me almost 7000 miles to get all the bugs out."—Florida, retired.

▶ **This is no fair-weather friend, either. He has owned 32 Cadillacs.**

Owners aren't too happy with the glove compartment. It's a minor item, granted, but one would think that in a Cadillac it would be both copious and efficient.

"It's awkward."—Michigan doctor.

"It's too small."—Iowa sales manager.

"Things tumble out when its opened."—California contractor.

"It's next to useless."—Maryland executive.

And so on, all pretty much in the same vein. So are comments about the front seat ashtray.

"It's unhandy."—Florida businessman.

"Inconvenient."—Michigan physician.

"Too small."—California businessman.

"The ashtrays up front are just terrible."—Illinois accountant.

Ranked sixth on the praise list by Cadillac owners was the car's quietness; again, something one would think comes with possession of the ignition key.

"The engine is very quiet."—Iowa executive.

"Car just whispers along at high speeds."—Pennsylvania designer.

"Road noise is minimal."—Tennessee sales executive.

Many owners had kind words for their cars' pickup and performance.

"Best performing car yet."—Kentucky businessman.

"Responds well when I step on the gas."—Virginia manager.

"Acceleration characteristics are superb."—Ohio supervisor.

Although, as mentioned earlier, many owners deemed the climate control system bad news.

Summary of Cadillac Owners' Reports

Excellent .. 67.2%   Good .. 26.8%   Fair .. 4.4%   Poor .. 1.6%

Best-liked features:

Handling	36.8%
Comfort	34.4
Ride	29.4
Styling	22.7
Reliability	14.1
Quietness	12.3
Performance	9.8
Climate control	9.2
Roadability	8.0
Workmanship	6.1

Least-liked features:

Wind noise	9.8
Rattles/noise	9.8
Climate control	8.9
Workmanship	8.7
Glove compartment	7.3
Finish/paint	7.3
Gasoline consumption	6.5
Styling	5.7
Window glass/lack of molding	5.7

Most liked to see changed:

Glove compartment (size/position)	11.9
Styling	10.4
Ashtrays, lighters (more)	9.0
Better climate control	7.5%
Headroom	6.7
Steering wheel position/size	3.7
Instrument panel/dash	3.7
Better fuel economy	3.7
Price (lower it)	3.0

Car traded in:

Cadillac	77.8
Oldsmobile	8.1
Pontiac	3.4
Buick	3.4
Thunderbird	3.4
Mercury	1.3
Others	2.0

Dealer service:

Excellent	61.9
Average	31.3
Poor	6.8

Buy from dealer again?

Yes	91.5
No	8.5

Buy another Cadillac?

Yes	98.1
No	1.9

Bought Cadillac because:

Value/trade-in	38.5
Past experience	21.2
Styling	13.5%
Prestige	11.5
Comfort	9.6
Availability	5.8
Different (something new)	5.8
Dealer/dealer service	5.8

Considered other makes?

No	68.7
Yes	31.3

Own another car?

No	68.3
Yes	31.7

Make of other car:

Chevrolet	28.1
Ford	16.5
Pontiac	14.0
Buick	12.4
Oldsmobile	9.9
Cadillac (another one)	7.4
Thunderbird	5.0
Mustang	5.0
Corvair	4.1
Dodge	3.3
Volkswagen	3.3
Mercury	2.5
Others	14.9

Total miles driven: 1,011,746

Cadillac Brougham

Lush and plush don't have to mean
mush as well; the best-kept
secret about Caddy is—it handles

MANUFACTURER Cadillac Division
General Motors Corporation
Detroit 32, Michigan

ENGINE
Type Water-cooled V-8, cast iron block, 5 main
bearings, pushrod-operated overhead valves
Bore & Stroke...................................4.13 x 4.0 in.
Displacement.......................................429 cu. in.
Compression ratio...............................10.5 to one
Power (SAE)............ ....325 bhp @ 4600 rpm
Torque.... ....480 lbs-ft @ 3000 rpm
TRANSMISSION...................3-speed automatic
WHEELBASE...133 in.
TRACK............................F: 62.5 in. R: 62.5 in.
CURB WEIGHT..N. A.
ACCELERATION **Seconds**
0-40 .... 5.5
0-60 .... 9.7
0-80 ....17.2
TOP SPEED...120 mph
SUSPENSION
F: Ind., unequal-length wishbones, coil
springs, anti-sway bar
R: Rigid axle, locating links, coil springs
BRAKES 12-in drums front and rear

What few people realize is that the Cadillac is a driver's car. People who consider themselves drivers would never consider the Cadillac, and people who buy Cadillacs probably don't care. Cadillac's advertisements are the tip-off—the car is never presented as a moveable object, rather as a stationary status symbol parked in front of some terrific mansion, but parked nevertheless. Which is a sadness. It was only the last decade when millionaire sportsman Briggs S. Cunningham took a relatively stock Cadillac coupe to the 24-hour race at Le Mans, France, and finished tenth overall with the beast. Maybe a '66 model would do as well. It could certainly rank with some of the more luxurious Grand Touring cars as a suitable device for getting

there from almost anywhere else, and it wouldn't take much more than a set of big tires, wide rims and Koni shocks (because it does tend to wallow around a bit on some surfaces).

It's sure comfortable enough. Our test car had the best seats (6-way power) of any non-sports car we ever drove. Plus the tilting and telescoping steering wheel, it adds up to a near-perfect driving position. The brakes were exceptional for an all-drum set-up (though not quite as good as the old Rolls-Royce or the old Corvette drums). The new variable-ratio power steering is particularly pleasant to use, with only 2.9 turns lock-to-lock. The system is similar to that used in the Jaguar 4.2 sedan, though it lacks the perfect feel of the English car's steering. And the 325-hp Cadillac gets around right sprightly for a car that weighs almost 5000 lbs. Responsive, very; but nimble, no.

But you'll never hear Thing One

from Cadillac about the Cadillac as a driver's car. They'll tell you that it's the best American luxury car made, which happens to be completely true. They'll go on about AM/FM stereo (new this year), power this, power that, hundreds of different interior combinations, and the completely automatic cruise control, climate control, and headlights that go on when it's dark and dim when a car approaches. Swell. But some of you well-heeled enthusiasts ought to get out there and drive the things—they really do go around corners and everything. Just ask Briggs S. Cunningham.